DAMMED INDIANS

Michael L. Lawson

FOREWORD BY VINE DELORIA, JR.

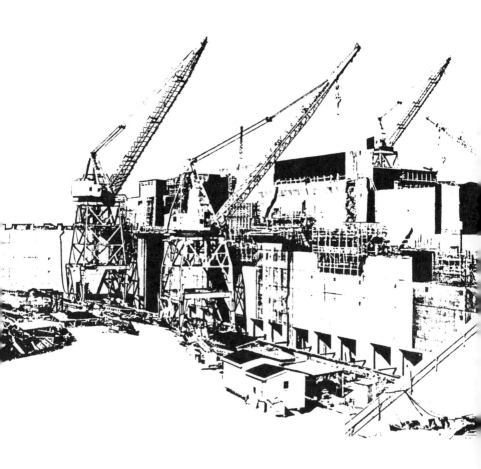

THE PICK-SLOAN PLAN AND THE MISSOURI RIVER SIOUX, 1944-1980

DAMMED INDIANS

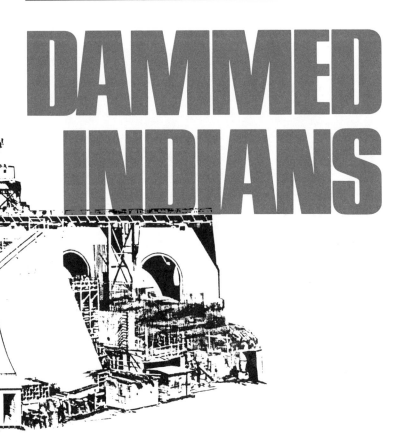

University of Oklahoma Press   Norman

Library of Congress Cataloging in Publication Data

Lawson, Michael L.
  Dammed Indians.

  Bibliography: p.
  Includes index.
  1. Dakota Indians—Land transfers. 2. Dakota Indians—Government rela-
tions—1934- . 3. Missouri River Basin project. 4. Indians of North
America—North Dakota—Land transfers. 5. Indians of North America—
South Dakota—Land transfers. 6. Indians of North America—Government
relations—1934- . I. Title. II. Title: Pick-Sloan Plan and the Missouri
River Sioux, 1944-1980.
E99.D1L33   978.3'00497   81-19721
                                                AACR2

To Richard N. Ellis
Scholar, mentor, friend

CONTENTS

ILLUSTRATIONS

MAP

FOREWORD by Vine Deloria, Jr.

There is something very sacred about the Missouri River to the Sioux Indians. Unlike traditions that extend far into the historical mists and are chronologically uncertain, our memories of the lands near the river are immediate and relate primarily to the last half of the nineteenth century when the tribe agreed to move to reservations. For a while the Santees and Yanktons were the only bands along this river, and the Missouri, together with the Niobrara, provided a measure of isolation and security to peoples who badly needed to be left alone to reflect on the radical changes they had experienced.

At Santee the Congregationalists founded their mission school, and several generations of Sioux learned to read and write and to worship in the Christian way in this little institution, which had influence far in excess of its modest setting. Below the Missouri at Santee were the grounds where the Sioux and Pawnees contended for hunting grounds before the white man came. At one particular spot, when the heat is dissipating in the evening coolness, one can still hear the death songs and smell the tobacco of the warriors who lost their lives on one of the hills overlooking the river. Although the Santees and Yanktons were agreeable to living in the white man's way fairly early after contact, the families who took up allotments along the river bank retained many of their own ways until the Corps of Engineers confiscated their lands and built enormous dams, which flooded both ancestral farms and ranches and memories, leaving the tribes materially and spiritually impoverished.

The area immediately surrounding Fort Randall Dam has special memories for my family which, I believe, are worth relating because they illustrate some of the spiritual loss that all Sioux families suffered in this bureaucratic disaster. My great-grandfather was Saswe, a noted medicine man of the Yanktons. His power was so great that stories still abound of some of his healings and mysterious feats. My grandfather was his favorite son from among the many sons that his three wives presented to him. Although it was something of a shock to the old man when my grandfather told him that he wanted to become a Christian missionary, Saswe felt that the course was proper and raised no objection. The old man, however, retained all of the traditional beliefs until he died, never once arguing with my grandfather about the differences in the two conceptions of spiritual things.

As the old man was nearing death, the sons and grandsons came to see him, and in the traditional manner some of the younger men were sent down to the river banks to seek out a sturdy cottonwood where Saswe's scaffold could be placed, since our people placed their dead in trees in those days. When Saswe heard his wives directing the young men to seek out a tree, he raised up his head and called to them, instructing them to take him outside his log cabin so that he could survey the landscape. Thinking that he had already chosen a tree, the relatives took the old man outside and propped him up so that he could see the bottomlands and the surrounding hills. He motioned for his bow and arrow. When he had them, with a new strength said to be an amazing throwback to his youth, the old man shot an arrow far up into the hills that raise themselves above the river bottomlands.

"Bury me there, in a hole six feet deep, covered with a nice thick layer of rocks from the river, and make sure no one can tell where I am buried," he told his stunned relatives. "Bury me in the manner of the whites because I want to sleep in peace when I go into the ground," he repeated. People could not have been more surprised by anything else that he could have done than by his asking to be buried like the whites. But, turning a deaf ear to all arguments, Saswe repeated that he wanted to rest in peace and he wanted to be buried high on those hills, which at the time were several miles from the actual banks of the river.

I know where the spot is because, from 1947 until the Fort Randall Dam was finished, I would often be traveling with my father to Santee and Yankton, and he would anxiously watch the progress of the dam construction and always would point out the place where Saswe was buried. My father was fascinated by the changing landscape because various estimates by people working on the dam projected how high the water would rise and, since these were scenes of my father's childhood, he wanted to remember every twist and turn of the river and its lands before they were lost from sight forever. When the dam's reservoir was finally filled with water several years later, we were driving across the finished dam and a happy grin spread across my father's face, because the waters rose to within fifteen feet of the place where great-grandfather had been buried. But, just like the old man had prophesied, he rested peacefully in the ground when all the ancient cottonwoods where he might have been laid to rest were under the waters of the dam. Even three-quarters of a century later it seemed that the old man had provided for himself through his spiritual powers.

Every Sioux family had similar losses as old homesteads and old memories were ruthlessly taken away. I remember about ten years ago standing on the western shores of Oahe reservoir and listening to Frank Ducheneaux, chairman of the Cheyenne River Sioux tribal council when the dams were authorized. He pointed out the various places, as best he could estimate, where the events of his childhood had taken place. With a trace of tears in his eyes, Frank showed me where the old agency road had come down from the breaks into the agency, where the boarding schools had stood, and where the cattle used to be issued during the first several years of reservation life. I chuckled a bit when he pointed out where he thought the old agency had been, because the very first window I ever broke with an air rifle was at Cheyenne Agency. This occurred when I was but a lad of eight years and unaware that air rifles could not be fired when one was smack in the middle of civilization—which is what the agency towns represented in those days.

In this book Michael Lawson eloquently and thoroughly chron-
icles the events, personalities, and agencies that were involved in
the massive Pick-Sloan Plan for "restructuring" the Missouri River.
Briefly, the Corps of Engineers wanted large dams on the river,
whereas the Bureau of Reclamation wanted small holding dams on
the tributaries. Rather than fighting each other, they simply co-
operated and built all of their proposed projects to the tune of
billions of dollars of taxpayers' funds. Indeed, the original estimates
of $1.75 billion had risen to $3.9 billion by 1952 and then to $28
billion by 1970, and one is afraid to ask for the final accounting,
if it can be rendered at all.

The Pick-Sloan Plan was, without doubt, the single most destructive act ever perpetrated on any tribe by the United States. If it had
simply been one act and had been committed only against the Sioux
with the violation of only one treaty, it would be viewed as gross
and unfair; but the projects eventually involved almost all tribes
living on the Missouri and its major tributaries in the states of
South Dakota, North Dakota, Montana, and Wyoming, and the
end is still not in sight. Recent discoveries of coal and other minerals
make certain that the Pick-Sloan mentality eventually will destroy
the High Plains of North America for both Indians and non-Indians
who live in this region.

In my opinion, three reservations suffered intensely: Crow Creek,
Lower Brule, and Fort Berthold. The larger reservations were able
to hold most of their grazing lands intact. Although they lost most
of their bottomlands, they had a sufficient number of communities
on the high plains west of the river so that the disruption of some
communities did not totally disorient the tribe. But Fort Berthold
was virtually destroyed, and the dam waters separated the reservation completely. The tracts that remained were left farther apart
by road than the people had originally been from the nearest white
settlements when the reservation was intact. The Crow Creek and
Lower Brulé tribes had almost all of their usable lands taken, and
their reservations were so drastically impacted that they have never
been able to establish viable communities since their lands were
lost.

Lawson shows how the Bureau of Indian Affairs, either by
trickery or misdirection, remained silent while this desecration

took place. This agency left the tribes helpless before the onslaught of the greedy and aggressive Corps of Engineers and Bureau of Reclamation. Although readers may be shocked by some of the revelations in this book that illustrate how unfair this project really was, the horrifying thing to realize is that the real treachery must always be a matter of supposition. Illegal activities of all kinds may never be documented, although it is almost certain that they occurred. That information that we do have is available for all the world to see and to understand, and it should be sufficient warning to all Americans about the absolute and dictatorial powers that federal agencies possess. One cannot, I would argue, read this book without a shudder of fear at bedtime that one's life and property may someday fall victim to ruthless, power-mad federal agencies.

A curious aspect of the financial settlements which may intrigue readers is the provisions for compensation for such intangibles as the little roots and berries that the people gathered along the river and creek banks on the reservations. Why, the reader may wonder, were these people compensated for the loss of bushes and trees with little or no commercial value? Well, the old people preserved their knowledge of traditional and natural medicine when they went on the reservations, and many of their herbs, berries, and roots grew along the banks of small, seasonal creeks. Traditional people used them to solve their health problems in traditional ways, and I can verify that many of them were more effective than any medicine from a pharmacy. But the medicines as well as the knowledge of how to use them died when the water rose. I know that the health of the people has declined significantly with the loss of these things, and I cannot help wondering what else must have been lost forever. A natural environment was completely wiped out without any consideration of what was there and was replaced by a mechanical electric grid system and large holding dams. The primary purpose of these structures, in my opinion, was merely to keep the Corps of Engineers busy between wars. This is a moral violation of ourselves as human beings.

I am particularly impressed with Michael Lawson as a scholar and as a person. His research, it seems to me, is thorough and takes into account the human foibles and failures, the arrogance and ignorance, and the optimism and pessimism that characterized all of the people who participated in this traumatic situation. More especially, however, I am impressed with his desire to plough entirely new ground. My opinion of historians is not high and ranks somewhere near that of my opinion of Congress, but Lawson's efforts represent a new wave of future historical writing and an awareness that bespeaks a return to the sensible and relevant topics and explorations that historians should pursue.

Let me explain further. In 1975 I was asked by a staff member of the Newberry Library to become their resident or, should I say, token, Indian. As part of the interview I was asked what I would recommend to make the Newberry's Indian Studies program more relevant. I suggested that they might make contact with the tribal councils of the midwestern region and make arrangements to microfilm the minutes of their meetings. Through such a project future students and historians would have an accurate and complete record of what Indians experienced and thought during this century.

I could not have made a more threatening suggestion as it turned out. The staff member, for whom I reserve a bit of anonymity because of his utter stupidity, grew exceedingly angry at my suggestion. He haughtily told me that they had very few documents that went beyond 1900 and that they should really not have these in their collection since no one in their right mind would consider the twentieth century to be history yet. When I tried to reply that Samuel Eliot Morison had done pretty well with the *History of United States Naval Operations in World War Two,* that Arthur Schlesinger, Jr., had seemed to regard the New Deal as history when he wrote his three-volume set, and that Winston Churchill's writings on the Second World War seemed to be accepted as history by a few serious people, his frozen smile, had I been able to bottle it, would have provided air conditioning for the southwestern deserts for many centuries to come. Needless to say, I am not a staff member of the Newberry Library.

Within this context Michael Lawson's writings are certainly a breath of fresh air. In my mind, he represents one of the finest and best scholarly traditions and one that must be recovered if we are ever to grasp our history away from the ashen-faced rodents who inhabit the archives of our institutions. The reading and writing of history should be returned to the people who have truly experienced it.

I am therefore delighted, enthusiastic, and honored to be asked to write this foreword. I think this is a splendid book and one worthy of everyone's serious attention. Furthermore, I would urge young scholars, both Indian and non-Indian, to look to this work as a model of the kind of research that must be done if we are ever to make sense of our past and understand our present. I hope that this book inspires the timid and conservative western historians to march into the twentieth century before it vanishes, to leave their fantasies of the West behind and to search for the West that is always changing, as well as the people who experience that change. We cannot turn the clock back, but we can certainly make note of the past as a prologue to the future.

This work is but one of countless volumes about American Indians and American communities. While one cannot begin to compare it with the other stories that have been written, because so many exist, one can certainly read this story and learn from it. We must sharpen our wits and determine that the future can and will be better.

PREFACE

Sioux writer Vine Deloria, Jr., once described federal-Indian relations in this country as a series of land transactions. Indeed, the government of the United States, in dealing with Native Americans, seems to have enjoyed its greatest success in reducing their original land base. Over two billion acres have passed out of tribal hands, much of it while under the supposedly protective surpervision of the Bureau of Indian Affairs.

The history of the application of the European doctrines of discovery and conquest to native tribes in the eighteenth and nineteenth centuries is well known, as is the evolution of policies which recognized them as "domestic dependent nations" under federal trusteeship. The subsequent saga of massacres, deprivations, and broken treaties, which resulted from the exercise of territorial imperatives on both sides, has likewise occupied the pens of many historians. It is less familiar that the struggle for land and sovereignty did not end in the bloody snowbanks of Wounded Knee in 1890, but has continued into the present century, for even greater stakes.

Preoccupied with the dramatic military confrontations of the nineteenth century, historians of federal Indian policy have, until recently, paid too little attention to the erosion of native land and water rights which has persisted to the present day. Because of the marginal nature of much of their remaining land and resources, this erosion of rights has become increasingly detrimental to Indian interests. The land has long constituted the very essence of tribal existence, and the future of many tribes today depends on their ability to utilize and control their own resources. Consequently these issues have become far too grave to be ignored.

Although the United States federal government has gradually become more subtle and sophisticated in its land acquisition methods, the consequences for Native Americans have changed but little. Treaty rights are now infringed on by statute rather than by brute force, and expanded federal administrative powers have replaced the militarily enforced reservation and land allotment policies of old. Tribes continue to be victimized by the fraudulence, ignorance, and deception with which the federal government conducts many of its Indian affairs. Tribal members still suffer from the conflict of interest that exists with the Department of the Interior between the Bureau of Indian Affairs and the other component land and water agencies. In exercising its trust responsibilities, the federal government persists in maintaining peremptory powers over tribal lands and continues to support white interests in decisions affecting native resources.

Increasingly in the twentieth century the United States has used its power of eminent domain to obtain large parcels of Indian land for public works projects. Because tribal groups have traditionally settled in river valleys, these appropriations have most often taken place as part of flood control and reclamation projects. Yet land has also been condemned for a variety of other federal purposes. The Department of Agriculture was allowed to establish a National Forest on land belonging to the Chippewas in Minnesota; the Bureau of Land Management permitted an airport to be built on property owned by the Quechan tribe on the Yuma Reservation in California; land of the Kansas Potawatomis was taken to allow a right-of-way for the Union Pacific Railroad; and a large portion of the Pine Ridge Sioux Reservation in South Dakota was turned over to the United States Army for use as a bombing range.

Since World War II several reservations have been adversely affected by the construction of federally administered dam projects on the nation's major rivers. Provisions of one of the oldest Indian agreements, the Canandaigua or Pickering Treaty of 1794, were broken when nine thousand acres of Seneca land were taken on the Upper Allegheny for the Kinzua Dam, which flooded the villages where the extraordinary Iroquois prophet Handsome Lake once held forth. The tribes of the Fort Mohave, Chemehuevi Valley, Colorado River, Yuma, and Gila Bend reservations in Arizona and California have likewise lost sizable parcels of land to reservoir projects in the Colorado River Basin.

While these projects claim to provide improved flood control, navigation, irrigation, hydroelectric power, recreation, and other benefits for the general public, Native Americans seem always to be the last to receive such advantages. Federal dams not only have produced immeasurable grief for the unfortunate people who lived within the reservoir areas but also have destroyed the natural ecology and aesthetic quality of their environment. The necessity of these projects, as well as their safety, increasingly has been questioned.

Concerned only with the greater accomplishments of these massive structures, developmentalists too often have ignored that smaller, more delicate matters of economic and human concern also are involved in the construction of the dams. It is precisely in regard to the emotion-laden problems of dislocation, with the individual and collective suffering that it brings to families and communities, that the federal government and the United States Army Corps of Engineers, in particular, has demonstrated an appalling lack of sensitivity.

The Pick-Sloan Plan, the joint water development program developed by the Corps of Engineers and the Bureau of Reclamation in 1944 for the Missouri River Basin, caused more damage to Indian land than any other public works project in America. The Chippewas, Mandans, Hidatsas, and Arikaras of North Dakota; the Shoshones and Arapahos of Wyoming; the Crows, Crees, Blackfeet, and Assiniboines of Montana; and virtually every other native group with land along the Missouri and its tributaries were made to suffer. In addition, three of the projects constructed by the United States Army under Pick-Sloan—the Fort Randall, Oahe,

and Big Bend dams—flooded over 202,000 acres of Sioux land on
the Standing Rock, Cheyenne River, Lower Brule, Crow Creek,
and Yankton reservations in North and South Dakota.

These five reservations provide material for an appropriate case
study of both the federal acquisition of trust land and the application of recent Indian policies. First, these Sioux people were forced,
in violation of their treaty rights and without prior consultation,
to relinquish their best land and resources, to evacuate their homes
and ranches in the wooded bottomlands along the Missouri, and to
take up new homes on the marginal prairie lands that remained
within their reservations. Hence, the disruption of their way of
life was more severe than is usually the case with people displaced
by public works projects. Second, the debate over what constituted
just compensation in their case became inextricably involved in
prevailing arguments over "termination" and other policies by
which the federal government hoped in the 1950s to conduct its
future Indian affairs. In addition, since the three Pick-Sloan projects have now been completed for several years, and since the
Indian policies so vigorously debated during that era have long
been rejected, sufficient time has elapsed since the Sioux were
dislocated both to place these events in perspective and to allow
an evaluation of their consequences.

As this study demonstrates, the damages suffered by the Missouri
River Sioux tribes far outweigh the benefits provided them to date
by the Pick-Sloan Plan. The chapters that follow offer a brief
historical sketch of the Missouri Basin, the Pick-Sloan legislation,
and the land and people of these five Sioux reservations. There is
a detailed summary of developments during the years in which the
impact of the federal water projects was most intensely felt by the
Sioux. An effort has been made throughout to provide a thorough
analysis of these developments, to show how they relate to the
continuum of federal Indian policy, and to demonstrate the inter-
action that took place at every level between tribal members, federal
representatives, neighboring white communities, and others who
came to play a part in this episode.

It is hoped above all that this work will encourage historians to
be more interested in recent Indian problems. Despite the great
variety and abundance of topics, materials, and resources available

to scholars, the list of good published works in this area remains pitifully small. This dearth of contemporary research, when coupled with the strong historiographical emphasis on nineteenth-century Indian affairs, has served both to distort the public image of modern Native Americans and their problems and to keep tribal members themselves ignorant of developments which impact drastically on their daily lives. As a result many of the most important events of the present century remain to be placed in historical perspective.

Finally, it should be pointed out that the views expressed in this volume represent the author's observations as an independent scholar and not as an official representative of the Bureau of Indian Affairs.

ACKNOWLEDGMENTS

I acknowledge and appreciate above all the cooperation of those tribal members whose openly shared observations made this work far more meaningful than it otherwise might have been. I am also indebted to the people of many agencies and institutions for generous assistance in helping me gather material for this study, although they are too numerous to mention individually. Special thanks must go to the professional staffs of several libraries and archives. These include the Library of Congress, the National Archives, the Department of the Interior Library, the Federal Records Center in Denver and in Kansas City, the Harry S. Truman Presidential Library, the State Historical Society of North Dakota, the South Dakota State Historical Society, the libraries of the University of Nebraska and the University of New Mexico, and the American Indian Research Project at both Northern State College and the University of South Dakota. My gratitude is similarly extended to personnel of the Office of Files and Records Research and the Aberdeen and Billings Area Offices of the Bureau of Indian Affairs, the Missouri River Division of the U.S. Army Corps of Engineers, and the Midwest Regional Office of the National Park Service.

I am eternally grateful for the continued encouragement and support of my major advisor, Professor Richard N. Ellis, who taught me more about being an active historian than most students ever have an opportunity to learn. Additional thanks must go to Professors Donald C. Cutter and Gerald D. Nash of the University of New Mexico and Vine Deloria, Jr., of the University of Arizona for reading the manuscript and offering valuable suggestions. Permission is gratefully acknowledged from Dayton W. Canaday, Director of the South Dakota State Historical Society, to publish the copyrighted material in this book, which previously appeared in a somewhat different format in *South Dakota Historical Collections* (1974) and *South Dakota History* (Spring, 1976); as is a grant from the Graduate Research Committee of the University of New Mexico, which helped defray research expenses.

Mere words can never adequately express or repay the debt to my wife Marcia for the hard sacrifices that permitted a soldier to become a scholar, the gentle patience that made hard times bearable, and the undying faith which assured that the established goal would be attained. Her more tangible contributions to this volume have included her skill in making editorial revisions and her invaluable assistance in conducting interviews.

Finally, I would like to thank my friend Albert Elkins of the Smithsonian Institution for designing the map.

DAMMED INDIANS

Chapter 1

THE MISSOURI: RIVER, VALLEY, BASIN

There is only one river with a personality, habits, dissipations, a sense of humor, and a woman's caprice; a river that goes travelling sidewise, that interferes in politics, rearranges geography, and dabbles in real estate; a river that plays hide and seek with you today and tomorrow follows you around like a pet dog with a dynamite cracker tied to its tail.

The Missouri River was located in the United States at last report. It cuts corners, runs around at night, lunches on levees, and swallows islands and small villages for dessert. Its perpetual dissatisfaction with its bed is the greatest peculiarity of the Missouri. Time after time it has gotten out of its bed in the middle of the night with no apparent provocation, and has hunted a new bed, all littered with forests, cornfields, brick houses, railroad ties, and telegraph poles. Later it has suddenly taken a fancy to its old bed, which by this time has been filled with suburban architecture, and back it has gone with a whoop and a rush as if it had really found something worthwhile. It makes farming as fascinating as gambling. You never know whether you are going to harvest corn or catfish. (George Fitch, American Magazine, *1907.)*

The Missouri River is an enigma. Despite over a century of human attempts to understand and control it, America's longest waterway remains perplexing and mysterious. The river eludes the efforts of

3

modern technology to tame it fully and continues to provide water of uncertain quantity and quality. It either furnishes too much of it, as it did during the disastrous floods of 1844, 1881,1943, and 1951, or too little of it, as was the case during the severe droughts of the 1860s, 1890s, 1920s, and 1930s. In the thirties farmers joked that the river's water was "too thick to drink and a mite too thin to plow." Although the reservoirs behind the six giant dams in Montana and the Dakotas are now as blue-green as Lake Superior, the greater length of the river is still murky, coffee-colored, and full of silt. Like the Indians who first discovered it, the modern residents of the Missouri Valley still call their river Big Muddy.[1]

Originating on the Continental Divide in Yellowstone and Glacier national parks and western Montana, the Missouri flows through seven states on its 2,465-mile course. From the town of Three Forks, where the Jefferson and Gallatin rivers unite with the Madison after rushing down from Montana's Bitterroot Range, this mad elephant of a river charges northward to Fort Benton and then eastward into North Dakota. From there it meanders on a southeast diagonal across South Dakota and along the Nebraska-Iowa and Kansas-Missouri borders, before shifting eastward again across Missouri to join the Mississippi just north of St. Louis. For most of its length the Missouri flows in a trench that measures as much as ten miles from bluff to bluff. This immediate floodplain is called the Missouri Valley. The river's huge drainage area, which covers 513,000 square miles in ten states, is properly termed the Missouri Basin.[2]

This is a land of great diversity. The lower basin, part of the Central Lowlands, is humid and green with lush farmlands and abundant rainfall. Most of the region's population and wealth is concentrated in this area. The upper basin is arid, brown ranch country with long, bitter winters and some of the harshest sweeps of empty land outside of the Russian steppes. This is the Great Plains that stretch eastward from the Rockies for 400 miles, sloping so gradually in elevation from 5,500 to 1,500 feet that they appear flat. This prehistoric seabed, whose significance in our nation's history has been so classically described by Walter Prescott Webb, is a no-man's-land of unpredictable moisture. Dry but fertile, this "Great American Desert" provided the stiffest challenge to America's frontier settlement.[3]

The physical extremes are extraordinary in the basin. There are boundless spaces and crowded metropolises, tall peaks and flat bottomlands, heavy rains and snows, destructive droughts and dust, intense cold and heat, dense forests and prairie wastelands, constant dry winds and suffocating humidity. Stream characteristics differ greatly. Tributaries vary from one hundred to one thousand miles in length, and there is wide fluctuation in seasonal flows. Falls are rapid on the Milk, Yellowstone, Little Missouri, Cheyenne, and other upper-basin streams. In the lower basin the current of the Platte, Kansas, Grand, Osage, and Gasconde Rivers is slow and sluggish. The James River, the only major eastern tributary in the upper basin, has a moderate flow.

Basin people also differ greatly, but they are generally an optimistic, pragmatic, proud, and determined lot. The constant rigors of this environment have endowed them with stoicism, patience, and perseverance. Although much of this land is dull, dreary, and inhospitable, it holds for many a compelling fascination—a love and lure perhaps best described in the classic works of Hamlin Garland, Willa Cather, Ole Rölvaag, and Mari Sandoz.

A colorful history is derived from these people and the varied landscape. This is the land of the stereotypical wild West with its trappers, explorers, and trail blazers; prospectors, drovers, and homesteaders; Indian chiefs and Indian fighters; steamboat captains and railroad engineers. Lewis and Clark, Long and Pike, Lisa, Astor, and Chouteau; Custer and Buffalo Bill, Crazy Horse, Sitting Bull, and Red Cloud; Wild Bill, Calamity Jane, and Jesse James; all carved out their historical niche on this ground. The challenge of this land profoundly modified American institutions and technology, just as the men and women who grew up there altered American politics. Missouri Basin people witnessed the rise of such important movements as the Populist Party, Non-Partisan League, and Farmer's Holiday Association. This area contributed such eminent figures as Jeanette Rankin, Thomas J. Walsh, Mike Mansfield, Gerald Nye, William Lemke, George McGovern, William Jennings Bryan, George W. Norris, and Harry S. Truman.

Great buffalo herds once fattened on the Missouri shores before drifting with the rains. The Sioux and other tribes wandered with the buffalo after the introduction of the horse, and this movement created a distinct aboriginal culture on the Plains. White settlers encroached on the region even before this culture reached its apex. Most of the land came under American jurisdiction with the Louisiana Purchase in 1803. Soldiers were dispatched from St. Louis to explore it, and an international group of fur trappers fought for trade advantages "across the wide Missouri." In 1820, Major Stephen H. Long looked out over the Great Plains and confirmed the observations of all previous explorers. He labeled it "The Great American Desert" because it was unfit for the kind of agriculture that was familiar in the more humid and timbered East.

Emigrants crossed these barren lands to the rich valleys of Oregon and California. Keelboats and steamboats ventured up the Missouri as far as Fort Benton. Silver brought settlers to Colorado in the 1850s while the slavery issue increased the population of Missouri and Kansas. A nation undivided by slavery refused to be split by geography, and the relentless progress of settlement continued. Steel rails converted the great desert into plains, cities sprouted on main transportation lines, and cattlemen discovered native grasses ideal for open grazing. As homesteaders advanced the farmer's frontier, it became apparent that new techniques were needed to cope with the special problems posed by transportation, construction, water, fencing, and Indians in this environment. Windmills, barbed wire, sod houses, dry-farming methods, new grains, and repeating weapons were ingeniously adapted, and social and economic institutions were tailored, to fit the subhumid climate. Native tribes were forcibly dispossessed and pacified, trees were planted, and family farms rapidly encroached on the open cattle ranges. Heated controversies arose between farmers, ranchers, packers, and railroad interests over some of the most important political and economic issues of the late nineteenth and early twentieth centuries. Speculation, overstocking, and the severe winter of 1885-86 destroyed the cattle bonanza, and by the turn of the century nearly all arable land had been settled.

In spite of new institutions and technologies that permitted settlement of the Missouri Basin, settlers were never prepared to cope with the cyclical periods of boom and bust, flood and drought, which have characterized the region since the fourteenth century.[4] Most farmers ignored Major John Wesley Powell's prudent observation in 1878 that large-scale irrigated farming offered the only safe means of agricultural livelihood in this area. They gambled instead that their fields would have adequate moisture. Over half of them lost, and America's agrarian frontier receded for the first time. Boom and bust persisted. In the early nineties farmers faced a severe drought in 1890 and 1891, a grasshopper infestation in 1892, and the financial panic of 1893. In the second half of the decade there followed the boom year of 1896 with its good rains and the immigrant explosion of 1899. The cycle returned with World War I. Because increased demand put millions of acres to the plow, record profits were enjoyed. Market contractions, over-production, and indebtedness burst this bubble in the 1920s, and the rapid extension of croplands only served to exhaust the soil and contributed to the Great Dust Bowl of the following decade.

The depression and drought of the 1930s had a profound effect on social, political, and economic life in the Missouri Basin. Hard times forced over 300,000 farmers out of the region, and the federal government poured in over a billion dollars in relief funds to aid those who stayed. Adversity sped acceptance of a large number of agricultural innovations, including modern farm machinery and improved irrigation techniques. Large commercial operations replaced subsistence farms in the years that followed, and more attention was paid to soil and water conservation and land-use planning. The public became aware of the region's serious social and economic problems, and the first federal programs were initiated to control and stabilize farm production and to improve the quality of rural life. New methods and programs not only increased productivity and efficiency but also reduced hardship and risk. Improved communication and transportation more fully integrated the region's population into the mainstream of American social and economic life. Nevertheless, some old problems persisted, and new ones developed.[5]

If the frontier was at least a psychological safety valve for urban masses in the East, the cities of the Missouri Basin have, since the 1930s, become a real safety valve for a rapidly declining rural population. Many migrants have successfully adjusted to urban life, and their migration has taken some pressure off those who remain on the land. For many who treasure the rural way of life, the transition has not been easy. This is particularly true of the region's

Indian population. The loss of the most productive element of the population, coupled with an increase in the proportion of elderly and indigent, has placed a severe strain on rural institutions. The increased dependence on urban tax subsidies and the inability of cities themselves to attract sufficient commercial and industrial revenues to sustain economic growth remain among the region's most profound problems.[6]

The most persistent problem in the Missouri Basin is the efficient use and control of water. The search for more and better utilization of this precious element has characterized the region since the Mandans and other settled tribes first diverted the Missouri to irrigate corn in the seventeenth century. The struggle continued as ranchers battled for choice water holes and the sodbusters tried to raise crops on the Plains. Lack of water has retarded industrialization and kept the population scattered. The problem is now heightened by the ever-increasing demands of commercial agriculture, industry, and municipalities for more and more water and hydroelectric power.

Controlling water has been a very serious problem. Floods have always plagued the basin, even centuries ago when nearly all the land was covered with timber and grass. The Missouri was in flood stage when Father Jacques Marquette discovered it in 1673. Heavy rains, ice jams, rapid spring thaws, and excessive runoffs have regularly sent the river and its tributaries crashing over their banks. This flooding has exacted an enormous toll in lives and money, carrying away homes and possessions, destroying crops and livestock, and rendering the land useless. Record crest stages and peak discharges occurred on the mainstream in 1844, 1881, 1903, and 1927. Serious floods also took place in 1917 and 1935. Between 1936 and 1950, 200 people were killed and 250,000 displaced by the river's rampaging yellow waters. But it was not until the destructive inundations of 1943 that the federal government decided to take the first large-scale measures to control the Missouri.[7]

Chapter 2

BIG PLANS FOR BIG MUDDY

On April 12, 1943, a sudden spring thaw caused the Missouri River to crest to its 1881 flood stage in Nebraska and southern South Dakota. Six lives were lost as the stream spilled over 70,000 acres of fertile bottomland, destroying $8 million in property and severely damaging the city of Omaha. In May torrential rains in the lower basin brought the Missouri to 1844 flood levels, inundating over 540,000 acres and causing $7 million in property damage. Rain accumulations of seven inches per day during the second week of June flooded an additional 960,000 acres and destroyed $32.5 million worth of property in Kansas and Missouri. The river jumped its banks again the next spring and flooded 4.5 million acres of rich farmland, bringing the two-year damage total to over $100 million.[1]

Basin residents cried for federal aid and relief. Congressmen from flooded districts demanded new flood-control surveys. Their requests pressed the federal government into action and touched off one of the decade's most hotly debated legislative issues; one that went far beyond the mere problem of controlling the Missouri.

On May 13, 1943, the House Flood Control Committee ordered the United States Army Corps of Engineers to survey flood-control needs in the Missouri Basin and to prepare a plan of action. Colonel Lewis A. Pick, Missouri Basin division engineer at Omaha, was specifically assigned this task. Though only slightly experienced in

9

flood-control construction, Colonel Pick wasted no time in carrying out his mission. Within ninety days he submitted to the chief of engineers in Washington a ten-page report, which became known as the Pick Plan.[2]

Since 1824 the Corps of Engineers had been authorized by Congress to regulate navigation of the nation's major rivers and harbors. This construction branch of the army became involved in flood control because local authorities proved unable to handle water problems and graduates of the U.S. Military Academy at West Point were found to be the only qualified government engineers who could. The federal government assumed this power under the commerce clause of the constitution. The corps' first involvement on the Missouri began in 1838 when two army boats were ordered to remove snags on the river. Congressional appropriations for channel improvements were first authorized in 1852. In 1912 the army engineers began a project to enhance navigation by providing an assured six-foot channel on the river from the Mississippi to Kansas City. This project was extended to Sioux City, Iowa, in 1925. By 1945 the corps had spent nearly $300 million to deepen the river for navigation.[3]

In the years following World War I federal control over the nation's waterways expanded liberally. The power of the Corps of Engineers grew because it was the oldest, most extensive, and most influential agency dealing with national water problems. The exigencies of war led to the establishment of dams at Muscle Shoals, in Alabama, in 1916. New and growing demands for public power production, comprehensive water-resource planning, and multiple-purpose dam construction brought about successive passage of the Federal Power Commission Act in 1920, the Boulder Dam Act in 1928, the Tennessee Valley Authority Act in 1933, and the extensive Rivers and Harbors Act of 1936. These enactments established policies that boldly extended federal power from the mere control of commerce on navigable streams to multiple-use authority over entire watersheds.[4]

Following a series of damaging floods in 1927, Congress directed the corps to conduct the most exhaustive hydrological study ever made of the Missouri River. Four years of extensive research resulted in the publication in 1933 of a 1,245-page document called the 308 Report. This study served as a technical source book for all future army developments in the basin, including the sweeping plans proposed by Colonel Pick in 1943. Under the influence of the chief of engineers, General Lytle Brown, the corps had given up its "levees-only" engineering philosophy and had withdrawn its seventy-five-year opposition to reservoirs as an orthodox method of flood control. Gradually the army had come to realize that reservoir storage was necessary to assure continuance of its navigation projects.[5]

The 308 Report concluded that the best site for a reservoir on the Missouri was at Fort Peck, Montana. Since navigation storage here meshed easily with New Deal public power goals, the army had little trouble in persuading President Franklin D. Roosevelt to authorize construction of Fort Peck Dam as a National Industrial Recovery Act project in 1933.[6] The corps wanted construction specifications to permit the depth of the Missouri navigation channel to be increased from six to nine feet. To accomplish this, they built the largest earth dam in the world and the biggest reservoir since Hoover Dam.[7] The army thus became firmly entrenched in the business of constructing massive multiple-purpose dam projects on the Missouri's main stem. The powers and techniques established at Fort Peck determined to a great extent the dominant role the Corps of Engineers would have in the future development of the entire Missouri Basin.[8]

Slowly the army learned that floods evoke more public support for specific projects than do navigation plans. After a flash flood raged down the Republican River in 1935, killing 105 residents of Nebraska and Kansas, Congress authorized construction of several local levee projects as part of the first nationwide Flood Control Act in 1936. Floods in 1937 brought about approval of nine reservoirs on lower Missouri tributaries to protect Kansas City and other towns. The first flood-control reservoirs in the headwaters of the Missouri system were authorized in 1941,[9] including two dams to protect Denver and an agricultural levee network stretching from Kansas City to Sioux City.

Before Colonel Pick began to devise his daring new plan for the Missouri in 1943, the Corps of Engineers had rapidly revolutionized its engineering techniques and philosophy and had greatly expanded its functions and powers beyond its constitutional limitations. The army was then involved in local projects totally unrelated to mainstream navigation and had cast aside its concern for maintaining a balanced budget. The concept of multiple-purpose dam construction had paved the way for these developments and had permitted the corps to bring power production, flood control, irrigation, recreation, and numerous other functions within the full range of its capabilities. The stage was now set for the broadest application of these new powers.[10]

The man who was the bold architect of the army's new plan was neither a hydrological engineer nor a product of West Point. His expertise was in the construction of airfields and arsenals; his degree was from Virginia Polytechnic Institute. Colonel Pick had served as senior engineer of the Missouri River Division for just one year when he was asked to design a water-development program. Later, after three of his Montana airfields had to be abandoned by the Air Force, he was described by General Thomas A. Robbins, deputy chief of engineers, as having the "sorriest record" in runway construction of any division commander. Pick redeemed himself and gained stature as the builder of the Ledo Road in Burma, which became known as Pick's Pike during the last days of World War II. This war accomplishment and the wide acclaim given his plan for the Missouri Basin catapulted Pick into the position of chief of engineers in 1949. He retired with three stars in 1953.[11]

Pick's plan for the river, completed in August, 1943, called for construction of three groups of projects by the Corps of Engineers. The first, an obvious response to recent floods, was the building of 1,500 miles of protective levees from Sioux City to the Mississippi. The second plan included construction of eighteen tributary dams, of which eleven had already been authorized by Congress. Of the seven new projects, five were on the headwaters of the Republican River in the lower basin and two were high on the Big Horn and Yellowstone rivers in Wyoming and Montana, respectively. Finally, the third and most dynamic proposal called for development of five huge multiple-purpose dams on the main stem of the Missouri above Sioux City. These giant projects would permit the army to apply liberally its new knowledge about earth dams and their construction. Cost for the total package was estimated at $490 million.[12]

Colonel Pick's proposals appealed openly to pervading New Deal ideas concerning multiple-purpose, basin-wide water development. They also took full advantage of the public alarm caused by recent flood damages. Unlike the prototype program established in the Tennessee Valley, the army plan did not relinquish power to an independent public corporation; it required full authority over all proposed projects. Many problems were deliberately left vague in the brief report. Exact flowage estimates, reservoir specifications, and procedures for the distribution of power and irrigation water were notably missing. No attempt was made either to justify project costs in terms of anticipated benefits or to address the important question of water availability for all intended purposes. As time passed the reasons for the colonel's vagueness and brevity became more apparent.[13]

From the army's point of view the Pick Plan was a stroke of genius. Although it set forth the most extensive set of proposals ever developed by the Corps of Engineers, it did so in simple language easily comprehended by the average layman. This made it easier to publicize and also facilitated congressional review. Because of its scope, the plan proclaimed army dominance over Missouri Basin waters and defiantly challenged the corps' closest rival, the Department of the Interior's Bureau of Reclamation, as well as advocates of an independent valley authority. It helped overcome the corps' "inactive" image in the region and greatly increased its visibility in the public eye. If not a brilliant engineer, Colonel Pick proved a master publicist. He was, after all, the man responsible for bringing the first public-relations experts into the corps, and he fully realized the advantages of political salesmanship.[14]

Seven months before the army submitted the Pick Plan to Congress in February, 1944, Colonel Pick, without authorization, began promoting his program on the banquet circuit throughout the basin. As a result his proposals gained nationwide publicity even before they received executive review. This raised the ire of President Roosevelt. On February 6, 1944, he ordered the director of the budget to return Pick's plan to the secretary of war for revision, pointing out, among other things, that it conflicted with existing Bureau of Reclamation plans in the upper basin and did not fit current presidential objectives. The president also criticized the proposal for failing to provide maximum power development and for neglecting to make provision for soil conservation or other watershed treatment programs. Without awaiting further executive action, the House Flood Control Committee began hearings on the army plan. Present at the proceedings were the governors of several upper-basin states, whose opposition to the corps proposals underscored the president's objections.[15]

To the people of the scarce-water states of the upper Missouri Basin it was obvious that the Pick Plan's greatest benefits would accrue to lower-basin residents. They feared that emphasis on flood control and navigation would interfere with their own desire to develop irrigation. The governors of Wyoming, Montana, and North Dakota were thus dispatched to Washington to protest army plans. After their arrival they were surprised to learn of a separate Corps of Engineers bill before Congress to deepen the Missouri navigation channel from six to nine feet.[16] The governors immediately claimed that this project, long proposed but never authorized, would leave no water at all for irrigation, and the Bureau of Reclamation soon affirmed their view. There was an attempt to protect upper-basin interests. Senators Joseph O'Mahoney of Wyoming and Eugene D. Millikin of Colorado introduced amendments to both the Pick Plan and the navigation-channel bill in the Senate Commerce Committee. They demanded that irrigation be given priority over navigation, that the arid states west of the ninety-eighth meridian be given superior rights to the use of basin water, and that Congress be required to submit all proposed legislation for watershed development to the states directly involved.[17]

Lower-basin residents attacked the O'Mahoney-Millikin amendments. They opposed any limitations that might retard plans to control and to prevent the floods from which they continually suffered, and they mustered enough support in the committee to defeat the amendments. Nevertheless, senators from the upper basin were still powerful enough to block eventual passage of the Pick Plan in Congress if irrigation rights were not assured. The need for compromise became obvious. After further debate the amendments were added to the pending bills, and irrigation was finally given theoretical primacy over navigation. While this controversy was being resolved, the Bureau of Reclamation came forth with its own comprehensive plan for the Missouri Basin.[18]

For five years the Reclamation Bureau had conducted an extensive study of the region's water needs. This research was aimed at the formulation of a comprehensive development plan by 1945. When the army unveiled the Pick Plan and asserted the authority of the Corps of Engineers over Missouri waters, Bureau of Reclamation engineers were caught off guard, as was the entire Interior Department. As a result a speedy completion of the Reclamation Bureau's plan was ordered in the hope that it could be introduced in Congress before the Pick Plan was approved. Responsibility for this task was given to William Glenn Sloan, a relatively minor bureaucrat, who had already done considerable work on the plan.[19]

Sloan was then the assistant director of the Bureau of Reclamation's regional office in Billings, Montana. Known as something of an engineering maverick, he was at the time held in disfavor by his immediate superiors. Like Colonel Pick, however, he proved an intrepid decision maker, a skilled politician, and a vigorous defender of his agency.[20]

Since 1902 the Bureau of Reclamation had been the federal government's primary water-development agency in the arid states of the West. Created in that year as part of Theodore Roosevelt's conservation program and established within the Department of the Interior, it devoted most of its efforts to irrigation, although flood control and hydroelectric power became important by-products of its dam projects. Hoover Dam on the Colorado River, Grand Coulee Dam on the Columbia, and other early marvels of the bureau's engineering contributed greatly to the development of the West. By 1944 the agency had spent over $900 million converting 16 million acres of dry wasteland into fertile farms. Eleven of its projects had been completed in the Missouri Basin, and nine more were under construction. Having concluded that irrigation alone could not pay for itself in this region, the bureau began in 1933 the Kendrick project, its first multiple-purpose structure in the basin.[21]

On May 4, 1944, the Reclamation Bureau submitted its Missouri Basin report to Congress. This 211-page document, labeled the Sloan Plan, was far more detailed and specific than the Pick Plan, which by then had been approved by the House of Representatives. Ninety projects were proposed with emphasis on irrigation and power development. Total reservoir capacity was nearly the same as that proposed by the army. But the Reclamation Bureau wanted its storage developed in smaller dams located in the headwaters rather than downstream and on tributaries rather than the main stem. Three large Pick projects on the Missouri were thus eliminated, and three other army structures, including Fort Peck Dam, were modified, giving priority to irrigation and power rather than flood control and navigation. Sloan kept two main-stem dams and added another to permit construction of massive diversion systems to irrigate the areas of the Dakotas hardest hit by drought.[22]

Sloan's plan promised, for an unbelievable $1.26 billion, to irrigate 4.8 million acres of land and to produce four billion kilowatt-hours of power annually. Yet other functions were not ignored. The Corps of Engineers' navigation channel was incorporated into the plan, sufficient flowage permitting, and ample municipal and domestic water supplies also were programmed. The Bureau of Reclamation, like the army, made no attempt to assure sufficient water for all project purposes, although it did admit that shortages might eliminate future navigation. Unlike the Pick Plan, Sloan's report presented economic justification for its proposals by estimating that federal sales of irrigation water and hydroelectric power would more than cover all project costs.[23]

Congress now had to consider two plans representing the contending claims, goals, and ambitions of two powerful federal agencies with fundamentally different dominant interests. Each plan was supported by an influential lobby in Washington and was backed by various regional interests within the basin itself. Major support for the Pick Plan came from the National Rivers and Harbors Congress, the Mississippi Valley Association, the Propeller Club of the United States, the American Merchant Marine Conference, and the Mississippi Valley Flood Control Association. The Sloan Plan was endorsed by the National Reclamation Association and the National Grange. Spokesmen from the lower basin charged that the Bureau of Reclamation plan disregarded their flood-control needs and ignored the economic importance of navigation. They thought it foolish to divert water from these purposes to create upper-basin farms, whose products eventually would compete with their own in the agricultural marketplace. Upper-basin residents argued against this view.

As the debate became more heated, Colonel Pick and Assistant Director Sloan grew to despise each other. The Reclamation Bureau engineer claimed that his agency was more familiar with basin problems and felt that his program offered a more comprehensive and balanced approach to eventual solutions than the army plan did. Pick and his supporters argued that the opposite was true. As chairman of the Missouri River States Committee, an unofficial body composed of the governors of the ten basin states, Governor Marcellus Quintas ("M. Q.") Sharpe of South Dakota endorsed the Pick Plan in a report to Congress. Governors of the other states soon protested that they had not approved the report. Battle was thus joined, compromise refused, and the plans of Pick and Sloan seemed irreconcilable.[24]

At this point, in the apparent stalemate, the *St. Louis Post-Dispatch* offered yet another proposal. A full-page editorial on May 4, 1944, urged basin residents to resolve their differences and to cooperate by bringing forth an even more unified water-development plan for the Missouri. It suggested that this be accomplished under the auspices of a Missouri Valley Authority (MVA).[25]

The establishment of an MVA had first been proposed by Senator George W. Norris of Nebraska in 1934. Norris was the creator of the Tennessee Valley Authority (TVA), which had been authorized the previous year. He had introduced legislation providing for a comprehensive program patterned after TVA, managed by an independent public corporation, and maintained by the Bureau of Reclamation. The urgency of a dynamic overall plan of water development and flood control was not apparent during the drought years. Support was lacking for the Norris bill, and Congress was content, for at least the next decade, to enact piecemeal measures for flood control in the basin.[26]

Revival of the MVA idea threatened the vested interests both of the Corps of Engineers and of the Bureau of Reclamation. Each agency wanted full authority over its own proposed projects. Colonel Pick had drafted legislation vesting complete federal responsibility over basin waters in an army-controlled Missouri Basin Commission.[27] The Department of the Interior was equally determined to have an expanded role in developing the region's postwar economy. The idea of an MVA, however, struck a responsive chord.

The success of TVA's experiment in "grassroots democracy" was almost universally acclaimed. The idea of extending the formula to their own region appealed to many basin residents, especially those suspicious of the intentions of existing federal water agencies. A pro-MVA campaign, spearheaded by the *Post-Dispatch,* gathered momentum during the summer of 1944. Support came from liberal Democrats, organized labor, and the National Farmers Union, which claimed over 140,000 basin members.[28]

On August 18, 1944, Senator James Murray of Montana, the MVA's leading political proponent, introduced the first of many bills for the creation of a Missouri Valley Authority.[29] Extension of the TVA principles of comprehensive planning, multipurpose development, decentralized administration, and expanded hydro-electric power was in obvious accord with the political philosophy of the New Deal. In a speech to Congress on September 21, President Roosevelt fully endorsed MVA and also recommended establishment of valley authorities for the Arkansas and Colorado river basins.[30]

Growing MVA support effectively dissolved the Pick-Sloan deadlock. No matter how much the Corps of Engineers and Bureau of Reclamation hated each other they hated the idea of another public corporation even more. As reluctant as the two agencies were to compromise, it soon became evident that political expediency demanded just that to forestall MVA. Elements of the water lobby, including the National Reclamation Association, the National Water Conservation Conference, and the Missouri River States Committee cried for the two organizations to resolve their differences and to combine their programs. Finally swayed by this argument, federal engineers established a committee for this purpose and scheduled a conference in Omaha to draft a "joint engineering report."[31]

On October 17, 1944, a one-page agreement rapidly produced at the Omaha Conference merged the Pick and Sloan plans. In just two days army and Bureau of Reclamation representatives pooled over 1,400 pages of technical data, specifying an exact number of projects and determining their precise jurisdiction. In effect, each group of engineers merely accepted the other's proposed projects. The Corps of Engineers was granted authority over all main-stem dams and those tributary projects primarily designed for flood control and navigation. Both were authorized to develop hydroelectric power and other benefits at their separate sites. The Reclamation Bureau accepted the army's five main-stem dams. The corps agreed to the bureau's plan for twenty-seven dams in the Yellowstone Basin, instead of the two it had proposed. Sites were also exchanged on the Niobrara, Platte, and Kansas rivers. Of the 113 projects proposed by the separate plans 107 were mutually accepted in this new "Missouri Compromise." Within a few days after the conference, legislation encompassing the joint Pick-Sloan Plan was introduced in Congress, where it was favorably received.[32]

The consolidation of the Pick and Sloan plans was described by James S. Patton, president of the National Farmers Union, as "a shameless, loveless shotgun wedding."[33] The reluctant partners of this unlikely union were certainly not motivated by an abiding affection. Pregnant with power, each of necessity was reconciled to accept the other's offspring. Together they approved $150 million worth of projects that one or the other had previously considered worthless. No attempt was made to consolidate or justify costs, exact project dimensions were never specified, and duplication remained. The problem of determining whether or not enough water existed to provide for both irrigation and navigation was ignored, even though W. Glenn Sloan himself publicly doubted that there was enough. Details concerning development and distribution of hydroelectric power and problems of administrative coordination were likewise left to the future.[34]

Despite its ambiguities the Pick-Sloan merger crippled MVA momentum. The separate plans received an extensive hearing on Capitol Hill and gained the support of strategic congressmen and powerful lobbyists, even before the Murray bill was introduced. That influential support now combined as one irresistible force offering a tangible program for basin relief. In comparison, MVA presented an administrative abstraction rather than specific projects, and its backers were not nearly as well organized. As a result, there was no real public debate on the alternatives in 1944. Representatives who stood to gain political benefits by offering public-works projects quickly aligned with Pick-Sloan and rushed it through Congress. Nevertheless, Senator Murray tried desperately at the twelfth hour to superimpose his administrative structure on the joint plan. He was persuaded to withdraw his opposition to the consolidated program only after Senator John Overton of Louisiana, the powerful chairman of both the Commerce Committee and the Irrigation and Reclamation Committee, assured him that MVA would receive full hearing in the next legislative session.[35]

In addition, President Roosevelt offered little guidance in the matter and refused to force the administrative issue on Congress, even though Pick-Sloan represented only a partial endorsement of his policy goals. The support of the New Deal leadership had clearly waned on this matter, preoccupied as the leaders were with the exigencies of the war, the election of 1944, and the growing conservative coalition in Congress.

In December, FDR approved the consolidated plan as part of the Flood Control Act of 1944, granting it an initial appropriation of $200 million.[36] He told Congress, however, that he still considered the administrative question open and that he wanted this "basic engineering plan" developed and administered by a Missouri Valley Authority. The next March, Roosevelt quietly authorized the army's nine-foot navigation channel as part of the Rivers and Harbors Act of 1945.[37]

The approved Pick-Sloan Plan, officially labeled the Missouri River Basin Development Program, included a total of 107 dams, 13 of which had previously been authorized. The five Corps of Engineers dams on the Missouri provided the key structures (Garrison Dam, in North Dakota, and the Oahe, Big Bend, Fort Randall, and Gavins Point dams, in South Dakota). Fort Peck Dam, in Montana, was also to be improved and incorporated into the plan. When fully developed, the Pick-Sloan Plan aimed at eliminating all inundations of any consequence on the Missouri and its tributaries. In addition to giant flood-control dams numerous earthen levees and concrete floodwalls were constructed on both sides of the river from Sioux City to the Mississippi to protect over 1.5 million acres of precious bottomland in the lower basin. The plan also aimed at irrigating over 5 million acres in the upper basin.[38]

After proposals for hydroelectric power were formulated, the plan provided for an output of 1.6 million kilowatts, one-third of which was produced by power plants at Garrison, Oahe, and Fort Randall. The nine-foot channel below Sioux City improved navigation. Programs were designed to enhance soil and bank stabilization and to reduce silt. Other programs were proposed to increase public recreation facilities, municipal and industrial water supplies, fish and wildlife, and mineral resource development. Extensive land surveys and detailed studies of the basin's history and prehistory were also included.[39]

Because the Pick-Sloan Plan touched on every aspect of life in the Missouri Basin, it was bound to be controversial. Unfortunately, effective criticism did not emerge until after its passage. Early critics, mainly proponents of the MVA concept, viewed the programs as "a loose joining of two already imperfect plans with all of the imperfections of both embraced under a single title."[40] They charged that Pick-Sloan failed in its objective of developing a unified water program because it was primarily concerned with protecting the vested and dominant interests of two entrenched bureaucracies. Opponents made a gallant effort in 1945 to place the program under centralized authority.[41]

Senator Murray and Congressman John J. Cochran of Missouri introduced new MVA bills in the Seventy-ninth congress.[42] Nationwide popular support for the measure appeared to be gaining strength, but legislative hostility had not weakened. The Cochran bill never made it out of committee, and the Murray bill was inadvertently killed by Harry S Truman, although the vice-president had previously endorsed MVA in the 1944 presidential election. When Murray's legislation came before the Senate, Truman allowed himself to be influenced by Senator Josiah W. Bailey of Louisiana, an avid MVA critic. Truman agreed to a resolution introduced by Bailey requiring the Murray bill to be dispatched to three separate committees for successive review: Commerce, Irrigation and Reclamation, and Agriculture and Forestry. This action effectively destroyed the measure. The antagonism of the first two committees was already assured. Each committee was allowed to review the legislation for up to sixty days, thus saddling it with further unnecessary delay.[43]

Murray protested but to no avail. He wanted his bill sent only to the committee of his own choice (Agriculture and Forestry), as was usually the author's prerogative. Senator Overton then broke his promise to give the measure a full hearing. He publicly expressed opposition to it even before the bill was received by his committees, stating that he considered the administrative issue solved with the passage of the Pick-Sloan Plan.[44]

As expected, both the Commerce Committee and the Irrigation and Reclamation Committee issued adverse reports. The Agriculture and Forestry Committee did not come forth with its modest endorsement until January 1946. Murray, completely discouraged at this point, did not press to have the bill considered further, and it died without floor debate. The issue itself did not die, however, because bills introduced by Murray and others kept it before Congress for the next ten years.[45]

Executive leadership for the MVA suffered a serious blow with the death of President Roosevelt in April 1945. In an attempt to assume the liberal mantle of his predecessor, Truman endorsed MVA as part of his Fair Deal program. He also voiced his support for the creation of valley authorities for the Columbia and Arkansas rivers and also for California's Central Valley. As a junior senator, Truman had faithfully supported TVA. As vice-president he had urged the extension of its principles to his native Missouri Valley. It was ironic that his unconscious action as president of the Senate destroyed the measure when it had its best chance for passage. In the years that followed, growing conservative opposition gradually brought a halt to the New Deal-Fair Deal continuum, and MVA never again marshaled the support it had in 1945.[46]

If MVA failed to have a fair hearing on Capitol Hill, it did receive a better one before the nation's public. Growing criticism of the Pick-Sloan arrangement brought unexpected support and generated vigorous debate. Favorable editorials in the *St. Louis Post-Dispatch,* the *Washington Post,* the *New York Times,* and the *Chicago Sun* kept the issue active in the press, as did the approving public comments of Senators William Langer and Milton Young of North Dakota, Hubert Humphrey of Minnesota, and Guy Gillette of Iowa, as well as those of Senator Murray. There was additional support in Washington received from the American Federation of Labor (AFL), the Congress of Industrial

Organizations (CIO), and the National Farmers Union (NFU). Regional MVA committees sprang up throughout the basin, and support also was mustered from such local organizations as the North Dakota Farmers Union, St. Louis Chamber of Commerce, Iowa Farmers Union, Missouri Federation of Womens Clubs, Veterans of Foreign Wars of Missouri, and Missouri Farmers Association. Finally, a national organization, Friends of the Missouri Valley, was established in Washington to coordinate the efforts of state and local MVA advocates.[47]

Nevertheless, the opponents of MVA were much stronger than its supporters. They included the influential Washington water lobby and its powerful congressional spokesmen, officials of most basin states, and 90 percent of the region's newspapers. The *St. Louis Globe-Democrat,* the *Kansas City Star* and *Times,* the *Omaha World-Herald,* and the *Denver Post* led the editorial vanguard against the measure. The United States Chamber of Commerce, the Missouri River States Committee, and the Farm Bureau also joined the ranks; and a new organization, the Missouri Valley Development Association, was formed for the sole purpose of directing MVA opposition.[48]

Critics of the MVA charged that it threatened private enterprise, state sovereignty, and congressional control. They felt its administrative structure represented a dangerous centralization of power that was unresponsive to local government and outside the control of the legislative branch. They feared creation of yet another New Deal supergovernment agency that, in their view, would be dictatorial in the use of its broad and discretionary powers. Their most effective argument was that MVA would conflict with the established governmental agencies that already had combined expertise and experience to devise a basic water-development program for the basin (the Pick-Sloan Plan). Formation of a new experimental agency, they argued, would seriously delay or drastically alter approved Pick-Sloan projects. MVA opponents also questioned the applicability of the TVA model to the Missouri Basin, an area thirteen times as large that had fundamentally different problems. Even TVA Director David E. Lilienthal agreed that it was possible for a region to be too large to be of "workable size" for a public corporation.[49]

In response, MVA proponents argued that a valley authority would stengthen private enterprise and would allow more local autonomy without surrendering legislative power. They pointed out that, because its administrative headquarters would be located in the basin itself, MVA would be easier to work with than separate agencies directed from Washington. They claimed further that MVA would break the hold of the large trusts on the river's resources, allowing lower power and freight rates and coordination, rather than elimination, of the activities of existing federal agencies.[50]

Critics of the Pick-Sloan Plan argued that MVA would ensure the priority of irrigation over navigation, provide more public power, and condemn less private land. A more comprehensive agricultural plan that included extension services, soil conservation, and reforestation programs was also envisioned. The most effective argument for MVA, however, was the great example of TVA's success in boosting the economy of the Tennessee River Basin. Increased agricultural production, industrial development, employment opportunities, and availability of low-cost public power could be counted among the positive achievements of TVA. Contrary to conservative views, southern governors testified that there had been no encroachment on states' rights, and they expressed pleasure with the arrangement whereby local governments received payments from TVA for tax-base reductions. Factions favoring MVA also considered the principles of TVA flexible enough to be adjusted to the particular needs of any river basin, including the nation's largest.[51]

Although residents of the Missouri Basin desired federal relief, they feared federal power. The plans of the Corps of Engineers and Bureau of Reclamation made them apprehensive, but MVA proposals were almost equally distrusted. Debate on the issue only seemed to cause public confusion about the relationship of local projects to overall program goals. There was a desperate need for more objective discussion by well-informed individuals who could weigh both sides of the issue, but such an exchange of ideas was apparently not forthcoming in 1945. As Pick-Sloan became law and made more headway toward its objectives, many came to feel that the development program under existing agencies would be adequate. As more ground was broken for real projects, momentum was lost for vague ideas. While the Murray bill was being defused in the Senate, a Gallup Poll in August showed basin residents three to one in favor of MVA. Outside the region, however, it was barely a public issue. Only 38 percent of those polled had even heard of the proposal, and among them 22 percent approved, 4 percent disapproved, and 12 percent had no opinion.[52]

Legislative backers of MVA did not ignore its critics. Proposals for the measure were continually altered over the years in hope of making it more acceptable. Provisions were added to protect more fully the rights and interests of individual states as well as to utilize more input from other public and private agencies. The board of directors was expanded to five members, three of whom had to be basin residents. An advisory board composed of federal agency representatives, basin state governors, and twelve private citizens was added. An adherence to the general outline of the Pick-Sloan Plan and to all existing water laws was assured. Finally, provisions were added to aid the readjustment of families dislocated by MVA projects and to allow rural communities to purchase electric power directly from the government.[53]

At the same time, Pick-Sloan critics were heeded, and federal engineers were particularly sensitive to the criticism that their plan lacked an integrated and dynamic view of the entire basin. In an attempt to remedy this, they sponsored the establishment in April 1945 of the Missouri Basin Inter-Agency Committee (MBIAC). This voluntary body was created to coordinate all federal and state activities and to provide administrative guidelines for the entire Missouri Basin Development Plan. Membership consisted of representatives from the Corps of Engineers, Department of Agriculture, Federal Power Commission, Federal Security Agency, Bureau of Reclamation and other Interior Department agencies, including the Bureau of Indian Affairs. The governors of four of the ten basin states were also representatives.[54]

Because MBIAC was not created by statute, its actions did not have the force of law, and it received no appropriations. Decisions could be made only by unanimous consent. The advantages of this arrangement to the Corps of Engineers soon became manifest, and MBIAC appeared to be the kind of coordinating agency envisioned by MVA. In reality, however, state representatives were dominated by federal agents, and army delegates easily dominated the other federal representatives. The organization served merely as a sub-committee of the Federal Inter-Agency River Basin Committee, which had been authorized under Corps of Engineers leadership in 1943. The Missouri River States Committee, which had already demonstrated its loyalty to army plans, selected state delegates but prohibited them from serving as chairman. Predictably, the first two heads of MBIAC were army engineers: Brigadier General R. C. Crawford was a force behind the Omaha Compromise of 1944, and General Lewis A. Pick himself served for over three years.[55] Glenn Sloan also held the chair between April 1949 and September 1950.

MVA advocates quickly saw through this camouflage. They charged that this loose federal-state confederation would never succeed in solving inherent controversies of the Pick-Sloan Plan. In their opinion MBIAC not only lacked teeth but also its piece-meal approach meant that each federal agency had to deal with several separate committees in both houses of Congress to gain approval for its part of the overall water-development program. Valley-authority advocates pointed out that MVA would have had the statutory power to enforce its decisions, to provide for more equal and effective representation, and to receive an annual appro-priation for its entire program in one legislative package. Pick-Sloan under MBIAC would only perpetuate army dominance while it ignored both the interests of local government and the impor-tance of irrigation. They held that one of the evils already apparent in the arrangement was that it was "trampling on the rights of Indians."[56]

Chapter 3

THE SIOUX: LAND AND PEOPLE

The original inhabitants of the Missouri Basin settled in the valleys of the Missouri River and its tributaries. When this Indian land was reduced to reservation size in the nineteenth century, most tribes managed to keep some of their riverside territory. In South Dakota, for example, the Sioux maintained possession of the greater part of the western shoreline of the Missouri River. As a result the Pick-Sloan Plan disrupted the lands of several native groups. Whether or not the Corps of Engineers and Bureau of Reclamation deliberately chose Indian over non-Indian land for their project sites as some tribal leaders charged, their plans ultimately affected twenty-three different reservations.[1]

The Corps of Engineers built five main-stem projects that destroyed over 550 square miles of tribal land in North and South Dakota and dislocated more than 900 Indian families. Most of this damage was sustained by the five Sioux reservations that are the primary concern of this study: Standing Rock and Cheyenne River, reduced by the Oahe project; Yankton, affected by Fort Randall Dam; and Crow Creek and Lower Brule, damaged by both the Fort Randall and Big Bend projects. In addition, the most devastating effects suffered by a single reservation were experienced by the Three Affiliated Tribes (Mandan, Arikara, and Hidatsa) of the Fort Berthold reserve in North Dakota, whose tribal life

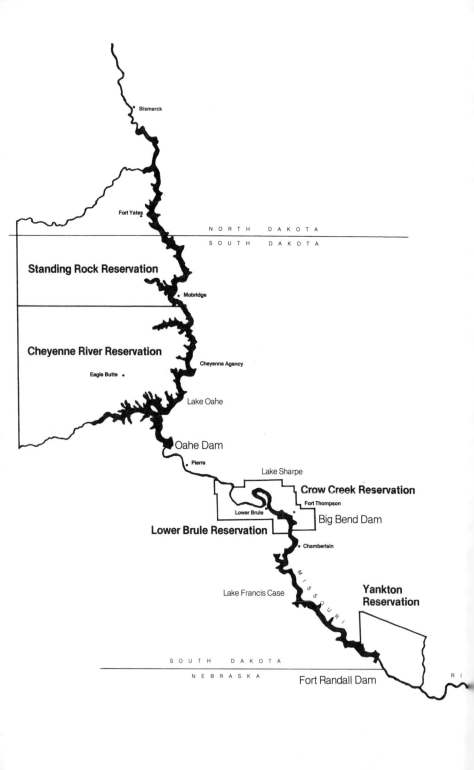

Bismarck

Fort Yates

N O R T H   D A K O T A
S O U T H   D A K O T A

Standing Rock Reservation

Mobridge

Cheyenne River Reservation

Cheyenne Agency

Eagle Butte

Lake Oahe

Oahe Dam

Pierre

Lake Sharpe

Crow Creek Reservation

Fort Thompson

Lower Brule

Big Bend Dam

Lower Brule Reservation

Chamberlain

M I S S O U R I

Lake Francis Case

Yankton Reservation

S O U T H   D A K O T A
N E B R A S K A

Fort Randall Dam

R I

was almost totally destroyed by the army's Garrison Dam. The corps' Gavins Point project also took a small portion of the land of the Santee Sioux in northeastern Nebraska. Other tribes were adversely affected by tributary projects of the Bureau of Reclamation, including the Chippewas in North Dakota, the Shoshones and Arapahos in Wyoming, and Crows, Blackfeet, Crees, Chippewas, Sioux, and Assiniboines in Montana.

Army dams on the Missouri inundated more than 202,000 acres of Sioux land. Approximately 580 families were uprooted and forced to move from rich, sheltered bottomlands to empty prairies. Their best homesites, their finest pastures, croplands, and hay meadows, and most of their valuable timber, wildlife, and vegetation were flooded. Relocation of the agency headquarters on the Cheyenne River, Lower Brule, and Crow Creek reservations seriously disrupted governmental, medical, and educational services and facilities and dismantled the largest Indian communities on these reservations. Removal of churches, community centers, cemeteries, and shrines impaired social and religious life on all five reserves. Loss not only of primary fuel, food, and water resources but also of prime grazing land effectively destroyed the Indians' economic base. The thought of having to give up their ancestral land, to which they were so closely wedded, caused severe psychological stress. The result was extreme confusion and hardship for tribal members.

The individual Sioux tribes sought in vain a generous federal settlement for their damages and for the violation of treaties that guaranteed the perpetual integrity of their land. They tried to gain for themselves the benefits promised by the Pick-Sloan program, as well as government assistance to help them overcome the hardships placed on them and to permit them to escape at last the vicious cycle of poverty and determine their own future. At nearly every turn their efforts were frustrated by an economy-minded government that too often proved insensitive to their needs.

The administrative structure of the Pick-Sloan Plan was largely to blame for this failure. Its piecemeal approach to basin problems and its preoccupation with engineering methods did not allow adequate consideration of the important human factors in condemnation of land and relocation of families. The army engineers who dominated the program, with whom the tribes had to negotiate first, had nothing in their training or background that prepared them to deal fairly and knowledgeably with Indians. The federal agency usually charged with that responsibility, the Bureau of Indian Affairs (BIA), was weakened at the time of the most crucial negotiations by a reduced budget and the threat of being abolished altogether. It was the aggressive tactics of the Corps of Engineers, coupled with the failure of the BIA to protect adequately the interests of its wards, that sparked criticism that the Pick-Sloan Plan was running roughshod over native rights.

The Indian victims of this bungled bureaucratic situation had for two centuries experienced a colorful history in their otherwise drab homeland. The five modern Sioux tribes affected by Pick-Sloan were descendent, of course, from those ennobled Plains warriors who have become the aboriginal stereotype for all North American Indians. The nomadic buffalo hunters, whose equestrian gallantry kept the advancing whites at bay for a time during the latter part of the nineteenth century, have long stood, with their feathered headdresses and beaded regalia, as the standard caricature of all tribes in both the literature of the West and contemporary media. Although the stereotypical Sioux culture was of relatively brief duration and did not apply equally to all of the Sioux tribes—not all were aggressive, nomadic, and nonagricultural—this popular image has continued to distort our vision of the Sioux. It is also grossly unfair to the traditions of other native groups.

The Sioux first drifted into the Missouri Basin in the mid-eighteenth century, after the pressure of better-armed enemy tribes and dwindling food supplies caused them to abandon their settlements in the Upper Mississippi Valley, where French explorers had discovered them a century before. As they migrated westward, three major divisions came to be recognized in the Sioux Nation: the Teton, or Western, Sioux, who were the first of the subtribes to migrate onto the plains and become buffalo hunters; the more sedentary and pacific Middle Sioux; and the Santee, or Eastern, Sioux, who were the last to break from the agricultural Woodland culture of the Great Lakes region.[2]

The gradual acquisition of the horse and gun enabled the Teton subtribes, in particular, to pursue effectively the great bison herds that roamed the Missouri Basin. These innovations profoundly touched the lives of these people and eventually shaped for them a migratory culture centered on the buffalo, their economic supermarket. This way of life may have been one dimensional, but it allowed them to become, for at least half a century, one of the most prosperous native groups in America.[3]

The advance of the mining frontier and the spread of transportation networks across the plains in the middle of the nineteenth century brought the Sioux into extensive contact with Anglo-Americans. Federal policy represented an attempt to halt the hostile confrontations that inevitably resulted from this clash of cultures and to allow the central portion of the Indian's territory to be opened for white passage. The United States gradually evolved a policy that concentrated the tribes into increasingly smaller "reserved areas," where, it was hoped, they might eventually become "civilized" and assimilated into the dominant culture. The Sioux, having evolved as a warrior society, were not at all inclined to submit passively to white encroachment. As a result various of the recalcitrant bands resisted the reservation policy by force of arms for nearly forty years—most notably during the attacks on the American forts along the Bozeman Trail known as the Sioux War of 1865-67, the ill-fated "Last Stand" of Colonel George Armstrong Custer at the Little Big Horn River in 1876, and the infamous 1890 "Battle of Wounded Knee."[4]

By 1889 the separate tribes of the Sioux nation had found themselves confined within the shrunken boundaries of their present reservations. On the west bank of the Missouri River the Standing Rock reserve, split by the boundary line between North and South Dakota, was set aside for the Hunkpapa and Blackfeet subtribes of the Teton Sioux and the Upper and Lower Yanktonai subtribes of the Middle Sioux. Just below this reservation, in north-central South Dakota, the Cheyenne River reserve was established to administer four of the Teton subtribes: the Miniconjous, Two Kettles, Sans Arcs, and remaining Blackfeet. The Lower Brulé subtribe (Teton) was placed on a reservation of the same name (but without an accent on "Brule") on the Missouri's western shore in central South Dakota, just opposite the Lower

Yanktonais (Middle) on the Crow Creek Reservation. In addition, the Yankton Sioux (Middle) had accepted, as early as 1858, a parcel of land just below Crow Creek on the eastern bank of the Missouri. The other major Teton subtribes, the Upper Brulés and Oglalas, were placed on the Rosebud and Pine Ridge reservations, respectively, in south-central and southwestern South Dakota. In addition, the Santee Sioux subtribes were concentrated on reservations in eastern North Dakota, South Dakota, and Nebraska.[5]

Having gradually been dispossessed of their sacred Black Hills, their western hunting grounds, and most of their fertile lands east of the Missouri, the Sioux were settled on some of the least valuable land in the entire basin. The physical characteristics of the reservations on the Missouri's western shore were typical of the Great Plains. This rolling prairie country, with its deep drainage and rough river breaks, was part of the Missouri Plateau. Elevation averaged about 2,800 feet. Canyons and buttes dominated the terrain, punctuated by vast expanses of almost level tableland. Short grasses and chestnut soils, capable of producing high grain yields, made much of this country ideal for grazing. Yet, heavy shale deposits and alkaline gumbo soils, which did not readily absorb the sixteen inches of rain that fell in an average year, made most of the land difficult to cultivate. Only the bottomlands along the rivers were consistently fertile and forested.[6]

The Crow Creek and Yankton reservations on the eastern bank of the Missouri fell within the Missouri Hills, or Coteau du Missouri, region. This undulating area is about thirty miles wide and lies like a passage between the fertile Prairie Plains of the eastern Dakotas and the semiarid Great Plains west of the Missouri. Grasses here were somewhat taller, and soils contained more humus and were less alkaline than those on the Great Plains. Yearly moisture was nonetheless unreliable, but farming was much less a gamble.[7]

The establishment of separate reservations blurred long-standing tribal distinctions. The old subtribal designations gradually became obsolete, and tribal members soon began to identify themselves according to their reservations. Hunkpapa descendants, for example, began referring to themselves as Standing Rock Sioux.

Life on the different reservations soon proved miserable. Ill fed
and clothed, the Sioux witnessed the destruction of the last ves-
tiges of their traditional culture. This proved a profound psychological blow, for it was not easy for even the more peaceful tribes
to accept white authority. Moreover, the methods used by the Indian Bureau did not help ease the adjustment. Local agents followed the stated federal policy of preparing tribal members for
American citizenship by undermining the power and influence of
their established leaders, by repressing their culture, and by making them economically dependent on the government dole. Thus
the Sioux were constantly victimized by corrupt political spoils-
men, morally debased and manipulative soldiers, and the constant
jurisdictional disputes that raged between the two.[8]

The policy of acculturation weakened tribal unity by recognizing Indians as individuals. This principle of individualism was
carried over into land ownership. Humanitarians had long demanded that each Indian be given a farm, where the civilizing
qualities supposedly inherent in tilling the soil could be readily
absorbed. Because this goal could also be used to justify a sizable
reduction of the Indian land base, speculators joined reformers in
supporting the Dawes Severalty Act in 1887. This law provided
that each Indian family head would receive a patent for 160 acres
of land, with lesser amounts going to other family members. The
patent would be held in federal trust for twenty-five years, and
full American citizenship would be granted to the allottees. After
all Indians on a particular reservation had accepted allotments, the
surplus land was to be opened for white settlement under provisions of the existing homestead laws.[9]

The procedures established by the Dawes Act were reversed
when applied to the Sioux. Surplus land was sold even before
surveys and allotments could be made. Although most of the Sioux
allottees were granted 320 acres instead of 160 acres or less, the
tribes lost 9 million acres in one fell swoop once the surplus land
was thrown on the open market.[10]

The Dawes Act was the most devastating piece of legislation
ever applied to the Sioux. It not only robbed them of considerable
property but also saddled them with land problems that continue
to wreak havoc even today. The ideal of little Sioux farms scat-

tered across the prairie was a pipe dream. Tribal members chose allotments not for their value as farms but for their proximity to their old homes and relatives. Most of the land was of marginal agricultural worth at best, and the Teton tribes had traditionally been adverse to farming of any kind. Moreover, the Indian Bureau reneged on its promise to provide adequate training and equipment. Some tribal members enjoyed success at stockraising, although 320 acres were hardly sufficient for a family ranch on the plains. For most of the starving Indians the land proved of little use. Once they could be judged "competent" under amended Dawes provisions, they were pressured to sell their holdings to whites. In this way speculators and crop farmers gained ownership of 80 percent of the allotments on some Sioux reservations. As a consequence, the reservations became "checkerboarded" between lands held in trust status for tribal members and those held by non-Indians with fee patents. This development further eroded the native land base and made it extremely difficult for the tribes to ever again consolidate their holdings.[11]

Because the Dawes Act failed to make adequate provision for settling the estates of deceased allottees, their property was merely divided equally among their heirs. This practice so fragmented ownership that, eventually, no individual tribal member owned enough of an original allotment to make effective use of the land. The full implications of these land problems will become even more evident in the chapters that follow.[12]

White encroachment on the reservations continued into the twentieth century. Large portions of Indian land were repeatedly opened to settlers or leased to ranchers. Christian missionaries gradually gained greater influence. The boarding schools that they established on or near the reservations emphasized vocational, but not agrarian, education. By removing Sioux children from parental influences during many of their formative years, these institutions played a key role in the acculturation process.[13]

Early attempts to develop a reservation economy failed miserably. Federal policies killed incentive and made effective land use impossible. Because the Sioux were influenced by culture and geography, they proved better at raising cattle than harvesting corn, and many of the tribes managed to increase the size of their herds each year. The lure of high prices during World War I, however, caused Indian ranchers to sell most of their stock. They chose immediate gratification and were plunged again into poverty during the inflationary postwar period. The depression and drought of the 1920s and 1930s forced many Sioux to sell their remaining allotments of land in order to survive.[14]

Ironically, it was at this time, in 1924, that Congress finally extended American citizenship to all Indians. This gesture was made principally in recognition of the number of tribal members who had distinguished themselves in combat during World War I. Thus, fifty-six years after the black man and four years after all American women, Indians were officially recognized as citizens in their native land.[15]

Living conditions on the reservations remained abominable for these new citizens. Their disgust with the inadequacies of federal supervision and the destruction of their native culture and land base sparked a white-sponsored reform movement in the twenties. Groups such as the Indian Rights Association and the American Indian Defense Association led the crusade. The Institute of Government Research in Washington conducted an extensive study of federal Indian policy and local reservation conditions. Its findings, submitted in the famous Meriam Report of 1928, confirmed the observations of reformers who had demanded abolishment of the land allotment system and had urged the immediate improvement of Indian health, education, and welfare services.[16]

Many of the reforms outlined in the Meriam Report, as well as those prompted by an investigation by the Senate Subcommittee on Indian Affairs, were enacted during the New Deal administration of President Franklin D. Roosevelt. Urged by reformist Indian Commissioner John Collier, congressional legislation was enacted that drastically altered the course of federal Indian policy. Legislative steps were taken to restore tribal community life, to halt the further alienation of native lands, and to provide new opportunities for economic development and self-government. The former policies of bureaucratic paternalism and forced assimilation were reversed, and for the first time, the unique aspects of native culture and religion were given full government recognition. The production of Indian artifacts, for example, was encouraged through a federal Arts and Crafts Board established in 1935. Appropriations for Indian health and education were increased, and the Johnson-O'Malley Act of 1934 permitted state agencies to extend social services to reservations for the first time. The groundwork was also laid for an Indian Claims Commission to adjudicate the many illegal or questionable treaties and transactions that had been foisted upon various tribes in the past.[17]

Most importantly, the so-called Indian New Deal brought about enactment of the Indian Reorganization Act (IRA), also known as the Wheeler-Howard Act of 1934, which established the concept of political self-determination for the tribes and permitted them to draw up constitutions providing limited powers of self-government. This law abolished the policy of land allotment and returned certain surplus lands to tribal control. It established a $10 million revolving credit fund to assist reservation development programs, as well as an annual $2 million appropriation for the purchase of new tribal lands.[18]

The IRA only applied to those tribal groups who voted in referendum to accept it. Among the Sioux, the Standing Rock, Cheyenne River, Lower Brule, Rosebud, and Pine Ridge reservations chose to draft constitutions and bylaws under the IRA provisions, while the Crow Creek reserve did not. Like many tribes across the nation, the Yankton Sioux accepted the law but never organized under it, preferring to continue the practice of conducting tribal business in general council. After the passage of the IRA, elected tribal councils and courts were established on most reservations, although small factions of each tribe opposed such changes. Credit was extended to cooperative livestock associations on the reservations and for farm and building projects. Long-range economic planning was instituted to promote and control tribal investments, and special funds were set aside for land consolidation and reservation development.[19]

The IRA was no panacea. Because it was patterned after the United States Constitution rather than tribal custom, the political structure it fostered was alien to tribes like the Sioux who had seldom functioned on a reservationwide level. This helps explain the intense factionalism that characterized the new tribal governments from the very beginning. Despite IRA claims for self-determination, tribal representatives soon found that they were constantly being monitored by federal authorities and could take little action without BIA approval. The new law granted more political and economic freedom, but did nothing either to extend the civil liberties of Indians or to remove oppressive and obsolete legislation. Neither did it guarantee fulfillment of treaty obligations nor the continuance of its own credit programs, which were reduced almost immediately.[20]

Yet, on balance, the Indian New Deal did prove to be a boon for the Sioux. The reforms of Commissioner Collier made it possible again to practice native customs and ceremonies. Expanded social services were extended to the tribes through the Public Works Administration, Works Progress Administration, Social Security Board, and other New Deal agencies. Emergency relief was provided those hardest hit by the Great Depression. Programs such as that of the Civilian Conservation Corps encouraged tribal leadership, improved reservation conditions, and provided steady employment to many tribal members for the first time in their lives. The luxury of a regular paycheck made more material comforts available. As author Vine Deloria, Jr., who grew up on Standing Rock, described it, "the Sioux climbed from absolute deprivation to mere poverty."[21]

The coming of World War II retarded this progress and reduced social services. Tribal members left the reservations to enlist in the armed services or to work in war industries. Once again the Sioux distinguished themselves in military combat, as well as in civilian service. After viewing the outside world, however, many found it difficult to accept reservation conditions when they returned home. From this group of more worldly tribal members emerged both the urban Indians who permanently detached themselves from native culture and the next generation of reservation leaders. Those who were determined to ameliorate reservation conditions faced a difficult task. Despite New Deal programs and the relative prosperity of the postwar years, most of the Sioux people still had not been able to escape the depths of their "invisible" poverty.[22]

In his work *The Other America,* which greatly influenced President Lyndon B. Johnson's War on Poverty, sociologist Michael

Harrington points out that poverty is largely invisible in this nation. Because the poorest of our people usually live "off the beaten path," they are removed from "the living emotional experience of millions and millions of middle-class Americans."[23] Urban ghettos and barrios are isolated from the casual observation of suburban residents who live in the same city. The plight of rural poor in regions such as Appalachia tends to be ignored because of our romantic preoccupation with their scenic environment. The inaccessibility of reservations and the isolation of Native American poor from mainstream America represent an extreme case of cultural invisibility. Among the poorest of the poor, Indians are the most invisible of all our citizens. Their poverty is outside the experience of most Americans, and it was not even reported by Harrington when his book was first published in 1962.[24]

Ironically, because of their status as wards of the federal government, the poverty, disease, and hunger of Native Americans has been more thoroughly documented than that of any other low-income group in this country. Most Americans, however, are unwilling to acknowledge that such conditions exist within their midst. As a result, the great reams of statistical reports compiled by the Indian Bureau and the many tomes produced by social scientists too often escape both the credibility and sensitivity of our affluent society.

The Sioux reservations are hidden among the windswept buttes and prairies of the Dakotas, one of America's most isolated rural regions. Like urban ghettos, they are usually visited only by those from the outside who cannot otherwise avoid them. Unlike Appalachia, the scenery of the plains only serves to emphasize their destitution. At a time when a renewed historical and sociological focus, coupled with the political activities of groups like the American Indian Movement, should be making Native Americans more visible, the Sioux reservations are becoming even more isolated. The population of the counties surrounding the reservations has been steadily declining since 1930, as has that of most of rural America. Small neighboring towns are dying. The interstate highway system running through the Dakotas does not pass through any Sioux land. Reservations only succeed in luring the few tourists whose curiosity is such that they cannot accept the popular, commercialized image of the "drugstore Indians" of the Black Hills. These tourists find a people who are both blessed with a glorious past and cursed with inhuman and almost inescapable living conditions at present. But there has been progress.

In the years just before construction of the Pick-Sloan projects, it seemed that the Sioux might never enjoy more than a marginal existence. Most tribal members lived with their extended families in one- and two-room log or frame houses with no electricity or plumbing. A few still lived in tents or the shells of old car bodies. On Standing Rock Reservation, for example, the average house had five occupants per room and only 13 percent of the homes had both electricity and running water as late as 1955. Nearly all Sioux households were dependent on wood stoves for both heating and cooking. The water supply, which was of questionable purity, often had to be hauled in unsanitary containers over long distances. Most homes lacked adequate outdoor privies, and some rural families were totally without toilet and garbage facilities.[25]

Transportation and communication facilities also were seriously lacking. Only half the families had cars, most of which were more than ten years old. Those who had none had to pay others to take them to the agency, to haul water, or to shop for groceries. Less than half the households had radios, few received newspapers, and still fewer had telephones. On the Yankton reservation, for example, only one family had a telephone in 1954.[26]

These living conditions contributed to very poor health for the Sioux. An especially high rate of tuberculosis existed on the reservations and was the principal cause of death. Gastrointestinal diseases and vitamin deficiencies related to a lack of adequate meats and vegetables in the diet were also prevalent. Forced to endure harsh Dakota winters with inadequate clothing and shelter, many tribal members died from pneumonia each year. There was a high incidence of acute alcoholism and extreme melancholia. These problems, common to many native groups, were clinically related to a variety of physical and mental disorders and socially related to the deterioration of native culture, family and financial difficulties, acts of violence, and an alarming suicide rate. Venereal disease and illegitimacy were also common.[27]

Health facilities on reservations were extremely limited. Lower

Brule Reservation had no medical facilities of its own, and the old hospitals on the other reservations were dilapidated and under-staffed. Although some tribal members lived as far as fifty miles from medical facilities, ambulance service was almost nonexistent. Doctors in neighboring white communities often refused to treat Indians or demanded payment in advance. Enrolled tribal members were entitled to free medical attention at Indian Health Service (IHS) clinics and hospitals but were often reluctant to take advantage of this benefit. They were either suspicious of the IHS doctors, whom they knew received comparatively low pay, or resentful of them because they were white. As a result, many Sioux preferred to have their ailments diagnosed and treated by family members or tribal elders known to be good medicine men. If traditional medicine failed to heal them, they then turned to the IHS hospitals as a last resort, often when it was too late for effective treatment. Federal clinics thus became feared as "places of death." It was difficult to overcome this notion because native cures often worked better than those of the white government physicians.[28]

The education situation was similarly unsatisfactory. Schools had been established on reservations for over half a century, yet the average Sioux tribal member had only a grade-school education. The overall education level increased by only three grades per generation. Attendance was irregular, and the dropout rate was high. There was no high school on Lower Brule Reservation, and the Yankton Sioux were without any schools of their own. The Standing Rock, Cheyenne River, and Crow Creek reservations had both day and boarding schools, but most facilities were sadly inadequate. Students not attending reservation schools were enrolled in nearby public schools, BIA schools out-of-state, or local boarding schools at Pierre, Flandreau, and Marty, South Dakota. Although the proportion of young Indians who were graduating from high school and attending college was slowly increasing, there were virtually no programs for adult education, and many older tribal members remained illiterate, unskilled, and unable to speak English.[29]

Despite an emphasis on vocational education, training received at Indian schools seldom brought regular employment. Only a small percentage of the adult tribal members on each reservation found steady work. On Standing Rock Reservation, for example, 74 percent of the heads of families were unemployed in 1955. Most Sioux who did find work were hired as cowboys, farmers, or construction workers or in nonsupervisory positions with the BIA. Some found seasonal work as migrant farm workers in the summer but were forced to seek welfare assistance in the winter after their savings were exhausted. As a result annual family incomes were extremely low. On Yankton Reservation, for example, the average income was only $730 in 1950, compared with an average of $3,073 for all American families and $2,771 for other families in South Dakota. A third of the families on Crow Creek Reservation made less than $500 in 1950. Economic conditions on the reservations were so bad that a substantial portion of Sioux family incomes was derived from government relief programs. On Standing Rock, for example, 47 percent of the population received some form of welfare in 1955.[30]

These conditions prevailed partly because the Sioux lacked natural resources necessary to sustain a rapidly growing population. In the 1950s and 1960s this scarcity became an even greater problem. The Pick-Sloan projects had destroyed a substantial portion of the most valuable Sioux resources, while Indian population growth began for the first time to exceed the national average. A lack of adequate training and investment capital and the crippling effects of federal Indian land policies made them unable to use effectively the limited resources that were available. Checkerboarded reservations and heirship lands made it almost impossible for tribal members to make use of their own holdings. On Crow Creek Reservation, for example, 87 percent of the grazing land and 50 percent of the cropland were leased to non-Indians. The Standing Rock Sioux used only 22 percent of their land, and 76 percent of the Yankton reservation was used by whites. Inherited interests in these leased tracts were often so divided that annual payments to some heirs amounted to only a few cents. Recipients of these tiny checks sometimes kept them as souvenirs. They symbolized the stupidity of government land policies that had been allowed to continue in chaos. Indian land owners often received checks that cost the BIA more to process than they were worth. Although the Indian Reorganization Act forbade further allotments, Congress has yet to provide a solution for the heirship problem, and the fragmentation of the Indian interests in inherited lands continues unabated to this day.[31]

Oil, gas, coal, and other mineral resources were known to exist on some reservations, but tribes generally lacked the money and skill to exploit them. Cultural and geographic isolation also made it difficult to attract industry. Tribal traditions further complicated economic growth. The give-away, the sharing of wealth with relatives and neighbors as a symbol of honor or mourning, was a common practice of classic Sioux culture. The tradition of hospitality and generosity carried over into the twentieth century. Families still were inclined to share their homes and belongings with less fortunate tribal members, even though reservation life and intermarriage had eroded traditional kinship ties and extended-family relationships. On Crow Creek, for example, 22 percent of the resident families in 1953 shared their homes and incomes with others. As a result of this practice, money coming into the reservations tended to be more evenly distributed than in white communities, and individual wealth was less valued. In some tribes there was considerable social pressure against conspicuous consumption or accumulation of wealth. On Lower Brule, for example, one anthropologist found that the most successful Indian ranchers were systematically cut off from community participation.[32]

Cattle raising was by far the most promising economic venture on the Sioux reservations. Nature tended to favor ranching in this region, and most tribal members preferred it as a way to make a living. The Standing Rock, Cheyenne River, and Lower Brulé tribes were especially successful in establishing cooperative live-stock enterprises. Utilizing Wheeler-Howard credit facilities, these tribes purchased cattle and equipment from local suppliers and loaned them to tribal members on a repayment-in-kind basis. The ability of Indian stockmen to increase the size of their herds each year made it possible for more and more tribal members to find gainful employment as ranchers. By 1951, for example, Standing Rock had established 234 cattle operators and a tribal herd of nearly 10,000 head. The Cheyenne River and Lower Brule Sioux coupled their enterprises with successful land consolidation programs. By 1950 tribal livestock programs accounted for over half of the total income on these reservations. Perhaps revealing their distinct cultural inclinations, the Crow Creek and Yankton Sioux made no effort to establish tribal programs but enjoyed greater success in raising poultry and harvesting corn.[33]

Despite initial progress, Sioux ranching operations faced a limited future. There was simply not enough land or money for tribal cattle enterprises to sustain or to employ more than a small proportion of the reservation population. The continuation of open-grazing methods and the practice of establishing small herds to include more tribal members was financially unrealistic and out of step with regional agricultural developments. Some areas required up to thirty acres of grazing land for each head of cattle. This placed severe limits on total herd size. Emphasis on increasing the number of Indian ranchers spread tribal programs too thin. Individual stockmen received inadequate equipment and had herds too small to ensure commercial success. On Standing Rock Reservation, for example, 71 percent of the Indian ranchers still used horse-drawn equipment to cut and to bale hay. On Cheyenne River Reservation only 10 percent of the ranchers had more than seventy head of cattle. It was impossible for these Indians to compete with neighboring white ranchers who used feedlot methods and more modern equipment. Unlike the Sioux, these stockmen tended to conform to the national trend that saw the concentration of more land and stock into fewer hands.[34]

Faced with the prospect of losing their most valuable land and resources, the Sioux affected by the Pick-Sloan Plan sought settlements with the government that would permit continued social and economic progress. Realizing they were powerless to stop the Missouri River dams, tribal leaders were determined to negotiate for payments and benefits that would allow them to make the most of their remaining resources. None of the tribes would deny that the loss of their homes, ranches, and forests hurt deeply. Neither did they pretend that they could ever be adequately compensated for this loss. If Pick-Sloan damages were inevitable, however, Pick-Sloan benefits might provide the means for a brighter future. A generous government settlement might allow development of new facilities and programs for health, education, housing, community growth, and employment. Direct benefits from the reservoir projects might also include irrigation, low-cost power, improved water supplies, and recreational and industrial development. Ranching programs could be enhanced, and the Sioux could take a giant step toward the goal of self-sufficiency.

Given the pattern of all past negotiations with the federal government, the Sioux had little cause to be optimistic. They had already been cheated and cajoled out of a vast empire. But this, they reasoned, was the twentieth century, not the nineteenth. The Sioux were now American citizens. A more humanitarian attitude had been made evident by the Indian New Deal. Had not an Indian Claims Commission been established to redress all past wrongs? Were not politicians in Washington discussing means by which the tribes could exercise even more control over their own affairs? The government could not be judged in the light of its past dealings. Surely the time was right for the first genuinely fair and generous federal settlement.

With this attitude in mind, the tribes dealt first with the Corps of Engineers and then with Congress, failing once again to realize fully what they were up against. For its part, the federal government, as in the past, did not fail to disappoint them.

Chapter 4

UPROOTED

The Sioux knew little of the Pick-Sloan Plan until long after it had been approved. Although existing treaty rights provided that land could not be taken without their consent, none of the tribes were consulted prior to the program's enactment. The Bureau of Indian Affairs was fully informed, yet made no objections to the plan while it was being debated in Congress in 1944. The Indian Bureau did not inform the tribes of the damages they would suffer until 1947. The Corps of Engineers was so confident that it could acquire the Indian land it needed through federal powers of eminent domain that it began construction on its dams, including those actually on reservation property, even before opening formal negotiations with the tribal leaders. The legislation establishing the Pick-Sloan Plan also ignored the Indians' water rights under the so-called Winters Doctrine.

The Winters Doctrine was propounded by the United States Supreme Court in 1907 in the case of *Winters* v. *United States.* The Fort Belknap Indians of Montana had brought suit against an upstream farmer, Henry Winters, to enjoin him from interfering with the flow of the Milk River, a tributary of the Missouri, through their reservation. The Court ruled that when the Indians gave up their rights to their former lands in exchange for the arid, unirrigated land of the reservation, sufficient water was reserved from the

Milk River to enable the tribe "to become a pastoral and civilized people." The court also held that the Indians' right to use the water could not be diminished by any rights created under state law. Later decisions, such as *Conrad Investment Company* v. *United States*, further extended the Winters doctrine establishing that Indians have prior and superior rights to both present and future beneficial uses of water. These early decisions were reaffirmed by the Supreme Court in the 1963 case of *Arizona* v. *California*, which granted five lower Colorado River tribes sufficient water to "irrigate the irrigable portions" of their reservations.[1] These legal complications, however, were resolved more equitably than other problems that arose.

The Pick-Sloan Plan was thus presented to the Sioux as a *fait accompli.* The federal government was determined to move them out, and there was nothing that they could do about it. Although the Sioux were angry and bitter that the United States again would break the faith of its treaty obligations and sacrifice their interests to satisfy white demands for progress, they realized that resistance was futile. Intertribal cooperation was virtually nonexistent, and the individual tribes were too politically fragmented to offer an organized opposition. Access to influential legislators and competent legal counselors was extremely limited, and tribal members were not inclined to take radical action. Federal officials ignored the protests that were made, and the Sioux were eventually forced to accept the inevitable consequences of Pick-Sloan. Gradually they resigned themselves to making the most of whatever alms might be offered in compensation, but their bitterness remained.

In 1947 the Bureau of Indian Affairs made its first effort to represent tribal interests within the Missouri Basin Inter-Agency Committee. To assess fully the damages to Indian land resulting from Pick-Sloan, the BIA organized the Missouri River Basin Investigations Project (MRBI) within the structure of its regional office at Billings, Montana. Initially this agency was given the task of conducting both extensive reservation surveys and appraisals to estimate replacement costs as well as social and economic damages resulting from inundation. Later MRBI was also assigned to help tribes gain equitable settlements and to assist relocation and reconstruction activities. BIA experts were brought in from various regions to serve the project for limited periods of time. Standard procedures were established for all the reservations, and staff members were assigned to the tribes on a circuit-rider basis. By 1948, MRBI had a full-time staff of forty-five people and an annual budget of $300,000.[2]

By the time when the first MRBI staff members had reached the field, the Corps of Engineers had spent approximately $28 million on preliminary construction of the Garrison, Fort Randall, and Oahe dams. The Fort Berthold reservation had been invaded by truck convoys and earth-moving equipment under army contract; the Corps of Engineers had condemned 3,349 acres of Yankton Sioux land in federal district court; and army survey crews had made aerial photographs and topographical maps of the other reservations. Initial MRBI findings on all Sioux lands were not published until 1949, by which time the corps had spent an additional $37.5 million on its three projects. Yet it was not until these early MRBI appraisals were made available that the Sioux learned the full effect of Pick-Sloan on their reservations.[3]

Construction of the Fort Randall Dam began in May 1946. This project was located near the Yankton reservation 100 miles southeast of the Crow Creek and Lower Brule reservations and just seven miles above the Nebraska line in south-central South Dakota. When it was completed in 1969, Fort Randall provided a water storage capacity of 5.7 million acre-feet and a maximum hydroelectric power output of 320,000 kilowatts. The reservoir behind the dam stretched over 107 miles and was named Lake Case in honor of the late Senator Francis Case of South Dakota. Fort Randall was built with compacted earth fill, as were other army projects on the Missouri. Like Garrison and Oahe dams, it featured a relatively high-head dam (160 feet) and a chute-type spillway designed to release excessive flows. Although the Corps of Engineers estimated this project would cost $75 million in 1944, it ultimately cost more than $200 million.[4]

The Fort Randall Dam flooded 22,091 acres of Sioux land and dislocated 136 Indian families. Hardest hit were the Crow Creek Sioux. The tribe lost 9,514 acres of precious bottomland, over one-third of which was forested. Eighty-four families, representing approximately 34 percent of the reservation population, were

General aerial view of Fort Randall Dam and Lake Francis Case, looking upstream toward the northwest, near Pickstown, South Dakota. Courtesy of United States Army, Corps of Engineers.

forced to evacuate their riverside homes and to accept land ill suited for houses, ranches, or farms. Fort Thompson, the reservation's largest community, was completely inundated. The BIA agency headquarters there, which also served the Lower Brulé Sioux, was moved thirty miles from the reservation to Pierre, the tiny capital city of South Dakota. The Indian Health Service hospital was moved twenty miles south to Chamberlain. These facilities were now located over ninety miles from remote parts of the reservations. Because tribal offices remained on Indian land, it was no longer possible for the Crow Creek and Lower Brulé Sioux to take

Aerial view of Fort Randall Dam, looking northeast, near Picks-town, South Dakota. In the foreground are the powerhouse, switchyard, and intake structure. Courtesy of United States Army, Corps of Engineers.

care of their BIA, public-health, and tribal business needs on the same day at the same location. For a people whose transportation facilities were severely limited, this situation created an immense hardship.[5]

The flooding of 7,997 acres of the Lower Brule reservation caused the dislocation of thirty-five Indian families or approximately 16 percent of the resident population. Nearly one-half of the lost acreage was sheltered pastureland. The Tribal Livestock Enterprise, the reservation's primary industry, suffered a serious blow. However, the town of Lower Brule, the main population center, was saved.[6]

The Yankton reservation lost 3,349 acres to the Fort Randall project. Here, however, the damage was less catastrophic. The nineteen families relocated represented only eight percent of the resident population. Because most reservation land was below the dam, only twenty percent of the tribe's river frontage was affected, and no major Indian communities were disturbed. Fort Randall also inundated 1,231 acres on the eastern boundary of the Rosebud Sioux reservation. The Corps of Engineers condemned the land of the six Indian property owners, but no tribally owned land was involved.[7]

In August 1948 at a site six miles northwest of Pierre, the corps began construction on the Oahe Dam, which was named after a nearby Indian mission established by the Reverend Thomas Riggs in 1873.[8] This construction project turned the muddy Missouri into a big blue lake, deeper than Erie and longer than Ontario. At a cost of over $346 million, Oahe became, next to Fort Peck Dam, the largest earth dam in the world. Stretching 250 miles northward to Bismarck, North Dakota, its reservoir, Lake Oahe, became the largest on the Missouri. The 245-foot-high dam produced the greatest power output (595,000 kilowatts) and the second largest storage capacity (23.5 million acre-feet) of any army project.[9]

The Oahe Dam destroyed more Indian land than any other public works project in America. The Standing Rock and Cheyenne River Sioux lost a total of 160,889 acres to this project, including their most valuable rangeland, most of their gardens and cultivated farm tracts, and nearly all of their timber, wild fruit, and wild-life resources. The inundation of more than 105,000 acres of choice grazing land affected 75 percent of the ranchers on the Cheyenne River Reservation and 60 percent of those at Standing Rock. Ninety percent of the timbered areas on both reservations were destroyed.[10]

Cheyenne River lost 104,420 acres to the Oahe deluge. Cheyenne Agency, the largest town on the reservation, and two other smaller communities were completely submerged. BIA and tribal facilities were moved sixty miles inland to the desolate prairie town of Eagle Butte, South Dakota. As in the case of Fort Thomp-

General aerial view of Oahe Dam and Lake Oahe, looking upstream to the northwest, near Pierre, South Dakota. Courtesy of United States Army, Corps of Engineers.

son, this relocation caused chaos and heartache for all tribal members. Over 180 families, about 30 percent of the tribal population, were forced to leave their homes.[11]

The Standing Rock tribe was somewhat more fortunate. Most of the agency headquarters at Fort Yates, North Dakota, remained above the reservoir pool level, but the town below, where the majority of nearby tribal members made their homes, was completely flooded. The filling of Lake Oahe made an island of the Fort Yates agency, separating it from the mainland area where most of the 170 families affected were eventually resettled. Standing Rock

Groundwork on the Oahe power plant, May 1960. Courtesy of
United States Army, Corps of Engineers.

Reservation lost 55,994 acres and was forced to relocate 25 percent of its residents.[12]

   While the Sioux were sustaining major damages from the Fort
Randall and Oahe projects, the Corps of Engineers began work on
the Big Bend Dam in September 1959. The project was located
near the new townsite of Fort Thompson on land belonging to the
Crow Creek and Lower Brulé tribes. The smallest of the army's
main-stem structures, Big Bend was developed primarily for hydroelectric power production. Taking advantage of the long bend in the
river for which it was named, engineers built a dam that produced
468,000 kilowatts and was just ninety-five feet high. The reservoir

Construction of the Oahe power plant, 1960. Courtesy of United States Army, Corps of Engineers.

behind it, only twenty miles long, was named for former South Dakota Governor M. Q. Sharpe. He was a leading advocate of the Pick Plan in 1944 who later served as tribal attorney for both the Crow Creek and Lower Brulé Sioux during their Fort Randall negotiations.[13]

The Big Bend project took an additional 21,026 acres of Sioux land. This time Lower Brulé suffered the most damage. The flooding of 14,609 acres, approximately 15 percent of the reservation land base, required the relocation of the town of Lower Brulé. The entire community was moved to a new site just one mile west of its former location. Sixty-two families, comprising 53 percent

Oahe Dam and powerhouse. Courtesy of United States Army, Corps of Engineers.

of the tribal population, were displaced. Most of the timber and pastureland not already destroyed by Fort Randall and nearly one-half of the remaining farms and ranches were inundated.[14]

The Crow Creek Sioux lost 6,417 acres to the Big Bend project and were forced to move twenty-seven families. These damages affected 5 percent of the reservation's land base and 11 percent of its population. Approximately one-fourth of the tribe's remaining farms and ranches were also deluged. The government's handling of the Fort Randall relocations had been so slipshod that families on both the Crow Creek and the Lower Brule reservations were relocated on lands within the projected area of the Big Bend Dam.

Closure of Oahe Dam, August 1958. Courtesy of United States Army, Corps of Engineers.

These unfortunate Indians were thus required to undergo the trauma of yet another move.[15]

The three Pick-Sloan projects reduced the total land base of the five Sioux reservations by about 6 percent. Because the native population was concentrated near the river, over one-third of the tribal members were forced to relocate. The natural advantages of their former homes could not be replaced on the marginal lands that remained. The shaded bottomlands had provided a pleasant environment with plenty of wood, game, water, and natural food sources. Livestock could graze on abundant grasses and take shelter under the trees. The barren upland regions to which these Indians moved were less hospitable, more rigorous, and presented far greater challenges to their survival.[16]

For those unfamiliar with Sioux culture and the geography of the Dakotas, it is perhaps difficult to appreciate how important the bottomlands were to their way of life. Trees along the river had provided the tribes with their primary source of fuel and lumber. The wooded areas also protected both man and beast from the ravages of winter blizzards and the scorching summer heat. The gathering and selling of wood helped supplement the Indians' small cash income. The inundation of the forestlands destroyed 90 percent of the timber on all of the reservations except the Yankton.[17]

The gathering and preserving of wild fruits and vegetables was a traditional part of Sioux culture. The many herbs, roots, berries, currants, plums, cherries, and beans that grew in the bottomlands added variety and bulk to the Indians' diet. These plants were eaten raw, dried and stored for winter, made into soups and sauces, or mixed with other foods to add flavoring. Traditionally they were also used for ceremonial and medicinal purposes. Buffalo berries, for example, were once used in female puberty rites, and chokeberries continued to serve as a cure for diarrhea and other ailments. A form of wild pea called a "mouse bean" was regarded in frontier days as one of the most palatable wild vegetables on the plains. This food source acquired its name because it was collected and stored by field mice and taken from their nests by Indians. According to tradition, the Sioux always replaced the beans they took with an equal amount of corn or other grain. Soup made from these beans was still considered a delicacy at the time of the inundation. The loss of these and other plants greatly reduced the Indians' natural food supply.[18]

The wooded bottomlands also served as a shelter and feeding ground for many kinds of wildlife. Deer, beaver, rabbits, and raccoons were abundant year-round, and thousands of pheasants and other game birds wintered there each year. The hunting and trapping of this game provided the tribes with an important source of food, income, and recreation. Destruction of this environment by the Pick-Sloan dams reduced the wild game and plant supply on the Sioux reservations by 75 percent.[19]

Although the Sioux fully exploited the resources of the bottomlands, the Missouri and other nearby streams were seldom used except as a water source. Fish had never become an important food for any of the tribes and was never a part of the reservation diet of Teton descendants. Furthermore, recreational fishing, swimming, and boating were uncommon activities for the Sioux.[20]

The loss of the bottomland grazing areas seriously crippled the Indian livestock industry. Ranching had become the primary economic activity on all of the reservations except the Yankton in the years prior to Pick-Sloan. The progress made by the Standing Rock, Cheyenne River, and Lower Brulé Sioux in establishing tribal cattle enterprises was greatly negated by the reservoir projects. A substantial portion of the Indian ranchers were forced either to liquidate their assets altogether or to establish smaller operations on the inferior reservation land that remained.[21]

In the bottomlands cattle were able freely to graze, water, and take shelter. On the upland prairies artificial shelters had to be built to replace the natural shelter of the trees, and the loss of the winter hay meadows meant open grazing was no longer possible. Fences had to be erected to confine the herds in smaller areas and to protect them from the waters of the wildly fluctuating reservoirs. Artesian wells, cisterns, and stock water ponds had to be dug, and feed supplements had to be purchased, to replace the natural water and food sources of the old habitat. Stock raising in the new environment thus proved more difficult, expensive, and risky.[22]

The upland regions also presented a stiff challenge for Indian homeowners. Houses built or relocated on this treeless land required better insulation and could no longer be heated by wood stoves. New sources of fuel, lumber, food, and water had to be developed or purchased. The necessity of finding new homesites and rangelands on the reduced reservations created a highly competitive and inflated real-estate market. The nature of the soil and terrain made irrigation impractical if not impossible. Paradoxically, Pick-Sloan flooded the most potentially irrigable lands. The Fort Randall and Big Bend projects, for example, destroyed the possibility of implementing plans proposed jointly by the BIA and the Bureau of Reclamation for sizable irrigation projects on the Crow Creek and Lower Brule reservations.[23]

Damage caused by the Pick-Sloan projects touched every aspect of Sioux life. Abruptly the tribes were transformed from a subsistence to a cash economy and forced to develop new ways of making a living. The uprooting of long-standing Indian communities disrupted and disorganized the social, economic, political, and religious life of well-integrated tribal groups and had a serious effect on the entire reservation population. It was an onerous imposition for tribal members to be forced to move their community halls, churches, and religious shrines. It was even harder for them to disturb the graves of their ancestors. Yet, on all except the Yankton reservation the largest cemeteries and most of the private burial grounds had to be excavated and moved elsewhere.[24]

Physical losses inflicted by Pick-Sloan were easily quantified. Psychological and aesthetic damages were more difficult to measure. Like any people forced to relinquish their homes, the Sioux hated not only giving up their property but also seeking unfamiliar places to live. Their particular circumstances made the situation even more difficult. Because of their close relationship with nature, the Sioux had a sacred attachment to their land. The areas along the river had afforded them a comfortable and relatively scenic environment with resources enough to sustain their way of life. The loss of this land and livelihood had a strong emotional impact on them. The disruption of both traditional communities and federal services created a great deal of anxiety, insecurity, and resentment. Feelings that they were being unjustly exploited made them sullen and bitter. Unlike others affected by public works projects, they were not able to duplicate their old way of life by moving to a similar environment. No Indian lands like the ones vacated existed after inundation. When measured in terms of the loss of federal services and close kinship ties, the disadvantages of leaving the reservation were much too great to make it a viable alternative.[25]

Many tribal leaders had been optimistic about the Pick-Sloan Plan until they learned of its full effects. The Crow Creek Tribal Council, for example, unanimously passed a resolution on May 2, 1947, welcoming the dam projects. Because they would provide "necessary benefits of flood control, generation of hydroelectric power, irrigation developments, and recreation and other opportunities," the council pledged to give federal agencies free access to their reservation and to fully cooperate in helping to bring about these objectives on Crow Creek. BIA Agency Superintendent Frell M. Owl later warned Tribal Chairman Vernon Ashley that the tribe would suffer severe damages from the Fort Randall and Big Bend projects and advised the council to reconsider its resolution.[26]

Once damage estimates were ascertained, the Sioux became more apprehensive about dealing with the government. They became more skeptical about the benefits promised by Pick-Sloan, and they waited cautiously to see what might happen on the other reservations.

The first native group forced to deal with the Corps of Engineers was the Three Affiliated Tribes of the Fort Berthold Reservation in western North Dakota. The construction of Garrison Dam on their land resulted in the taking of 152,360 acres. Although this was less than the total amount of Indian land destroyed by Oahe Dam, the effects on Fort Berthold were far more devastating. Over one-fourth of the reservation's total land base, including the agency headquarters at Elbowoods, was deluged by the dam's reservoir. The remainder of the Indian land was segmented into five water-bound sections. Because the bottomland population was even more concentrated than on the Sioux reserves, the project required the relocation of 325 families, or approximately 80 percent of the tribal membership. For many years successful as ranchers and farmers, these industrious people lost 94 percent of their agricultural lands.[27]

Without prior warning the Corps of Engineers entered Fort Berthold Reservation to begin construction on the dam in April 1946. The first of the army's Pick-Sloan projects on the main stem of the Missouri River was Garrison Dam, which became America's fifth largest dam at a cost of over $299 million. The 212-foot-high structure provided a storage capacity of 24.2 million acre-feet and a generating capacity of 400,000 kilowatts. Its long reservoir, Lake Sakakawea, was named for the famous Shoshone woman who helped guide Lewis and Clark on their expedition up the Missouri in 1804.[28]

The Corps of Engineers, without authorization from Congress, altered the project's specifications in order to protect the city of Williston, North Dakota, and to prevent interference with the Bureau of Reclamation irrigation projects, but nothing was done to safeguard Indian communities. When the army threatened to confiscate the land it needed by right of eminent domain, the Fort Berthold Indians protested in Washington. There they succeeded in having Congress halt all expenditures for the Garrison Dam project until they received a suitable settlement. This legal action was based on the Fort Laramie Treaty of 1851, which provided that land could not be taken from the tribes without their consent and that of Congress.[29]

Negotiations with the army subsequently began in earnest. The Tribal Council offered an alternative reservation dam site free of charge. This optional site, whose selection would have caused considerably less damage to the Indians, was rejected by the Corps of Engineers because it would not permit adequate storage capacity. Army negotiators did offer to purchase an equal amount of land in the Knife River Valley to replace that lost to the Garrison project, but the Indians found it unsuitable for their needs.[30]

Further talks were marred by an unfortunate incident. Crow Flies High, an opponent of the incumbent tribal government, managed to gain the support of a small faction of the tribal members by circulating a petition opposing all negotiations. At a reservation conference attended by General Pick, who had returned to the post of Missouri Division Engineer, members of this dissident group appeared in full ceremonial garb, denounced the talks, and publicly insulted the army officers present. Pick lost control of his emotions, flew into a rage, and promised never to forget the incident. In retaliation he promptly broke off negotiations and repudiated all agreements reached to that time. By his failure to understand the situation, the general clearly revealed his basic ignorance of the people with whom he was dealing. Pick's contention that the Indians were belligerently uncooperative was used by him as a reason to dictate his own settlement terms to Congress.[31]

In 1947 the Three Affiliated Tribes finally had to accept the $5,105,625 offered by Congress and the corps for their losses. This settlement, considered generous by many on Capitol Hill, meant that they received about $33 for each acre of their land with improvements and severance damages. From this amount they were expected also to pay relocation and reconstruction expenses. The agreement did permit them to claim additional compensation through Congress or the courts. The Indians were determined to exercise this option, and they petitioned for more money and additional benefits, such as exclusive rights to a small portion of Garrison's hydroelectric power production at a reduced rate. After a private appraisal claimed damages to the tribe were $21,981,000, legislation requesting that amount was introduced in Congress. Following two years of debate the House and Senate finally agreed to a compromise figure of $7.5 million. Legislation for this final settlement received President Truman's signature on October 29, 1949.[32]

The total compensation of $12,605,625 was over $9,000,000 less than the Indians felt was the fair market value of the damages they sustained. The final piece of settlement legislation denied their right to use the reservoir shoreline for grazing, hunting, fishing, or other purposes. It also rejected tribal requests for irrigation-development and royalty rights on all subsurface minerals within the reservoir area. The petition for a block of Garrison Dam power was denied on the grounds that the granting of exclusive rights to the Indians would violate provisions of the Rural Electrification Act of 1936. The legislation provided for distribution of funds on a per capita basis and its failure to bar the collection of previous individual debts from this money proved to be a serious handicap. Because the law stipulated that it was a final and complete settlement of all claims, the Three Affiliated Tribes were unsuccessful in their twenty-year struggle to have its deficiencies corrected by amendatory legislation.[33]

Within a few years the Fort Berthold Indians were obliged to move to new homes. Relocation and salvage procedures established by the Corps of Engineers proved unsatisfactory. Private movers contracted by the army were unreliable, and tribal members were denied permission to cut most of their timber prior to inundation. Flooding of the bottomlands rendered the residual reservation useless. Settlement payments were too low to provide full reestablishment for most families. The uprooting of kinship and other primary groups destroyed the community life so fundamental to the Indians' culture. Farms and ranches were liquidated, unemployment rose as high as 79 percent, and many tribal members were driven to a life of despair in nearby urban centers. Millions of dollars in federal funds were pumped into the reservation to counteract social and economic damages. After a generation of hard work the tribes began to show signs of recovery, but psychic scars from their ordeal remained evident.[34]

The Fort Berthold experience was a meaningful one for the Sioux. Negotiations with the first native group affected by Pick-Sloan established many important precedents. Most important, Congress had demonstrated its recognition of the federal government's extraordinary obligations regarding the taking of Indian land. If the tribes had been left merely to the devices of the Corps of Engineers, they would have received a cash settlement equal only to the amount of the army's appraisal of their property, subject to court appeal. This, after all, was the procedure established for the acquisition of all other lands required for public works projects.

Because of the Indians' special treaty rights, their status as wards of the government, and their inability to replace lost resources, Congress saw fit to provide the Fort Berthold tribes with additional money and assistance for relocation and reconstruction. Although the additional $7.5 million was too little to be fully effective, and the help provided by the army was unsatisfactory, these gestures symbolized an attempt by Congress to acknowledge its moral and legal duty to the Indians. The Sioux tribes succeeded in extending this obligation, and each of them received a more satisfactory settlement in the years to come. The Corps of Engineers, however, like the oblivious ostrich, continued to ignore the special responsibilities of the federal government toward Indians and repeatedly violated the principles established by Congress.

The Sioux kept a close watch on Fort Berthold developments. Delegates from several tribes were sent to Elbowoods and Washington to attend negotiations and to learn how special problems were being resolved. Most of the tribes learned more of what they might expect when dealing with federal officials, and the incident with General Pick made them particularly wary of the Corps of Engineers. Unfortunately, when it came time for their own negotiations, it was their weakest member, the uninformed and disorganized Yankton Sioux, who first had to confront the army.[35]

When construction of the Fort Randall Dam began a month after Garrison Dam, the Corps of Engineers was soon faced with the necessity of acquiring 3,349 acres of Yankton land. Tribal members on this reservation were badly split into five separate political factions, none of which could muster enough support to provide effective government. The Yankton Sioux therefore lacked a constitution and representative council, even though they had voted to accept Wheeler-Howard provisions. The tribe met in general council if it met at all, and at other times anarchy prevailed. They had not displayed any special concern over Pick-Sloan as a group and had not sent delegates to Fort Berthold. The Corps of Engineers took advantage of this situation and decided to proceed as if their land were like any other private property by condemning the parcels it needed in federal court.[36]

Without prior consultation with either the tribe or the Bureau of Indian Affairs, the army condemned thirty-one separate tracts of Yankton land between April 1947 and April 1948. After the corps deposited $132,324 with the federal district court, an amount equal to its appraisal of the Yankton property, it took immediate possession of the land and began charging rent to the nineteen Indian families living there. In a letter to Acting Indian Commissioner William Zimmerman, Jr., General Pick advised that, unlike developments at Fort Berthold, special legislation would not be needed for the Yankton Sioux because, in his view, the army could settle all problems "in the field."[37]

The confiscation of Yankton land by the corps was illegal. The army not only violated the Yankton Treaty of 1858, which provided that land could not be taken without the prior consent of the tribe and Congress, but also ignored legal precedents established by the Supreme Court. In such cases as *Cherokee Nation* v. *Southern Kansas Railroad Co.* (1890), *Thomas* v. *Gay* (1898), and *Choate* v. *Trapp* (1912), the court had determined that Congress could abrogate Indian treaties in order to exercise its sovereign right of eminent domain. In the case of *United States* v. *North American Transportation and Trading Co.* (1920) the court had ruled that a federal agency could not exercise this right without prior congressional authorization. Nothing in the Flood Control Act of 1944, which approved the Pick-Sloan projects, or in any subsequent legislation had authorized the Corps of Engineers and Bureau of Reclamation to condemn Indian land. The army's decision to do so in the case of the Yankton Sioux seemed to be based on a calculated risk that it could get away with it. Unfortunately, time proved the generals to be correct.[38]

The corps' condemnation suits went unchallenged. The Yankton tribe was not aware of its legal rights, and district court magistrates apparently did not research thoroughly before making their decisions. The Bureau of Indian Affairs also failed to legally challenge the army, although it did choose to haggle with the corps over certain provisions of the court settlements. For example, the BIA questioned the adequacy of army land appraisals, claiming that they had undervalued farm improvements and timber. They also objected to the policy whereby impoverished tribal members were required to lease their formerly owned land until forced to relocate. At a conference with BIA officials in Omaha on April 28, 1948, corps representatives agreed to allow the Yankton Sioux to use their land and salvage all timber and improvements without charge. When the Indian Bureau tried to implement this policy, army officials refused to acknowledge their earlier concessions. In frustration the BIA decided to turn the entire matter over to Congress.[39]

Faced with the possibility of again having to justify its actions on Capitol Hill, the Corps of Engineers pleaded with the BIA to renegotiate a local settlement. Pick suggested to Zimmerman that additional compensation might easily be obtained through the district court. Agreeing to a final conference in Omaha on October 15, 1948, bureau officials accepted corps promises to abide by its previous concessions to allow free occupancy, to honor salvage rights, and to permit an impartial board to reappraise land values. At the same time the BIA proceeded with its plans to request an additional $85,000 from Congress to cover relocation costs. It justified this action by pointing out that the army settlement was insufficient to allow Indian families to purchase substitute lands and to reestablish their farms elsewhere. Congress, however, refused to act quickly on this legislation, and the Yankton Sioux families were forced to move with only the funds they had received through the court, with six years passing before additional compensation was received.[40]

In the meantime the Corps of Engineers began construction on its third main-stem project, the Oahe Dam. Commissioner Zimmerman hoped to avoid the kinds of problems created at the Fort

Berthold and Yankton projects. In another letter to General Pick he asked that the army refrain from condemning the land of the Standing Rock and Cheyenne River Sioux tribes and cooperate with the BIA in establishing more humane procedures. To help assure that this would be done, protective legislation was introduced in Congress by Senator Chan Gurney and Congressman Francis Case of South Dakota. Both congressmen proposed bills that would not only establish legal guidelines for negotiations with the separate tribes but also require the two federal agencies to work together in reaching an agreement comparable to the final Fort Berthold settlement.[41]

Congress was receptive to the measure. It recognized, as it had in the Fort Berthold case, that the government was obliged to negotiate a fair settlement with the tribes. It also candidly acknowledged that the Oahe project would be of greater benefit to people below the dam and that "no benefits will accrue to the Indians." "These Indians are opposed to the construction of the reservoir," noted Congressman Case in presenting his measure, "but realizing that they cannot prevent such action, urge the enactment of this bill."[42]

The legislation, as enacted in September 1950, made the army chief of engineers and the secretary of the interior responsible for negotiating favorable settlements with tribal representatives. It required that the final settlement not only provide payment for Indian land and improvements but also cover the costs of relocating tribal members "so that their economic, social, religious, and community life can be reestablished and protected."[43]

President Truman proclaimed in signing the act that "the United States government must make certain that these groups of American Indians, who will sacrifice their best lands and their homes for the benefit of the nation, will be dealt with on a basis commensurate with their sacrifices."[44] To assure an equitable settlement, the law required both the Corps of Engineers and the Bureau of Indian Affairs to prepare detailed appraisals to determine the fair market value of all Indian property within the reservoir area. Tribal members who rejected these appraisals were given the right to have the value of their land determined in federal district court at army expense.[45]

Settlement contracts were to be negotiated, approved, and submitted to Congress for final determination within eighteen months. They were to take effect only after ratification by an act of Congress and by approval of three-fourths of the adult tribal members on each reservation, as stipulated by treaty. If an agreement could not be reached in the field, Congress itself would arbitrate a final settlement. The law stated, however, that under no circumstances would negotiations be allowed to interfere with construction schedules of the Oahe project. It also declared that the final agreement would represent a complete legal settlement of all Indian claims regarding the loss of their land. To make sure everyone understood these terms, the legislation was translated into Lakota and was distributed throughout the reservations.[46]

When news of this law reached the tribes, officials on Standing Rock and Cheyenne River breathed a sigh of relief. Congressional protection eased fears that the Corps of Engineers would treat them as it had the Yankton Sioux. Still they were not completely satisfied with the legislation.

The original bill had requested that a block of Oahe's electric power be set aside for the exclusive use of the tribes, and the Department of the Interior had endorsed the request. The House Committee on Interior and Insular Affairs dropped the provision, and the subject was thus open for negotiation. The legislation as finally amended provided that the Sioux tribes, like the Fort Berthold Indians, would receive electric power on an equal basis with all other users under provisions of the Rural Electrification Act of 1936. Congressman Case pointed out to his colleagues that for the Indians to be able to purchase electricity on the same basis as rural cooperatives and other public bodies was equivalent to "no compensation at all."[47]

Other important considerations were also ignored. The law made no provision for attorneys to represent the tribes in negotiations. The question of shoreline access rights was also left unresolved. Unlike the Fort Berthold settlement, the law failed to address the problem of payments to members of other tribes and nontribal members who held inherited interests in tracts covered by the reservoir.[48]

The Cheyenne River and Standing Rock Sioux felt that the Fort

Berthold Indians had been robbed by the government and were determined to negotiate settlements more favorable to tribal interests. Legislation in 1950 helped pave the way for this development, even though it denied hydroelectric power provisions and ignored other important considerations. The Lower Brulé and Crow Creek Sioux were encouraged to seek legislation that would protect them in the Fort Randall negotiations, and all tribal officials were determined to fight for maximum benefits. Little did they suspect how long and hard the battle would be.

Chapter 5

EARLY DISPUTES

Negotiations with the separate Sioux tribes followed a similar pattern. It was inevitable that army, Indian Bureau, and tribal officials arrived at different estimates of damage. The BIA was often willing to compromise with the Indians; the Corps of Engineers consistently refused to offer concessions and ultimately failed to reach a satisfactory agreement with any of the tribes. Negotiations dragged far beyond established time limits, and Congress was extremely slow in considering contract provisions. The Crow Creek and Lower Brulé tribes, like the Yankton Sioux, were actually forced to move before agreeing to a settlement, and the Standing Rock Sioux received funds at the last possible moment. Only the Cheyenne River Indians, who managed to settle four years before the others, were afforded enough time and money to prepare an orderly retreat.

The unversed and unwary tribal representatives were simply outgunned in negotiations. They were forced at every turn to do battle with experienced federal experts, while the BIA hampered their efforts to secure competent legal advice. The individual lawyers who eventually were allowed to represent each tribe found themselves pitted against teams of government attorneys. Settlement demands drawn up by the Indians very often were circumvented or ignored by federal negotiators. In every case the Corps of Engineers used strong-arm tactics by posing the threat of its assumed powers of eminent domain. Local congressmen did what they could for the Indians but too often exhibited split allegiances and shifting loyalties. The result was a half-a-loaf settlement for each tribe, although in turn each tribe gained more money and better terms. None of the Sioux tribes received anything close to what they considered just compensation.

In accordance with congressional guidelines established in 1950, the Standing Rock and Cheyenne River tribes selected committees to represent them at federal negotiations. Most of the delegates were chosen from the ranks of tribal councils. Tribal leaders Josephine Kelly of Standing Rock and Frank Ducheneaux of Cheyenne River appointed themselves to head the committees. Both were political veterans.[1]

Kelly had been one of the first Indian women elected to tribal office under provisions of the Indian Reorganization Act. Ironically, she had once hitchhiked to Washington in the early thirties to protest passage of this law. She was strong willed and stubbornly independent and had proved herself an outstanding tribal leader. Unfortunately, her tenure in office ended before serious negotiations were undertaken.[2]

The Cheyenne River chairman, Ducheneaux, proved a tough negotiator throughout the Oahe ordeal. He had served on the original tribal council chartered in 1934 and was elected to the top post in 1950. He weathered the often vicious infighting of tribal politics and managed to keep the top position for sixteen years, an enviable tenure for any Indian leader.[3]

While waiting for Congress to provide negotiation guidelines for the Fort Randall settlement, the Crow Creek and Lower Brulé tribes also appointed negotiating committees. Chairmen Abel Bad Moccasin of Crow Creek and Richard LaRoche, Jr., of Lower Brule headed these delegations. The Yankton Sioux declined to select a tribal committee and relied solely on the efforts of local congressmen to secure a settlement for them. Legislation to provide additional payments to the Yankton tribe, first introduced in 1949, had received little consideration on Capitol Hill. The Interior Department decided to combine the Yankton compensation bill with proposals to establish legal settlement procedures for the Crow

Creek and Lower Brulé tribes, but this legislative package met with considerable delay. The first of the new bills, introduced by Congressman E. Y. Berry of South Dakota, was not presented to Congress until June 19, 1952. Although amended and approved by the House Interior Committee, the Senate failed to consider it before the Eighty-second Congress adjourned. As a result Berry was forced to reintroduce the bill in 1953.[4]

To aid in negotiations, the Cheyenne River, Standing Rock, and Lower Brulé Sioux retained the services of Ralph Hoyt Case, a local attorney. Case had a long record with Indian claims, having first been engaged by the Cheyenne River tribe in 1922. He had served as counsel for nearly all of the Sioux tribes at one time and had previously represented them in the early years of the long-pending Black Hills suit before both the United States Court of Claims and the Indian Claims Commission. In 1949 he had worked for the Fort Berthold Indians in negotiating the Garrison settlement, but criticism of the terms of that agreement brought Case under fire. As complaints against him were spread from reservation to reservation, one after another of his tribal contracts was canceled. The Standing Rock and Lower Brulé Sioux eventually succumbed to the pressure and released Case before any talks began. Case continued to be retained by the Cheyenne River tribe throughout their negotiations because he was a close friend of the Ducheneaux family.[5]

Efforts on the part of the Standing Rock Sioux to hire another attorney ran into difficulty. Tribal leaders sought to employ James E. Curry, a noted Washington lawyer and an outspoken critic of the Bureau of Indian Affairs. Rather than following the standard procedure of having the BIA pay for their legal services, the tribe wanted to use its own funds to retain Curry on a four-year contract to assure that their counsel would be completely independent of Interior Department politics. Indian Commissioner Dillon S. Myer would not hear of the idea. He and Curry were bitter enemies. Myer refused to approve more than a one-year contract on these terms, requiring the lawyer to gain his favor in order to keep his contract. Because the Standing Rock tribe wanted to retain the same attorney throughout the extended period of the Oahe negotiations, they immediately protested Myer's decision to Interior Secretary Oscar Chapman.[6]

For seven months the tribe waited patiently for Chapman to answer their charges. In the meantime Myer publicly attacked Curry, accused him of being an opportunist and a sham, and charged that he deliberately misled the Indians by improperly soliciting their claims while bartering solely for his own gain. Myer was a curious appointee of the Truman Administration. He had previously administered the Japanese internment-camp program during World War II. Lest anyone doubt that the New Deal spirit was dying within the BIA, Myer also refused to approve Curry's contracts with the Crow Creek Sioux as well as those with twelve other tribes. Others in Washington, including members of the Senate Indian Affairs Subcommittee, applauded his stand. His vendetta against the Indian claims lawyers was also extended to seven other attorneys, including Felix S. Cohen, a leading authority on federal Indian law and a primary architect of the Indian Reorganization Act.[7]

After it became apparent that the Interior Department was ignoring Standing Rock complaints, a tribal delegation headed by Josephine Kelly was sent to Washington with orders to stay there until they received a hearing. For twenty-six days the Indians camped out in Secretary Chapman's office, lobbied in Congress, and were interviewed by radio broadcasters, newsmen, and columnists in their effort to present their case. Congressmen from the Dakotas were pressed to urge the Interior Department to "end all obstructions and delays."[8] The tribe also succeeded in gaining the support of former Interior Secretary Harold L. Ickes, anthropologist Gene Weltfish, and author Oliver LaFarge, who was the director of the Association of American Indian Affairs. Groups as diverse as the American Bar Association and the Daughters of the American Revolution also pleaded the Standing Rock case.[9]

Finally, on May 17, 1951, Secretary Chapman overruled Myer and approved the tribe's contract with Curry. The Standing Rock Sioux had won a significant victory for all of America's Indians. The Interior Secretary's decision meant that for the first time tribes could select their own attorneys and could make contracts with them on their own terms. Chapman's action, although slow in coming, demonstrated his ability to rise above the petty controversies generated by the Indian commissioner in order to protect the civil liberties of tribal members.[10]

Myer soon retaliated. He openly criticized his boss in statements to the press. He also moved to place new restrictions on the tribe through his ultimate power over its purse strings. Even though forced to approve their contract with Curry, he refused to let the Standing Rock Sioux spend more than $300 a year for his legal services, thus severely limiting their chances for adequate representation. To the chagrin of tribal leaders, it took another long Washington battle before this new restriction was lifted.[11]

Curry's contract with the Crow Creek Sioux never was approved. Myer also blocked tribal attempts to hire a local attorney, Ramon Robideaux. A protest led by the Indian Rights Association and the Association of American Indian Affairs produced no results. The American Civil Liberties Union provided funds for lawyers to serve as unofficial tribal representatives in preliminary negotiations that began in 1952. Eventually, however, the tribe felt compelled to find an attorney who met Myer's approval. It settled on M. Q. Sharpe, a local lawyer previously engaged by the Lower Brulé Sioux. Sharpe, the former governor of South Dakota, had no trouble gaining approval for his contract. As chairman of the Missouri River States Committee, he had been a leading advocate of the Pick Plan during the congressional debate of 1944.[12]

Meanwhile, the Standing Rock and Cheyenne River tribes were forced to confront the Interior Department on yet another Oahe project issue. In September 1951 the BIA announced plans to consolidate its separate facilities on the two reservations and to move them to the predominantly white community of Mobridge, South Dakota.[13]

The proposal immediately produced a storm of protest. Both tribes claimed that consolidation would create endless hardship for the Indians and would violate their treaty rights. Delegations under Josephine Kelly and Frank Ducheneaux again went to Washington to confront Chapman. The National Congress of American Indians and the General Federation of Women's Clubs lobbied for their cause, and the tribes' position was eloquently defended by Francis Case, who now served in the United States Senate. Hearings were scheduled on the issue, during which Myer defended his decision in light of BIA budget cuts. Although Chapman faced overwhelming opposition, he again moved to override bureau administrators and ordered discontinuation of the consolidation plans.[14]

The Curry case and the consolidation plan demonstrated to Indian leaders that tribal self-government was clearly a myth. The first showed the strict limitations imposed by the Indian Bureau on tribal autonomy. The second, in contrast, emphasized the continued dependence of the Sioux on federal services. In the years following World War II, which were characterized by a general retreat from Indian New Deal principles, the terms "Indian self-determination" and "Indian self-sufficiency" were frequently bandied about in government circles. Officials in Washington began to discuss ways by which the government might untangle itself from "the Indian business" and might terminate both BIA subsidies and controls. These "termination policies" were aimed at the eventual abolishment of the Indian Bureau and the establishment of county-type governments on reservations. Such innovations were given serious consideration during the latter years of the Truman administration, largely under the impetus of Commissioner Myer. Consequently, during the early Eisenhower years, legislation implementing termination for the Menominees, the Klamaths, and four other comparatively prosperous tribes was introduced and approved.[15]

Most tribes welcomed self-determination but were not prepared for self-sufficiency. Because of the nature of their historical development, few tribes were endowed with economic resources sufficient to support such essential government services as welfare, education, and police protection. Yet many were confident they had tribal leaders capable of handling the challenge of complete self-government. Influenced by talk of termination, the Standing Rock Sioux rejected the consolidation plan and issued a statement that the tribe was prepared "to assume all authority, responsibility, and obligations that may arise in the administration of tribal property and affairs."[16] Ironically, the entire focus of their protest was to prevent reduction or elimination of existing federal services, which they considered vital.

The idea of terminating the reservation structure with its federal supervision influenced nearly every aspect of Indian affairs throughout the 1950s. It was paradoxical that policies shaped by this

idea took two directions regarding the Pick-Sloan negotiations.
On one hand, both Congress and the BIA recognized that in
light of probable termination the tribes were justified in receiving
settlements that would help them become self-sufficient. That
recognition accounted in part for the government's willingness
to offer payments beyond the usual scope of federal land acquisition procedures. On the other hand, if the BIA eventually was
to be abolished, many government officials could see no need to
take any further interest in Indian affairs. Consequently, appropriations for the bureau were reduced, tribal problems received
less attention in Washington, and termination advocates gained
even greater strength in Congress. Such developments accounted
for the many obstacles and long delays placed in the path of tribal
efforts to secure timely and equitable settlements.

Soon after negotiating committees were appointed at the Cheyenne River and Standing Rock reservations, the Corps of Engineers
hired a private Denver firm, Gerald T. Hart and Associates, to
prepare an appraisal of all Indian land within the Oahe project area.
The Hart appraisers began their work in the spring of 1951. A team
of Missouri River Basin Investigations Project (MRBI) foresters
surveyed timber resources on the reservations, and other staff
members monitored the army-sponsored appraisals. In November
the Hart firm submitted its valuations to the tribal councils.[17]

In the meantime the Standing Rock committee held its first
open conference at Fort Yates with representatives of the Corps
of Engineers and Bureau of Indian Affairs. Tribal members wanted
to know what consequences they could expect if they refused to
move from their land. Tribal leaders in attendance immediately
asked the critical question of what action would ensue if they
refused to give up their title. Army spokesmen were mortified.
They had come to discuss matters of compensation and were in
no way prepared to explain the necessity for the dam itself. They
had assumed that everyone already understood that the project
would be completed regardless of what the Indians thought or
did, but tribal members soon reminded them that they had special
property rights protected by treaty. "Let me tell you folks," said
corps representative Lloyd Atchley in reply, "there is little difference in the taking of land from Indians and others regardless
of race."[18]

Angered by the obvious reference to the army's broad powers of eminent domain, tribal attorney Curry reminded Atchley that the corps had as yet no legal authorization to take the Indians' land by force. Tribal negotiator Leo Cadotte then stated that, if the army intended to use condemnation, it was in for a fight. The Sioux, he declared, would no longer "give up their land as easily as they did the Black Hills."[19]

In the face of hostile opposition the corps representatives were gradually compelled to assume the posture of a supplicant asking the tribe for permission to take its lands. When the corps representatives continued to be interrogated about the necessity of the project, they could only reply in terms of its potential benefits to the Indians. Tribal members were generally unimpressed by the arguments. W. L. Gipp explained that it was no benefit to be moved to land that was so desolate that even "the jackrabbit carries a box lunch."[20] Skeptical of the army's glowing descriptions of future recreation and tourism, tribal negotiator James McLean replied that the tribe would be much better off if tourists "went swimming in some other lake."[21]

It was ironic that the increasingly heated discussion of benefits was interrupted by a power failure that caused the conference to be adjourned until morning. Corps spokesmen were forced again the next day to defend the entire Pick-Sloan Plan and to explain in particular the necessity and location of the Oahe project. One tribal member asked why the army did not build more dams in the lower basin. Before the corps representative could offer an explanation, Chairman Josephine Kelly replied, "Because there are no Indians down in that country."[22]

The Hart appraisers determined that damages to Indian property would amount to $1,605,410 for the Cheyenne River Sioux and $1,320,000 for the Standing Rock tribe. These estimates were based on an agreed definition of "fair market value" previously determined by the Corps of Engineers and Bureau of Indian Affairs.[23] Land values were based on a summation of the worth of selected tracts and not on a detailed tract-by-tract evaluation. Improvements were appraised according to their replacement costs less depreciation for obsolescence. Severance damages were limited to specific tangible elements on the ground as they affected particular tracts. The Hart appraisal accepted MRBI estimates on timber values, but it did not include mineral values because the army did not expect to gain full title to those resources.[24]

As soon as they received the Hart appraisal, the Cheyenne River Negotiating Committee began an investigation of the findings. The Hart valuations were checked against tribal and agency land records, information furnished by property owners, and their own field inspections. The committee was assisted in the review by one of its members, Sidney Claymore, who was a professional land appraiser. With his help the negotiators soon discovered some errors in property descriptions. Certain buildings, fences, stock ponds, and other improvements had somehow been overlooked, and some cropland and timber were not included. In many cases the committee concluded that property and damage estimates were much too low. Because of these discoveries the committee requested a conference with federal officials to discuss ways of correcting the errors.[25]

On January 7, 1952, Cheyenne River negotiators met with Commissioner Myer in Washington. In response to their request for a conference with corps officials, he arranged a meeting with General Pick, then chief of engineers, for January 11. At the meeting tribal delegates presented an eight-page list of appraisal errors. After reviewing their findings, the general agreed that corrections would have to be made before negotiations could proceed. He promised that the army would reevaluate the appraisal and correct all mistakes. Tribal Chairman Frank Ducheneaux then suggested that a conference be held at Cheyenne River in the spring to resolve appraisal differences and to begin discussion of other matters related to settlement negotiations. General Pick agreed and expressed hope that final contract talks could be initiated by September 15, 1952. In light of similar complaints emanating from the Standing Rock negotiators, the chief of engineers also agreed to review their appraisal and to confer with them in the spring too.[26]

The two tribes were not alone in their criticism of army appraisal methods. Other property owners affected by Pick-Sloan projects objected to corps procedures and made their complaints known in Washington. They, like the Indians, were dissatisfied with techniques that one writer described as the army's "land inquisition policy."[27]

In the taking of private property for public purposes, the Corps of Engineers and other federal agencies were required by the Constitution to provide landowners with "just compensation" as determined by due process of law. The meaning of this rather vague legal requirement had been variously interpreted. The courts defined just compensation as an amount equal to the "fair market value" of the property. This value was further defined as "the price a willing buyer would pay a willing seller." But the courts maintained that the property owner should be placed in the "same pecuniary position" after the taking as before. Both the army and the Department of Justice, which handled most federal condemnation cases, insisted on a narrow interpretation of their legal requirements, emphasizing the willing buyer–willing seller concept.[28]

Corps appraisals were usually conducted by its own real-estate division. Property owners were supposed to be notified in advance and were invited to accompany army appraisers, who were usually civilians. Valuations were based on the present market value of similar local property, but appraisers were not allowed to discuss specific items or values with property owners. After estimates were checked by a reviewing appraiser, the corps offered its appraised valuation as the basis of settlement, without offering an explanation of the method used to obtain that single figure. Owners thus had no idea if all of their property had been included or properly evaluated. If they rejected the offer, the army filed a condemnation suit against them in federal district court. They were then forced to undergo the lengthy and expensive ordeal of having the fair market value of their property determined by a judge or jury or both. For those who could afford to follow this route, the usual result was a much higher settlement.[29]

Once a settlement had been reached, the Corps of Engineers took full title to all property. If owners wanted to remove their houses, improvements, or other resources, they were required to pay the appraised salvage value of such items. Property not moved on time was confiscated by the army. If owners wished to make use of their former land prior to inundation, they were compelled to lease it from the corps at variable rates.[30]

Dakota farmers affected by the dam projects complained that the Corps of Engineers never gave them advance notice of appraisal dates. They objected strongly because neither were they allowed to see a breakdown of separate valuations once appraisals were completed nor were their legal rights adequately explained to them. They charged the army appraisers with being unfamiliar with local lands, with being extremely inconsistent evaluators, and with basing their valuations on the least valuable land in the area. Also, they resented the corps' policy of buying only the tracts it needed instead of entire farms, because loss of bottomland often rendered the remaining property useless.[31]

Several landowners reported being intimidated into signing contracts and continually threatened with condemnation of their land. They claimed that procedures that allowed the Corps of Engineers to take title to the land merely by depositing a sum of money equal to its own appraisal with the court violated both the spirit and the letter of constitutional due-process requirements. In some early cases the army refused even to reveal its appraisal findings in the hope that it could bargain for a lower price. Outrage at this policy, however, soon forced the corps to prohibit its agents from offering settlements below the final appraisal figure. In 1952, Congress also forced the army to recognize its obligation to provide payment for relocation costs. For the first time, the corps was required to offer owners an amount equal to 25 percent of the appraised property value to help defray moving expenses.[32]

The hostility and insensitivity that characterized Corps of Engineers land acquisition policies did little to enhance its rapidly sagging public image in the Missouri Basin. That such human callousness was entirely unnecessary had been demonstrated by the experience of the Tennessee Valley Authority (TVA). Emphasizing the "same pecuniary position" concept, TVA had consistently shown its concern for the human consequences of dam construction. Appraisals were carried out in a friendly and cooperative manner by local committees. Property owners were offered generous settlements that took into consideration both inflation factors and replacement costs. When owners accepted the offers, as 97 percent of them did, they were paid quickly and were allowed to use their land and to salvage their property without further charge. If they did not accept, their appeal was heard by a special committee established for the sole purpose of adjudicating such settlements.[33]

TVA made every effort to accommodate displaced families. The agricultural extension services of several state universities were engaged to assist them in finding new homes and adjusting to new circumstances. Steps were taken to prevent land inflation, and state and local governments were reimbursed for the loss of property tax revenues. As a result of these policies most landowners affected by TVA enjoyed a more desirable living situation after they were relocated than they had known before.[34]

TVA acquired over 1,000,000 acres and displaced about 20,000 farm families, yet only 3 percent of its land was taken through condemnation. In contrast, the corps took over 1,600,000 acres for Pick-Sloan projects and forced more than 25 percent of the 4,000 families involved to go to court for settlement. The hostility generated by army methods, coupled with the fact that owners received on the average 44 percent more money from the courts, tended to encourage litigation. In contrast, owners who rejected TVA appraisals received only 18 percent more funds, and the settlements were far more uniform. For owners, the process of condemnation was usually lengthy, frustrating, and expensive (costing at least $1,000) but it generally rewarded those who had the patience and money to persevere against the army.[35]

In dealing with the Corps of Engineers, the Sioux tribes had an advantage over non-Indian property owners. Because of their treaty rights and special status as wards of the government, Congress was obliged to require the army to negotiate more equitable settlements with them. The Bureau of Indian Affairs was also charged with the responsibility of protecting tribal interests, and this allowed the Indians to operate from a much better bargaining position. Negotiating as a tribe, they were more organized than independent rural families and were also better represented on valuations, because the army was required in their case to make a breakdown of its appraisals for review. The Corps of Engineers did not acknowledge its obligation to provide for relocation and reconstruction expenses as required by Congress. It continued to proceed as if the Indians had no special legal status. Yet in the end the Sioux tribes generally received better settlements than their non-Indian neighbors, although they certainly did not have the same opportunity to move to land of comparable value.[36]

Chapter 6

EARLY DEMANDS

Local meetings between Standing Rock and Cheyenne River negotiators and federal representatives began in May 1952. Whitney J. Agard, now Standing Rock chairman, requested permission to amend the tribe's contract with James Curry and to provide him with an additional $500 to enable him to attend the Fort Yates negotiations. Myer refused the request, calling it another tactic in the lawyer's "highjacking game." When Agard threatened to halt further talks until the tribe had adequate legal counsel, Myer again found himself overruled by the secretary of the interior.[1]

By the time of the May conferences the negotiation time limits established by Congress had already been exceeded. Fourteen months of discussion and research had failed to bring an agreement on land appraisals, which were only the first order of business. When tribal representatives were forced to ask for more time, Congress accepted their request on April 8 and extended the contract deadline to January 31, 1953.[2]

Talks at Cheyenne River opened on a somber note on May 13. "This is not a happy occasion," said Frank Ducheneaux. "We are here to participate in the gutting of our reservation."[3] As discussion proceeded, it soon became apparent that army, BIA, and tribal negotiators had each arrived at a different estimate of damages. Despite General Pick's earlier assurances Corps of Engineers spokesmen maintained that the original Hart appraisal was without error.[4]

The congressional guidelines established for negotiations in 1950 stated that the army appraisal would be used to assist negotiators in determining the amount of just compensation. It did not hold that these valuations would constitute the final property settlement. Despite these stipulations, the Corps of Engineers proceeded at all tribal conferences as if its appraisal results were the final word and not merely the basis for negotiations.[5]

BIA representatives strongly objected to the army's position. In their own investigations MRBI staff members had discovered numerous errors in the Hart valuations, but not quite as many as were claimed by tribal negotiators, although both were extremely critical of the procedures Hart had followed. They objected that the appraisal was neither based on a comprehensive soil survey nor conducted on a tract-by-tract basis by appraisers familiar with Dakota lands. They felt that it should have included potential mineral and irrigation values. Clearly the Indians were neither willing nor informed sellers under the eminent-domain concept, which held that fair market value was "the value agreed upon by a willing and informed purchaser." MRBI spokesmen held that the appraisal of the tribes' land should be based on "the highest and best probable use of their property."[6]

Once it became evident that negotiators could not resolve their differences, Ralph Case, the tribe's attorney, suggested that a joint committee be established to conduct a new appraisal. Federal officials reluctantly agreed to the proposal. A six-member review committee, consisting of two representatives each from the tribe, the army, and the BIA, was appointed to prepare a new survey. MRBI personnel also resolved to conduct their own separate evaluation.[7]

Meetings with Standing Rock representatives on May 15 and 16 produced similar results. Because agreement between the parties could not be reached, new surveys were scheduled. When Pick learned the results of these relatively unfruitful conferences, he charged that the MRBI had sabotaged the talks by releasing its confidential damage estimates to the tribes without army approval. MRBI Director Walter U. Fuhriman quickly refuted these accusations. He explained that the Indians' complaints were based solely on their own investigations and denied that the MRBI had leaked any information. He suggested, as an afterthought, that the tribes probably should have had access to the MRBI data.[8]

The reviewing committees began their work in June. Meeting again in Omaha, Nebraska, on August 7, federal and tribal representatives agreed to begin final negotiations in Washington on November 10 and to continue talks for as long as was necessary to reach an agreement. Results of the reviewing committee's appraisal on Cheyenne River were made available in September, but complications developed at Standing Rock, where appraisers became bogged down in a dispute over land valuations. The situation was further complicated by the untimely death of Tribal Chairman Agard. Consequently, further progress was indefinite until a new tribal leader could be elected in November.[9]

On November 10, Cheyenne River delegates again were in Pick's office in Washington. Procedures for the final contract talks were established, and actual negotiations began in the Interior Department hearing room on November 12. Despite Pick's previous promises and the reviewing committee's discovery of a 1,573-acre error in the Hart firm's land description, army spokesmen again pronounced that the original appraisal figure of $1,605,410 represented their official offer. The $2,053,177 appraisal of the reviewing committee was then presented as the official offer of the Bureau of Indian Affairs.[10]

Announcement of these figures sparked vigorous debate between federal representatives, but tribal spokesmen had not yet had the floor. When Chairman Ducheneaux rose to speak, he announced that tribal negotiators had found errors in both appraisals and would present their own proposals on November 14. Federal negotiators were given copies of the Cheyenne River requests on that date. Because they wished to have more time to study the Indians' demands before continuing the talks, the federal representatives asked that negotiations again be adjourned until November 17.[11]

The contract proposed by the Cheyenne River Sioux was designed to guarantee to the tribe certain rights, privileges, and benefits from the Oahe project. The Indians also asked for a cash settlement of over $23 million. Of this amount $2,614,779 represented the tribal appraisal of land, improvements, and severance damages within the reservoir area. The sum of $8,316,092 was requested for what negotiators termed "tangible future damages" that included the loss of grazing leases, timber, wildlife, wild fruits, and other resources. Finally the tribe asked for $12,599,432 to establish a rehabilitation program for the entire reservation.[12]

The tribe felt its request for tangible future damages was based on a reasonable premise. Because all tribal members would suffer from the loss of land and resources, it was felt that the entire tribe, and not just individual property owners, should receive compensation for future as well as present values. The tribe's demand for rehabilitation funds was a logical extension of this same idea.[13]

In 1950, Congress had provided that the final settlement with the Cheyenne River Sioux would pay the costs of "reestablishing the tribe . . . so that their economic, social, religious, and community life can be reestablished and protected."[14] Tribal negotiators broadly interpreted this provision, since they realized that their requests were based on important precedents.

The term "rehabilitation" was carried over from Indian New Deal days. Loans and grants established to improve social and economic development on the reservations during that period were called rehabilitation programs. A new emphasis on the goal of tribal self-sufficiency caused Congress to revive this concept in the late 1940s. For example, the Fort Berthold Indians received additional funds for that purpose in 1949 as part of the Garrison settlement. Tribes unaffected by public works projects also received support. In 1950, Congress appropriated $88,570,000 to establish a ten-year rehabilitation program for the Navajo and Hopi Indians. During the period of the Oahe negotiations, the Papagos, the Pine Ridge Sioux, the Turtle Mountain Chippewas, and other tribes were also considered for rehabilitation funds.[15]

Because the termination policies were being discussed in Washington, the Cheyenne River negotiators thought the federal government might be willing to offer a settlement that would allow them to take a giant step toward self-sufficiency. Their rehabilitation estimates were based on a socioeconomic survey prepared by MRBI experts in June 1951 and showed the amount they estimated would be necessary to establish self-help programs to bring the entire reservation to a level of common decency. The estimate was broken down as follows:

Repayment Cattle Program	$ 3,288,000
Domestic Water Supply	600,000
Farm Program	210,000
Land Purchase Program	1,000,000
Industrial Assistance Program	297,500
Rehabilitation Housing Program	1,000,000
Rehabilitation Road Program	2,153,932
Educational Loan Program	500,000
Tribal Welfare Program	2,800,000
Business Enterprise Program	750,000
Total	12,599,432[16]

In addition to tribal requests for monetary compensation, negotiators specified other contract provisions. They wanted all relocation and reconstruction costs charged against the army appropriations for the Oahe project and not against their own settlement funds. They requested that the tribal council be given exclusive jurisdiction over such matters and that all facilities "be
restored to a condition not less advantageous than the condition
they are now in."[17] Furthermore, they asked that tribal members
be allowed to retain all mineral rights within the reservoir area,
that they be given a reasonable amount of time to salvage timber
and improvements, and that they be permitted to reside on their
property and make use of it without charge until the gates of
the dam were closed.[18]

Once the project was finished, the tribe wanted to retain grazing
rights along the shoreline and to have unrestricted access to the
reservoir. They also asked permission to develop recreational facilities near the water. Similar shoreline provisions had been denied
the Fort Berthold tribes in 1949, but the Cheyenne River negotiators agreed from the outset that the only acceptable settlement
would guarantee shoreline rights. Because the negotiators were
aware of the hazards to livestock caused by the reservoir, they
also declared that the federal government should be held responsible for any herd losses resulting from shoreline fluctuations.
They were determined to succeed where the Three Affiliated Tribes
had failed and also requested a 20,000-kilowatt block of power
from the Oahe Dam to be provided at low cost for their exclusive use.[19]

The proposed contract, principally drafted by Chairman Ducheneaux, contained provisions designed to protect settlement funds once they were appropriated. It maintained that the tribal council should have complete control over the money, that individual tribal members should receive credit and not cash for their interests, and that use of the money for substitute land purchases would be guaranteed. In addition, it demanded that the funds should be tax-exempt, should draw interest at a rate of 5 percent per annum until expended, and should not be encumbered by either administrative costs or outstanding liens and debts. The tribe wanted to assure that nothing in the settlement would interfere with financial benefits already received under Wheeler-Howard programs. An additional provision requested that the negotiators be reimbursed up to $100,000 for expenses incurred during the negotiation of a settlement.[20]

The federal government was asked to assist the tribe in finding new property. The contract demanded that all new lands, both inside and outside the reservation, come under federal trust status, thus allowing the tribe to consolidate its holdings as it saw fit. It also requested that all surplus federal lands on the reservation be restored to tribal ownership. The committee proposed that all legal fees be assumed by the army whenever individual owners rejected the appraisal value of their land in federal court. Finally, it asked that the Interior Department provide new survey markers on all reservation land to facilitate relocation, that it undertake reforestation and coal development programs to help replace lost fuel supplies, and that it study further the irrigation potential of tribal lands.[21]

The negotiating conference reconvened on November 17 to discuss these contract proposals. Army representatives, growing increasingly impatient with the course of the talks, declared they would make their final offer on November 21. In the meantime the corps decided to review the separate appraisals to determine if a higher payment could be justified. Realizing that the tribe would not accept an amount substantially below the BIA's offer, Major General G. J. Nold, acting for General Pick, authorized a final offer of $2 million. Although this figure was nearly $400,000 above the Hart appraisal, it was about $53,000 less than the reviewing committee's damage estimates.[22]

After tribal negotiators considered the army offer on November

21, they asked for additional time to prepare a counter proposal. On November 26 they submitted an offer of $2.5 million for property damages, but with the stipulation that, if the army failed to accept this compromise figure, it would not prevent the tribe from returning to its original request of $2,614,779.[23]

General Nold politely told the Indians that their counteroffer was unacceptable. BIA representatives declined to make another bid, and the property appraisal stood once again in disagreement. Nold then asked if the tribal committee wished to discuss other provisions of their proposed contract. In disgust Frank Ducheneaux replied that, since it was evident that an agreement could not be reached on the fundamental issue of property damages, he considered further discussion useless. The stalemate could not be broken. After a long silence a BIA representative moved to adjourn the conference. His motion was quickly seconded, and tribal negotiators stormed out of the hearing room. As committee member Lloyd LeBeau later recalled, "the tribe just couldn't deal with the Corps of Engineers at all."[24]

Having failed to reach agreement with the army, the Cheyenne River Sioux were now compelled to deal directly with Congress in accordance with the 1950 negotiation guidelines. Members of the South Dakota congressional delegation were asked to submit bills incorporating tribal contract demands. Senator Francis Case and Congressman E. Y. Berry agreed to sponsor legislation only after tribal leaders promised to scale down their cash demands and to omit certain contract proposals. As a result the Indians decided to trim their requests for future tangible damages from $8,316,092 to $6,871,467 and their rehabilitation program from $12,599,432 to $12,289,432.[25]

The tribe's request for hydroelectric power was dropped when legislators advised that Congress would not consider it because of its Fort Berthold decision. The congressmen also demanded withdrawal of proposals that would exempt settlement funds from both taxes and administrative costs. Also, provisions were omitted that would have restored surplus lands to tribal ownership, established exclusive rights for shoreline recreational development, and held the Interior Department responsible for replacement fuel supplies and survey markers. Legislation incorporating the amended tribal proposals and requesting a total settlement of $21,715,678 was finally introduced in the Eighty-third Congress on January 29, 1953.[26]

The Standing Rock Sioux had just begun their new negotiations at that time. A conference with federal representatives, the first in many months, took place at Fort Yates on January 13. Earlier, in October 1952, BIA officials had made a new offer of $1.7 million for the tribe's property damages and relocation expenses. Although this was substantially higher than the Hart figure of $1,320,000, tribal attorney James Curry advised negotiators to reject the offer, because it was not equitable with the Fort Berthold settlement and contained no rehabilitation provisions. He also urged tribal officials to protest vigorously that property owners were being asked by corps representatives to sign documents attesting to the accuracy of the Hart appraisal. While under constant harassment from BIA officials, Curry encouraged the tribe to fight as diligently for an adequate final settlement as it had for the right to counsel. He warned against falling under federal domination.[27]

The lawyer's advice went for naught. In November the Standing Rock Sioux elected a new chairman, F. David Black Hoop. Even before taking office, this new tribal leader turned Curry's confidential correspondence over to BIA officials and declared his complete opposition to the Washington attorney. Commissioner Myer was not saddened by this development. Consequently Curry soon found himself without a contract, and a local lawyer, J. K. Murray of Bismarck, North Dakota, was hired to represent the tribe in negotiations that began in January 1953.[28]

Army representatives again opened the talks with a discussion of land values. As in the case of the Cheyenne River negotiations they offered an amount equal to the Hart appraisal. The reviewing committee's estimate of $1,650,000 was then submitted as the BIA offer, despite its earlier bid of $1.7 million. Although tribal negotiators had previously arrived at an estimate of $1,815,000, under J. K. Murray's advice they asked for $1,720,000. When Brigadier General W. E. Potter asked the tribal committee if that was their final offer, they recessed for further consultation with their attorney. When they returned, they requested an amount equal to the most recent BIA offer. Potter countered with

$1,460,000, which the Indians rejected, and the first day's meeting adjourned without agreement.[29]

Tribal negotiators opened the January 14 conference by returning to their original offer. Spokesman Louis Gipp justified this action by explaining that the tribe had to consider the inflation of land values between the time of appraisals and the time of payment. Potter found this unreasonable, because he felt it was the tribe's fault that a settlement had not been reached. Hoping to avoid a hostile confrontation, counsel Murray advised the Indians to accept a figure somewhere between the BIA and army offers. In private he then told corps negotiators to raise their offer a little and he would take the Indians aside and "shake them down a bit."[30]

As a result of these maneuverings Potter was coaxed to offer $1,575,000. The tribe was then persuaded to accept the amount, even though it was 15 percent less than their original bid, on the condition that the tribe would also receive a satisfactory payment for intangible damages and rehabilitation. Potter agreed to these terms but made it clear that the additional valuations would have to be determined by Congress, since the corps had no authority to consider them. As in all of its talks with the tribes, the army insisted that its regulations did not permit compensation for anything other than property, although Congress had in each case authorized the corps to negotiate settlements that included provisions for relocation and reconstruction.[31]

No other issues were resolved in the January conferences. Because no contract could be completed before the extended deadline of January 31, another time extension was requested. Although no official action was taken on that request, negotiations continued throughout the spring. Unlike the Cheyenne River tribe, which had presented all of its contract demands at the first conference, the Standing Rock Sioux held extensive talks with federal representatives on each of the various settlement issues before drawing up their requests. The tribal negotiators drafted a contract in March, amended and approved it by a tribal-council vote in May, then submitted it to Washington for further consideration.[32]

The proposed contract asked for a cash settlement of $20,753,630. This figure approached the sum requested from Congress by the

Cheyenne River Sioux, even though the Standing Rock tribe would suffer considerably less damage. More than one-fourth of the total demand, $5,178,630, was asked for intangible damages. Specifically, the money was for the kinds of losses categorized by the Cheyenne River tribe as "tangible future damages," and an additional $14 million was for rehabilitation. MRBI officials previously had endorsed an appraisal of $3,834,146 for these losses. Independent of Oahe negotiations, the tribe had requested $10 million for rehabilitation in 1949. Included in their latest bid, however, was a $1,973,000 demand for per capita distribution.[33]

The wording of their demands was similar to the Cheyenne River contract and asked that the federal government cover all relocation and reconstruction costs out of separate funds and grant hydroelectric power, mineral, salvage, and shoreline access rights. Federal funds were also requested to pay the court expenses of tribal members who had rejected appraisal values and to reimburse the tribe for all negotiation expenses, but the Standing Rock contract was less specific about substitute land provisions and the protection of settlement funds. It said nothing, for example, about interest payments or the trust status of new property, although it did demand that the final settlement in no way restrict future tribal efforts to obtain additional rights and damage payments.[34]

Standing Rock negotiators hoped their contract would be approved quickly by the chief of engineers and secretary of the interior so that legislation could be introduced in Congress. Because the extended time limits for talks had expired, the negotiators felt that the federal government would want to ratify an agreement rapidly. They anticipated that congressional hearings soon would be initiated. Such was not to be the case. Five months passed and no word came from Washington. After eight months had passed, local congressmen were called on to investigate the matter. Finally, after taking no action for more than a year, the army and BIA announced in May 1954 that more time would be needed to study the tribal proposals.[35]

In the meantime the Standing Rock Sioux succeeded in getting Congressman Berry to introduce on June 11 a bill incorporating tribal demands. To their chagrin this legislation requesting a cash settlement of $26,370,663 was held in abeyance by the House

Interior Committee, pending passage of a final agreement with the Cheyenne River tribe. Consequently, the Standing Rock contract was not given serious consideration until 1955, and several additional months passed before the tribe received a final settlement.[36]

Agreements with the other tribes were also delayed by congressional procrastination. The Crow Creek and Lower Brulé Sioux had petitioned as early as 1951 for the prompt initiation of settlement talks, but Congress did not heed their proposals for settlement procedures until 1954. In the meantime the tribes were not idle. Meetings were held on the reservations to discuss contract terms, negotiating committees were appointed, and contracts for legal counsel were finally approved. Damage appraisals were prepared by both the army and the BIA; MRBI staff members conducted socioeconomic surveys; and tribal lands were inspected by Commissioner Myer.[37]

In 1951 the Bureau of Indian Affairs announced that because of the Fort Randall project it planned to move its facilities at Fort Thompson, which served both the Crow Creek and Lower Brulé tribes, to the white community of Chamberlain, South Dakota. It also proclaimed that all schools on the reservations would be closed and students would be transferred to nearby public institutions. Hospital facilities at Fort Thompson had already been moved to Chamberlain the previous year.[38]

Both tribes vehemently opposed those decisions, which they viewed as an initial step toward termination. Tribal leaders protested that the relocation plan would create undue hardship, especially since the citizens of Chamberlain were known to be deeply prejudiced against Indians. In a petition to D'Arcy McNickle of the BIA's Tribal Affairs office, they asked that the decision be reconsidered. The tribes trusted McNickle, a noted Flathead Indian novelist and historian, who later became head of the Newberry Library Center for the History of the American Indian. In October 1951, Myer was moved by McNickle to help put tribal fears to rest.[39]

In a letter to Herbert Wounded Knee, Crow Creek tribal chairman, Myer denied that an official decision had been made concerning the Fort Thompson facilities. He assured the tribal leader that the Bureau of Indian Affairs had no intention either to ignore tribal desires or to deprive the Indians of their rights, but in executive conference with other BIA administrators on February 1, 1952, the commissioner reaffirmed the earlier decisions. Fortunately no further action was taken on this matter during Myer's term of office. Under the direction of Glenn L. Emmons, President Eisenhower's appointee for Indian Commissioner, plans were altered slightly. The Fort Thompson facilities were moved to Pierre instead of Chamberlain, and grade-school children were allowed to stay in reservation schools.[40]

On July 21, 1952, the gates of Fort Randall Dam were closed, and by the end of the year portions of the reservations were under water. Still the tribes awaited the initiation of settlement talks. Finally, negotiations with the Crow Creek and Lower Brulé Sioux were opened at Fort Thompson on March 9, 1953.[41]

The Corps of Engineers offered the Crow Creek negotiators $375,613 for their land and improvements. This settlement was based on an appraisal made by the corps' own real-estate division. BIA officials offered $399,313, an amount reached by MRBI appraisers. The Lower Brulé tribe was then offered $233,756 by the army and $270,611 by the BIA. When attorney M. Q. Sharpe, who was representing both tribes, asked corps officials if they would accept the higher MRBI figures, they flatly refused. The corps then threatened to take the land by condemnation if an agreement could not be reached quickly.[42]

Several other meetings were held during the next few months, but all failed to bring the parties closer to settlement. Members of the Crow Creek Indian Rights Association complained to Eisenhower's Interior Secretary Douglas McKay. The Indians felt that tribal members were systematically denied both information about the Fort Randall project and participation in the ongoing talks. BIA spokesmen also expressed disgust with the army's reluctance to compromise, but corps officials remained unmoved.[43]

The Army began preparing condemnation suits on the Indian land without waiting for further developments. They claimed that the rising pool level of the Fort Randall reservoir and the long delay of Congress in establishing settlement guidelines left them no alternative. The tribes were assured that 90 percent of the appraised value of their property would be made immediately available to them through the federal court, and that this legal action would in no way affect the eventual settlement from Congress. In effect, the Indians were being asked to give up their land before agreeing to a price.[44]

On June 1, 1953, army spokesmen agreed to accept BIA appraisal figures as the basis of their condemnation suits. M. Q. Sharpe did not challenge the army's right to take tribal lands, but he did remind corps representatives that the tribes had not yet agreed to accept MRBI valuations. After long discussion with their lawyer, Indian negotiators were persuaded to accept the army offers provided that certain rights could be guaranteed. These included the right to use the land free of charge until a final settlement could be reached and the retention of all mineral rights within the reservoir area. Corps representatives expressed pleasure that a land agreement had finally been reached, but they gave no assurances that tribal conditions would be met.[45]

On August 4, 1953, the army filed suit in the United States District Court of South Dakota in an attempt to obtain title to lands on the Crow Creek and Lower Brule reservations. The action went unchallenged, the court passed favorably on the condemnation request, and the Corps of Engineers again succeeded in circumventing its legal obligations to the Indians. Despite previous agreements an amount equal to the army's land appraisal rather than that of the BIA was deposited with the court, but this money was never distributed to the tribes. The United States District Attorney's office failed to file a declaration of taking, which would have given the army full title to the land, before Congress finally passed a law establishing legal guidelines for the Fort Randall negotiations in July 1954. This act required federal representatives to open new talks with the tribes. When these negotiations failed to bring about an agreement by 1955, the Justice Department permitted the army to carry through its original condemnation suits.[46]

The year 1953 proved a fallow one for negotiations. Tribal efforts to reach settlements were constantly frustrated during this first year of the Eisenhower Administration. The Congress was already preoccupied with the Korean War and the anti-Communist crusade of Senator Joseph McCarthy but, with a view towards termination, undertook a massive investigation of the Bureau of

Indian Affairs. Consequently, little consideration was given the Sioux tribes' pending legislation. Further administrative action became tangled in the web of Washington bureaucracy. The change in executive leadership prompted further delay, and the Standing Rock tribe, for example, waited eighteen months for an administrative review of their proposed contract. Although most Indians favored the Democratic Party and feared Eisenhower's termination policies, they could take some pleasure in the departure in 1953 of two dreaded government officials. In March, Dillon S. Myer resigned as Indian Commissioner to allow President Eisenhower to appoint his own man, Glenn L. Emmons; and in February, General Pick resigned from the post of Chief of Engineers to return to civilian life.[47] Unfortunately, these personnel changes were not accompanied by any significant new developments in policy.

Chapter 7

NEGOTIATIONS AND SETTLEMENTS, 1954–1957

Legislation for the Cheyenne River Sioux that was introduced by Congressman Berry on January 29, 1953, was finally reviewed and passed by the Eighty-third Congress in 1954. Members of the Tribal Negotiating Committee were called to Washington to appear at lengthy hearings conducted by the House and Senate subcommittees on Indian affairs.

Chairman Ducheneaux later recalled that the Indians learned two important lessons from these hearings. First, to accomplish anything in Washington the tribal committee had to pay its own expenses. The BIA would only reimburse Indian delegates for official visits up to five days, and that did not allow sufficient time to "cut through the white tape," as they put it. Second, members of Congress wanted to talk to "real Indians" and were obviously more comfortable in dealing with stereotypic full bloods in native regalia than with tribal leaders who, like Frank Ducheneaux, wore business suits, smoked cigars, and clearly articulated their demands. In response to the second lesson Cheyenne River negotiators resorted to a strategy of theatrics. It was decided that the two full bloods on the committee, John Little Cloud and Alex Chasing Hawk, would do most of the talking. Thus Little Cloud was instructed to speak in Lakota at the hearings, and Chasing Hawk was to translate his remarks into broken English, even though both men spoke their adopted language fluently. The Congressmen were delighted.[1]

While tribal negotiators succeeded in putting on a good show at the hearings, they were far less successful in persuading Congress to approve their compensation requests. They were constantly pressured to compromise their benefit requests and to scale down their cash demands. When it came to a showdown on these issues, the Indians found themselves compelled to rely on their own resources. Their official defenders, the Bureau of Indian Affairs and congressional representatives, tended to abandon their cause when the going got rough. Despite their loyalty to him, their lawyer, Ralph Case, proved much too willing to "go along with the boys on Capitol Hill," and E. Y. Berry, their chief legislative patron, suffered an acute case of that familiar malady, "the forked tongue syndrome."[2]

Berry, whose membership on the House Indian subcommittee should have been an advantage, came to be considered a "liability" by the tribe. Although he lived in McLaughlin, South Dakota, on the northern edge of the reservation and publicly proclaimed himself their loyal neighbor, the Cheyenne River Sioux considered the Republican leader hostile to their interests. At home he was influenced too much by local white ranchers to be objective about Indian problems and was too paternalistic toward the tribes when he did consider them. In Washington he quickly fell under the influence of other GOP policymakers, especially Senator Arthur V. Watkins of Utah. Watkins was the controversial chairman of the Senate Subcommittee on Indian Affairs and recognized leader of the termination movement in Congress. He was considered by many tribal groups to be the government's "number one Indian hater."[3]

In remarks before the House, Berry clearly linked the Cheyenne River settlement legislation with prevailing views on termination. He stressed that the rehabilitation program was a step toward self-sufficiency and self-determination and emphasized that its main features had been designed by tribal leaders themselves. But he mistakenly assumed from the Indians' expressed desire for self-improvement that they also favored termination. "I hope that this Congress will see fit to go along with them," he told his col-

leagues, "and to help get them in shape, financially, and economically, and intellectually, so that they, too, may be able to get
out from under the yoke of the Indian Bureau before too long."[4]

Left without an effective voice to represent them, the Cheyenne
River delegates could do little but watch as Congress methodically
shrank the settlement amount. In its recommendations to the
House, the BIA, their official guardian, advised that their property
payment be reduced from $2,614,779 to $2,234,934. The bureau
also suggested that their rehabilitation request be separated from
the property settlement and made the subject of separate legislation, that all subsurface mineral rights as well as all substitute
land purchased outside the reservation be declared taxable, and
that the interest rate on the final settlement be reduced from 5
to 4 percent.[5]

In its recommendations on the Berry bill the Corps of Engineers
echoed its previous hard-line stand. Army Secretary Robert T.
Stevens suggested that the Indians be given only $2 million for
their property and no more than 25 percent of that amount for
relocation and rehabilitation. He demanded that the tribe be forced
to pay a fee for the privilege of using their former lands until
they were flooded. The fee would also be payment for the salvaging
of timber, removal of improvements, and retention of shoreline access rights. He denied the tribal council's right to have any authority over reconstruction activities and the distribution of settlement
funds. Stevens objected to the proposed procedure whereby court
judgments for higher individual property settlements would be
taken out of the army's project funds. Finally, he suggested that
tribal mineral rights be restricted solely to gas and oil and that
the federal government disclaim any responsibility for livestock
hazards created by the reservoir.[6]

After evaluating these recommendations, the suggestions of its
own members, and the testimony of the Indians, the House Interior Committee issued its final report on the Cheyenne River
proposals on June 23. The committee conceded the tribe's demand
for a property settlement of $2,614,779, but it drastically reduced
the other cash requests. Compensation for additional severance
damages was cut from $6,871,467 to $3,973,076; the rehabilita-

tion program was slashed from $12,289,432 to $6,044,500; and the interest rate on the tribal settlement was reduced from 5 to 4 percent as the BIA had suggested. Thus, in one swift stroke, the Cheyenne River Sioux lost more than $9 million.[7]

Although House members were tightfisted when granting cash to the Indians, they were more generous than might have been expected in providing certain other benefits. Despite army recommendations, the tribe was permitted to retain all the salvage, mineral, and shoreline rights it had demanded without payment of fees. The Interior Committee retained those provisions of the original bill that protected settlement funds from prior claims and held the federal government responsible for all hazards to cattle created by the dam. The BIA was directed to give full assistance in finding suitable new land for tribal members. The Indians, however, were denied their request to have all land purchased by them outside the reservation included under the trust status.[8]

Tribal members were given the right to have their individual property settlements determined in federal court at government expense, but the committee declared that additional awards would be charged against the tribe's own compensation for severance damages and not against the army's Oahe project appropriations as the tribe had demanded. Finally, the congressmen granted the Indians the $100,000 they had requested as compensation for negotiation expenses, but stipulated that not more than one-half could be used for attorney fees.[9]

When the Cheyenne River legislation, as amended in committee, was passed by the House and referred to the Senate on August 3, 1953, Senator Francis H. Case of South Dakota was expected to carry the ball for the Indians. Case was more highly regarded than Berry by Sioux leaders and previously had been adopted as an honorary member of the Standing Rock tribe, but like his congressional colleague he tended to be a paternalistic fair-weather friend. A vigorous promoter of Pick-Sloan, the senator never allowed his sense of responsibility toward his Indian constituents to outweigh his other allegiances. He was predisposed to follow whatever the prevailing view toward Indian policy might be in

Washington and had lent support to both the New Deal reform effort and to the termination movement. Yet in nearly all cases he served best the interests of his non-Indian supporters.[10]

The Cheyenne River bill, which had languished in the House for eighteen months, was reviewed by the Senate during a two-week period. Watkins vehemently attacked the legislation, and Case did little to defend it. The Indian subcommittee chairman voiced strong opposition to the amount requested for severance damages and rehabilitation. Senator Case merely stated that he would not accept the amount of money offered the tribe for similar land he owned along the Missouri.[11]

After brief deliberation the Senate trimmed another $2,088,341 from the tribal requests. The property payment was cut from $2,614,779 to $2,250,000, the amount of the revised MRBI appraisal. Responsibility for the distribution of this money was denied the tribal council and given to the BIA. Payment for severance damages was further reduced from $3,973,076 to $3,134,014, and the rehabilitation program was reduced from $6,044,500 to $5,160,000. The Interior Committee added a provision requiring the Corps of Engineers to pay the costs of relocating tribal property out of its Oahe appropriations, but they deleted language that directed the army to carry out this activity "in such a way as will best serve the Indians." To reduce the amount of interest paid to the tribe, a stipulation was added requiring all settlement funds to be expended within a ten-year period.[12]

Finally, the Cheyenne River legislation, amended beyond the recognition of the tribal negotiators, was passed by the Senate on August 18, concurred with by the House the next day, and signed into law by President Eisenhower on September 3.[13] After four arduous years of negotiations the Indians at last had a settlement, but tribal negotiators were keenly disappointed with the results of their efforts. They were especially disgruntled that the final award of $10,644,014 was more than $13 million less than the amount they considered just compensation for their losses. In bitterness and frustration they thought about launching a campaign to reject the settlement, but Ralph Case advised against such a maneuver. Realizing that the tribe would face certain condemnation if it refused to ratify the agreement, he told tribal leaders that they could best carry on their fight through amendatory legislation, despite a provision in the act that stipulated it represented "the final and complete settlement of all claims, rights, and demands . . . arising out of the construction of the Oahe project."[14]

The Cheyenne River Sioux decided to follow their lawyer's advice, but future events proved Case wrong. Repeated attempts over several years to gain additional compensation and benefits from Congress ended in failure. Tribal leaders ultimately were forced to accept the 1954 settlement as the best possible under the circumstances. Given the inevitability of the Oahe project and the nature of their representation before the government, they could find solace in the success of gaining one of the highest cash-per-acre settlements of any tribe to that time. They had reached a far more satisfactory agreement than had the Fort Berthold Indians in 1949, and had established a precedent for later settlements that would provide other Sioux tribes with proportionately more money. The Cheyenne River Sioux, unlike other tribal groups, found consolation in managing to reach an agreement and receiving settlement funds before their land was flooded and their people forced to move.[15]

In addition to the cash settlement of $10,644,014, the 1954 legislation guaranteed that the costs of relocating and reconstructing all BIA and tribal facilities would come out of the army's Oahe budget. The law also stipulated that the economic, social, religious, and community life of the tribe would be "restored to a condition not less advantageous . . . than the condition said Indians are now in."[16]

Congress allowed the tribe to retain the mineral, salvage, and shoreline access rights it had requested and also agreed to have the federal government take responsibility for all livestock hazards posed by the project. Substitute lands purchased within the reservation continued under federal trust status, holders of inherited land were allowed to consolidate their interests as they saw fit, and the tribe was promised federal assistance in its relocation and reconstruction activities. The tribal council was granted $100,000 for its negotiation expenses, and the law also guaranteed that no part of the settlement funds could be used to offset or counter any previous tribal claim against the government or to interfere with any federal benefits the tribe already received. Finally, the legislation upheld the right of individual tribal members to reject the amount of their appraised property value and to have a final settlement determined in federal district court. In such cases the government pledged to pay all court costs if the tribe deposited an amount equal to the appraised value of the property as a sign of good faith, but the individual litigants would have to pay their own attorney's fees.[17]

Despite provisions which seemed generous when contrasted with the Fort Berthold settlement, the Oahe legislation was most remembered by the Cheyenne River Sioux for what it did not give them. It did not grant their request for $23 million at 5 percent interest. Demands for a block of hydroelectric power, for exclusive shoreline recreation facilities, and for certain tax exemptions were also systematically eliminated. Congress also denied federal trust status to substitute lands purchased outside the reservation and refused to return all surplus federal land to tribal ownership. A prohibition against the hiring of administrative personnel out of settlement funds was dropped, and the secretary of the interior, not the tribal council, was given final authority over the disbursement and expenditure of all appropriations, including those designated for the tribal rehabilitation program.[18]

Tribal members who rejected their property appraisals were denied free legal representation in court as had been requested and were discouraged from litigation by the elaborate procedures established for such cases. Pleas for the Interior Department to assist the tribe with financial problems, fuel resource development, surveying markers, and irrigation projects on the reservation were ignored.[19]

In addition to denying these requests, Congress placed certain restrictions on the rights and privileges it saw fit to grant the Indians. Mineral rights, for example, were made subject "to all reasonable regulations which might be imposed by the Corps of Engineers."[20] This meant that the army might arbitrarily prohibit not only the extraction of tribal mineral resources within the reservoir area if it could find justification in its own regulations but also might place shoreline hunting, fishing, and grazing rights under "regulations governing the corresponding use by other citizens of the United States."[21] Congress again made the tribe subject to the rule of such federal agencies as the Corps of Engineers and Bureau of Reclamation and, in effect, gave equal shoreline rights to non-Indians within the reservation.

Tribal salvage rights were also restricted by army regulations and placed under strict time limits. The Corps of Engineers was required to give a one-year notice before the Oahe Dam was closed, after which the tribe had six months to salvage all timber, improvements, and other property within the reservoir area. The law held that the federal government could not be held liable for any loss of life or property after closure of the dam gates.[22]

In late December the Cheyenne River Sioux were asked to vote whether or not they wanted to accept the final settlement offered by the Eighty-third Congress. In accordance with treaty provisions, the law required ratification by three-fourths of the adult tribal enrollment. Chairman Ducheneaux urged acceptance as the only viable alternative. A count of the ballots in January 1955 revealed that 92 percent of the tribe had followed his advice. On April 6 the secretary of the interior officially declared the Oahe settlement act to be in effect.[23]

After observing hearings on the Cheyenne River legislation and witnessing the final outcome, the Standing Rock Sioux asked Congressman Berry and Senators Case and Karl E. Mundt of South Dakota to introduce new legislation for them in the Eighty-fourth Congress. In June 1955 extensive hearings were held on these bills before the House Subcommittee on Indian Affairs. In September the subcommittee toured the reservation.[24]

The Standing Rock tribe requested a settlement of $26,370,663 in tax-exempt funds based on a private appraisal conducted for the tribe by the William Davis Company, a reputable Kansas City firm. Of this amount $2,799,633 was asked for direct property damages, $7,571,000 for indirect and severance damages, and $16 million for rehabilitation programs. With the exception of hydroelectric power rights the tribe asked for benefits identical to those demanded by the Cheyenne River Sioux in their original proposals, and it based its appraisal on similar kinds of damages. In addition they requested compensation for the loss of their interest in the riverbed as well as the value of the tax immunity of all trust land within the reservoir area. A provision was also included to require the government to return to the original owners all former Indian land found unnecessary for project use.[25]

The Hart appraisal of the Standing Rock property had been $1,320,000. The Corps of Engineers had finally raised its offer to $1,575,000 but had refused to grant any further concessions. Because of a new range and soil survey conducted by the MRBI staff in 1954, the Bureau of Indian Affairs offered $1,613,454 for direct property damages and $3,904,559 for all indirect damages, including rehabilitation costs and intangible future losses. The amount proposed as a total settlement was $5,518,013.[26]

Following hearings in Washington and visits to Fort Yates in 1955, members of the House Interior Committee decided to amend the Standing Rock legislation to bring it into line with the Cheyenne River settlement. The final property payment to the Cheyenne River tribe had been 9.6 percent higher than the original MRBI appraisal, which allowed for an increase in land values between 1951 and 1954. It was decided to use this same formula for Standing Rock, even though more time had elapsed. The property settlement was thus set at $1,769,168, 9.6 percent higher than the official BIA offer.[27]

The committee used the same per capita sum granted the Cheyenne River Sioux in arriving at a figure of $8,500,000 for rehabilitation. On the issue of indirect damages it decided to compromise between the separate estimates presented by the BIA and the tribe and to offer $5,575,000. The recommended settlement was thus reduced to $14,075,000.[28]

The Interior Committee made a favorable report based on that amount to the Committee of the Whole on June 27, 1956, although a dissenting opinion was issued by seven members of the committee led by Chairman Clair Engle of California. The dissenting members took a position similar to that held by representatives of the Corps of Engineers. They declared that the final settlement should be determined in court rather than by Congress, just like any other matter of "condemnation." They accused the tribe and its lawyer of seeking a "political settlement" and further stated that the amount recommended by the Interior Committee was "not only unfair but exorbitant." They especially opposed payments for indirect damages and rehabilitation and charged that a settlement on these items was discriminating, since it gave the Indians "different, preferential, and more generous treatment . . . establishing a precedent for further and even worse raids on the Treasury."[29]

The debate stirred up by this minority opinion effectively blocked further consideration of the Standing Rock legislation in the Eighty-fourth Congress. Tribal officials were incensed because their rehabilitation program had been placed under BIA administration. They had previously urged that the bill be allowed to die and were adamant about maintaining tribal supervision over such funds. They feared that BIA control would permit that agency "to perpetuate its functions upon the tribe for another 150 years."[30]

As a result of these developments, a third set of legislative proposals for the Standing Rock Sioux were introduced in 1957.[31] Tribal negotiators, who had experienced difficulty in getting their demands before Congress, now realized that they faced an even tougher battle keeping their proposals intact. The minority opinion had clearly jarred them. Already with too few friends in Washington, this open declaration of hostility toward their interests made the Indians realize more fully the impossibility of their task. To these pressures was added the lack of time. Construction of the Oahe Dam was continuing rapidly, and most of the non-Indian property needed for the project had already been obtained. The Corps of Engineers announced that closure of the dam gates would begin in the spring of 1958. The Standing Rock negotiators seriously doubted that they would have a settlement by that time.[32]

The factor of time proved even more detrimental to tribes affected by the Fort Randall project. Closure of that dam took place in June 1952. In 1954 construction was 84 percent complete, all non-Indian land had been acquired, and the pool level of the reservoir was rising rapidly, while Indian property owners still awaited Congressional action. Finally legislation providing a settlement for the Yankton Sioux and establishing contract guidelines for the Crow Creek and Lower Brulé tribes was approved on June 6, 1954.[33]

The Yankton Indians, who had already been forced to relocate, received a payment of $106,500 in addition to the $132,324 pre-

viously granted the tribe for condemnation of land. Congress directed that these funds would be appropriated from the BIA budget rather than the army's project funds. The Indian Bureau was
therefore charged with the responsibility of programming this
money in a manner that would "protect their economic, social,
religious, and community life."[34]

Shoreline rights similar to those granted the Cheyenne River
Sioux were also provided the Yankton tribe, but mineral rights,
at the urging of the Corps of Engineers, were limited to oil and
gas only. Property owners had previously been allowed limited
salvage rights and free use of their former land until it was needed
by the army. Because of their inability to adequately represent
their own interests and to fight for a more beneficial settlement,
the Yankton Sioux failed to receive any general rehabilitation
funds. A golden opportunity to improve the social and economic
life of the entire reservation, no matter how slight, was thereby
missed.[35]

Negotiation guidelines established for the Crow Creek and Lower
Brulé Sioux were similar to those provided for the Cheyenne River
and Standing Rock tribes in 1950, with some important exceptions.
The growing urgency of the situation caused Congress to shorten
time limits for further talks; BIA and army representatives were
given only a year to obtain a contract agreement. Despite treaty
provisions and precedents established by the Fort Berthold and
Cheyenne River settlements, tribal ratification requirements were
lowered from three-fourths of the adult tribal members to a simple
majority. The Interior Department had recommended this action
in order to expedite approval. Finally, the retention of tribal mineral rights, as in the Yankton settlement, was limited to gas and
oil.[36]

New talks with the Crow Creek and Lower Brulé tribes were
rekindled in the autumn of 1954 but ended again in deadlock. The
BIA raised its offer for a property settlement to allow for the
increase in land values since 1951, the year of the last MRBI
appraisal. The Corps of Engineers refused to offer any more than
the amount it had previously deposited with the federal court in
its condemnation suits of 1953. Although the tribes were increasingly pressured by the impending flood, they were determined to

hold out for better terms. Lower Brulé negotiators, for example, demanded a property settlement of $508,493, which was 82 percent higher than the best BIA offer. In the meantime tribal leaders were compelled by circumstances to make plans for the evacuation of their lands.[37]

Crow Creek and Lower Brulé families within the Fort Randall reservoir area faced the prospect of having their homes inundated during the spring runoff of 1955, yet they still had no money with which to move. Condemnation funds deposited with the court were not available because the Justice Department had not yet filed a "declaration of taking" on the land, and the chances for a timely congressional settlement appeared increasingly dim. Because it was anticipated that favorable agreements could not be reached with BIA and army representatives, Senator Case and Congressman Berry were asked to introduce settlement legislation for the tribes in the Eighty-third Congress. These bills, which asked $5,686,036 for Crow Creek and $6,348,316 for Lower Brule, were never given consideration. As a result, the tribes expected that they would have to use their own meager funds to help families relocate. During the fall of 1954 tribal leaders began planning for this eventuality.[38]

In the meantime BIA officials were still debating where to move the agency facilities at Fort Thompson. Most of them preferred Chamberlain. Although the Indians wanted all government services to remain on the reservation, they overwhelmingly preferred Pierre to Chamberlain if an outside location had to be selected, and they petitioned Congressman Berry to make their wishes known in Washington. Because the mayor of Chamberlain had on several occasions demonstrated his prejudice against Indians, the BIA finally decided to yield to tribal requests and to establish the Pierre Agency as the new administrative headquarters for the Crow Creek and Lower Brulé Sioux.[39]

Following the breakdown of negotiations in November 1954, both the army and BIA requested the Justice Department to carry out the condemnation suits filed in 1953. The Corps of Engineers wanted clear title to the land, and the Indian Bureau wanted some money dispersed to tribal members before they were forced to move. Consequently, an official declaration of taking was filed on

January 20, 1955. The court allowed the army to take the Indian land it needed, and no one questioned the legality of the suit itself. The Corps of Engineers later claimed that its action was legal because the settlement guidelines, established by Congress the previous year, had stipulated that negotiations would not be allowed to interfere with the scheduled construction of the Fort Randall project. The army, however, had filed suit before legislation was passed, and nothing in the act itself specifically authorized the Corps of Engineers to exercise the right of eminent domain as required by law.[40]

On March 22, Indian landowners on Crow Creek Reservation received $399,313 from the court, and those on the Lower Brule received $270,611 as partial payment for their property. The army had been required to deposit an additional $23,700 for Crow Creek and $36,855 for Lower Brule in order to bring payments up to the MRBI appraisal figures. BIA assistance was requested in the distribution and expenditure of these funds, and tribal committees were formed to plan relocation activities.[41]

Efforts on the part of tribal leaders to tap other money sources proved unsuccessful. Several families who lived within the reservoir area were not legally entitled to receive condemnation money because they did not actually own property there. The Corps of Engineers was compelled to pay these Indians a certain amount for relocation, but they refused to release the funds until actual costs of moving had been incurred. The tribes were forced to create hardship funds out of whatever surplus monies could be found in order to assist these tribal members. Because of the limited funds available to the tribes and because of their constant need to hurry, the relocation and salvage operations on the two reservations, which were carried on throughout the remainder of 1955, proved to be very inadequate.[42]

The Crow Creek and Lower Brulé tribes, like the Standing Rock Sioux, were compelled for three more years to fight for a settlement from Congress. New legislation incorporating tribal demands was introduced in the Eighty-fourth and Eighty-fifth congresses by Senator Case and Congressmen Berry, Harold Lovre, and George S. McGovern of South Dakota.[43] Hearings were conducted on these bills by the Indian subcommittees in 1957. Despite the obvious urgency of the settlements Congress felt no compunction to move quickly, and no further action was taken until 1958. In the meantime, the Fort Randall project, 99 percent complete according to army reports, was officially dedicated on August 11, 1956.[44] As the waters of the reservoir began to inundate the bottomlands and former homes of tribal members, the Indians went down to the shore to watch. As Lower Brulé leader Richard LaRoche recalled, "It was a sad moment."[45]

Chapter 8

THE FIRST DECADE

In 1954 settlements were reached with the Yankton and Cheyenne River Sioux. Congress had finally provided negotiation guidelines for the Crow Creek and Lower Brulé tribes, and both had succeeded in getting settlement legislation introduced by the end of the year. The progress of settlement with the Standing Rock Indians, however, continued to be impaired by executive delays. The tribe finally had its requests submitted to Congress in 1955, but they did not receive a settlement until after the gates of the Oahe Dam were closed in 1958. Following the breakdown of new talks in 1955, the Crow Creek and Lower Brulé tribes were also forced to wait three more years for a final agreement. In the meantime the federal government took title to their property by condemnation and relocated tribal members without proper compensation. Within a short time their land was inundated by the waters of the Fort Randall reservoir.

The year 1954 also marked the tenth anniversary of the Pick-Sloan Plan. In the decade since its passage the basic program had undergone important changes. It had also withstood formidable challenges both from within and without the federal government. In the wake of growing criticism and controversy concerning program goals and methods, the Corps of Engineers and Bureau of Reclamation managed, nevertheless, to have both the number of projects within the plan and its overall appropriations liberally increased.

The original Pick-Sloan Plan authorized 107 reservoirs; 1,500 miles of protective levees; irrigation systems for 4.7 million acres; supplemental water for an additional 500,000 acres; and 1.6 million kilowatts of electric power. By 1954 the program had been expanded to include over 150 reservoirs, irrigation for 7 million acres, and 3,200,000 kilowatts of power. The total cost of the plan, originally estimated at $1.75 billion, jumped to $9.3 billion by 1952. The latter figure had tripled by 1970.[1]

The Missouri Basin Inter-Agency Committee, which administered the program, gradually expanded in membership although not in the scope of its program. Representatives from the Commerce Department were added in 1947, and delegates from the Labor Department and the newly created Department of Health, Education, and Welfare joined in 1952. The United States Public Health Service previously had been brought into Pick-Sloan with the passage of the Water Pollution Act of 1948.[2]

State representatives, originally four in number, were gradually given equal representation and voting rights, although they were still prohibited from chairing the committee. By 1952 their delegation was expanded to include representatives from all ten basin states. Several of the states also established local coordinating committees, such as the North Dakota Natural Resources Council, to protect and promote local interests. Despite these developments MBIAC continued to be thoroughly dominated by the federal water agencies in general and the Corps of Engineers in particular.[3]

The greatest outside challenge to Pick-Sloan continued to come from advocates of a Missouri Valley Authority. Die-hard proponents of MVA managed to keep the issue alive in Congress until 1956. By 1951 the advantages of the established program over the proposed one were almost irrefutable. While MVA spokesmen continued to talk in vague terms about specific projects, Congress proceeded to fund a substantial portion of the Pick-Sloan structures. To stubborn basin farmers the prospect of MVA thus seemed analogous to "buying a pig in a poke."[4] In addition, their political loyalties, like those of most of their neighbors in the region, had become overwhelmingly Republican, and they were therefore sharply opposed to any further "New Deal nonsense."[5] Because basin residents did not accept Pick-Sloan without criticism and suspicion, they were less willing to support creation of another supergovernment agency. Predictably, their views were also influenced by the anticommunist hysteria generated by cold-war tensions. The socialistic overtones of MVA were exaggerated, and conspiratorial plots were implied. An Iowa congressman, for example, claimed that he had evidence proving that the entire valley-authority idea had been masterminded "by the Communist Party of America in 1928."[6]

Negative public opinion eventually combined with the powerful Washington water lobby to drown MVA once and for all, but critics of Pick-Sloan, including MVA partisans, were momentarily heartened by two critical studies which appeared in the late 1940s. The first was prepared in 1948 by the Public Affairs Institute, an independent, nonprofit, and presumably nonpartisan research center based in Washington, D.C. The second was published in 1949 by the famous Commission on the Organization of the Executive Branch of Government chaired by former President Herbert Hoover. The latter investigation was conducted by the Hoover Commission's Task Force on Natural Resources under the direction of former Wyoming governor Leslie A. Miller.[7]

Both studies accused Pick-Sloan of inadequate planning, uncoordinated action, and ineffective administration in approaching basin water problems. The army and Reclamation Bureau were harshly criticized for failing to provide a more comprehensive water-management program. MBIAC was also chided for its unwieldy and inflexible structure, its basic weakness in providing effective coordination, and its inability to solve such critical questions as the availability of sufficient water for irrigation and navigation. Duplication of effort and inflation of costs on the part of the federal water agencies were also challenged. The studies even questioned the necessity and feasibility of several individual projects, including the army's navigation channel, its Garrison and Gavins Point dams, and the Bureau of Reclamation's diversion projects in the Dakotas.[8]

The Public Affairs Institute recommended that an engineering review board be established to investigate thoroughly all Pick-Sloan projects before further construction was allowed. It also expressed the urgent need for the development of a national water policy. Recommendations of the Hoover Commission were even more sweeping. Its report suggested that the Corps of Engineers civil water functions be turned over to the Interior Department, that the Reclamation Bureau be streamlined, and that a new water development service be established to coordinate all federal water programs. In addition it urged creation of a cabinet-level Department of Natural Resources.[9]

Both studies implied that Pick-Sloan would be vastly improved if brought under an administrative structure similar to the Tennessee Valley Authority. This finding should have been expected from the Public Affairs Institute, whose sponsors included many leading MVA proponents. That it was not a predictable result of the Hoover study gave new credibility to the MVA campaign. Although the major suggestions of the Task Force were never implemented, and the federal water agencies again managed to ride out the storm of criticism, the Task Force's investigation gave new life to the valley-authority debate. It also caused the disenchantment of several former Pick-Sloan supporters.[10]

Federal engineers had not recovered from the impact of the Hoover study before the Agriculture Department unveiled its own supplemental program for the Missouri Basin, the so-called Young Plan. Scientists, farmers, and other concerned observers had long been critical of Pick-Sloan for neglecting soil conservation and watershed management techniques as means of achieving both increased productivity and flood control. In 1949 former MBIAC chairman Gladwin E. Young, the Department of Agriculture's Missouri Basin field representative, devised extensive plans whereby these methods could be integrated into the existing Pick-Sloan program.[11]

The Young Plan was aimed primarily at holding more water in the soil by retarding runoff and erosion. Its methods included scientifically improved ways of cropping, seeding, terracing, reforesting, and draining land. Its cost was estimated at $8.5 billion over a thirty-year period, which approached the sum then being projected for the Pick-Sloan engineering structures.[12]

Federal water agencies and their lobbyists resisted the Young Plan. "Soil conservation is all right and necessary to protect the land," proclaimed General Pick in summarizing their views, "but it has no place in flood-control planning."[13] Congress was also less than enthusiastic about the program. Consequently, the Young Plan, like the MVA proposals, languished for several years on Capital Hill until even its most zealous supporters were compelled to give up hope. The Agriculture Department managed to implement it in some local areas, but its broad program was never approved.[14]

In 1950, Pick-Sloan came under the gun of President Truman's newly formed Water Resources Planning Commission. This body was directed to make an extensive study of America's ten largest river basins with a view toward development of a national water policy. It echoed the criticisms expressed by the Hoover Commission and others. Its report, however, was the first to castigate the Corps of Engineers and Reclamation Bureau for abusing the rights of Indians. The commission recommended steps to minimize physical and psychological damages to the tribes. These included prompt and generous payments for their property, full financial and technical assistance in relocation and reconstruction, and greater fringe benefits, such as development of hydroelectric power and irrigation for their exclusive use.[15]

The findings of the presidential commission were preceded by the stinging assessment of a joint council of America's leading civil, metallurgical, and chemical engineers. These experts reviewed Pick-Sloan from a more technical standpoint and recommended that the entire program be halted until more sound engineering and administrative policies could be implemented. Unfortunately both of these appraisals, together with the MVA proposals, the Hoover study, the Young Plan, and all previous challenges to the existing Missouri Basin water development program, effected no change whatsoever in the Pick-Sloan Plan. The Corps of Engineers and the Reclamation Bureau merely disregarded their critics while their supporters in Congress worked to neutralize any and all threats. But federal water agencies and their legislative cronies could not ignore the protests that spewed forth from nature itself in 1951 and 1952.[16]

Catastrophic floods on the lower Missouri River during those years brought Pick-Sloan critics out in full force. Angry basin residents demanded to know why, for example, the Corps of Engineers' $41 million levee project had failed to protect Kansas City from extensive flooding. No appreciable results had been effected by the $1.25 billion appropriated to the army for basin flood control since 1944. Basin residents also pleaded with President Truman to commission a more extensive investigation of the region's water problems and programs, an idea that had originally been proposed by Senator James Murray in 1948.[17]

Both the MVA and Young proposals gained adherents with the floods. New lobbying groups, such as the Associated Missouri Basin Conservationists, were formed to prevent completion of the Pick-Sloan Plan, and old antagonists, such as the Congress of Industrial Organizations (CIO), Nebraska MVA Committee, and the *St. Louis Post-Dispatch* stepped up their campaigns. Truman was finally pressured to order the creation of a Missouri Basin Survey Commission in January 1952. This eleven-member body was composed of various regional experts and congressmen, including Senator Murray, and was directed to make a thorough investigation of the basin's land and water resource problems and to report its findings by January 1953.[18]

These developments caused some Pick-Sloan proponents to have second thoughts. They began to talk in terms of reevaluating the program and building more upstream reservoirs, but the army stood firm. When attacks became too intense to be ignored or easily parried, the Corps of Engineers decided to take the offensive. Pick again led the charge. His tactic was to blame Congress for being stingy with its appropriations during the Korean War. If all Pick-Sloan structures had been in place, he claimed, no flood damage would have resulted. The solution he urged was not new projects or programs but increased support for existing ones.[19]

Scientists, engineers, and other experts immediately questioned the logic of these statements. They pointed out that the major floods had been caused by heavy rains in areas where no Pick-Sloan projects had been planned, but the Chief of Engineers was not deterred. Using the same weapons that had brought him success in the legislative war of 1944, he took his campaign to the basin itself. General Pick appeared before various local groups to fight for increased appropriations.[20] He managed to convince flood victims of the wisdom of the army cause and to gain both their support and that of several regional newspapers, including the *Kansas City Star* and the *St. Louis Globe-Democrat.*

For allegedly misrepresenting facts, Pick was censured by the Joint Engineering Council for a violation of the engineering code of ethics.[21] A more skeptical Kansas editor described his appearance in Topeka as a "stampede tactic" and commented: "Pick should be reminded of another general who was recently demoted because he dared to step over into the realm of civilian decision. Pick has made MacArthur look like a small town operator in that regard."[22]

Meanwhile the Missouri Basin Survey Commission carried out its work. Public hearings were held in seventeen basin cities, project sites were inspected, and state and federal agencies were consulted. An official report of its findings was issued on January 3, 1953. Because major deficiencies were discovered in the administrative structure of Pick-Sloan, the commission recommended a thorough reorganization. The solution it finally developed was a compromise between Senator Murray and the pro-MVA faction and those who favored a federal-state compact.[23]

First, the commission recommended the creation of a Missouri Basin Commission, consisting of five basin residents appointed by the president to provide better direction and coordination. This group was to be headquartered within the basin itself and was clearly the idea of valley-authority proponents. In accordance with the compact proposal, however, local participation was to be voluntary, and states were given the right to reject operation of the commission within their boundaries.[24]

Second, the report also urged that state and local interests bear a greater share of Pick-Sloan project costs and that navigation be given lowest priority for the use of water. The completion of the army's main-stem dams on the Missouri was approved, but the commission questioned the need for a nine-foot navigation channel, as well as certain tributary dams in the lower basin. Finally, the report urged immediate implementation of the Young Plan and encouraged a more thorough investigation of the entire Missouri Basin program.[25]

Like all previous suggestions to improve Pick-Sloan, the recommendations of the Missouri Basin Survey Commission went for naught. Truman left office before receiving the report he had initiated, and the Eisenhower administration paid little attention to it, although it did attempt to reorganize federal resource agencies. A Presidential Advisory Committee on Water Resources Policy and an Inter-Agency Committee on Water Resources were thus established at the subcabinet level in 1954. As a result the MBIAC charter was revised and expanded to include more intensive resource development programs. The basic deficiencies of the committee itself were not corrected, and in 1955 it was again attacked by a Hoover Commission Task Force on Water Resources and Power.[26]

Throughout the first decade of the plan's existence, it was generally acknowledged that the administration of Pick-Sloan was a disappointment, if not a failure. Critics continuously introduced proposals for expanded responsibilities and more centralized control. Yet the Corps of Engineers and Reclamation Bureau managed to keep the original program intact. Taking the offensive at times, spokesmen, such as Pick, finally succeeded in winning the majority of the regional population to their side. Disaster and army rhetoric combined to convince most basin residents of the soundness of individual projects and the acceptability of MBIAC as an administrative body. Consequently, the federal government was pressured to reject MVA, the Young Plan, the Missouri Basin Commission, and all other alternative proposals.

By the close of the Truman Administration, the Corps of Engineers and Bureau of Reclamation had come through the worst of it. Their greatest challenges had been weathered. Flood victims in the basin now cried for the original Pick-Sloan Plan to be accelerated and expanded, and Washington was anxious to oblige. New projects were added in 1954, and the army received its second largest appropriation for the program: $217,700,000. In the meantime the Sioux tribes had a much more difficult time in getting money from Congress.[27]

Chapter 9

NEGOTIATIONS AND SETTLEMENTS, 1958–1962

After eight years of negotiation the Standing Rock Indians succeeded in gaining a settlement from Congress in September 1958, a month after the gates of the Oahe Dam were closed. At the same time compensation was received by members of the Crow Creek and Lower Brulé tribes who had been forced by the Fort Randall project to evacuate their homes, although these people were denied funds for rehabilitation. Shortly thereafter these two Sioux groups were again compelled to brace themselves for battle. Construction of the Big Bend project on their land began in May 1960, after the Corps of Engineers was again allowed to condemn tribal property. Legislation for the Indians was introduced only two months earlier, yet moved relatively quickly through Congress. Final settlements, including money for rehabilitation programs, were approved in October 1962, and this time the Crow Creek and Lower Brulé Indians received their money before sustaining further damages.

Legislation for the Standing Rock Indians' settlement had not been reported out of the House Interior Committee during 1957. In an attempt to pressure Congress to act more swiftly, tribal leaders acted against the advice of their new counsel, Marvin J. Sonosky of Washington, D.C., and filed an injunction in the United States District Court of South Dakota in January 1958. This would halt further construction of the Oahe project until an adequate settle-

A Corps of Engineers publicity photo of Chief Eldest Son at the Oahe Dam construction site, 1958. Courtesy of United States Army, Corps of Engineers.

ment was negotiated.[1] Convinced that the army would take their land through condemnation if the Indians tried to work through the court, their lawyer at first scoffed at this tactic. "You can no more stop the dam," he had told them, "than you can stop the sun."[2] By February he had changed his mind. After researching the case more thoroughly, he became firmly convinced that the Corps of Engineers did not have the legal authority to condemn Standing Rock property.[3]

As the court was considering action, the army decided in March to file suit to condemn a large parcel of South Dakota land needed

*The dismantled Cheyenne River Agency prior to its inundation
by the Oahe reservoir, 1960.* Courtesy of United States Army,
Corps of Engineers.

for the Oahe project, six acres of which belonged to the Standing
Rock tribe. Seizing this opportunity to challenge the corps and
to present his new evidence, Sonosky filed a motion on behalf of
the tribe to dismiss the suit because Congress had not given the
army specific authorization to condemn tribal land.[4]

To support his case, the Standing Rock attorney cited the Sioux
treaty of 1868, which was reaffirmed by acts of Congress in 1877
and 1889. The acts proclaimed that land could be taken from the
tribe only upon payment of just compensation and the consent of
three-fourths of its adult membership. He then established that,

even though the Supreme Court had determined that Congress had the right of eminent domain over Indian land as long a just compensation was provided in accordance with the Fifth Amendment, the Court also had ruled in at least two cases that this power rested only with Congress and could not be extended to other federal agencies without the expressed authorization of that body.[5]

The presiding judge was George T. Mickelson, a former governor of South Dakota. He reviewed the arguments at length and decided on March 10 to uphold the tribe's motion to dismiss the army's suit. In doing so he ruled that Congress had not authorized the corps to take Indian lands by any legislative act, including the Flood Control Act of 1944, which had authorized the Pick-Sloan Plan, and the 1950 law that established settlement guidelines for the Standing Rock and Cheyenne River Sioux tribes. "It is clear to this Court," he remarked, "that Congress has never provided the requisite authority to the Secretary of the Army to condemn this tribal land. Such action is wholly repugnant to the entire history of Congressional and judicial treatment of the Indians."[6]

In effect Judge Mickelson ruled that the army could not take possession of Standing Rock property until after it had been purchased by Congress. Once again, as in their earlier dispute with Indian Commissioner Myer, the tribe, determined to fight for its rights, had gained a significant victory. If this same reasoning had been applied in the case of the Fort Randall takings a decade earlier, it certainly would have saved the Yankton, Crow Creek, and Lower Brulé Sioux considerable grief. Speedier settlements would have been provided those tribes, and more money for relocation would have been made available before the Indians were forced to give up their land. The entire relocation process, unpleasant at best, could have been made less painful and more beneficial.

Although condemnation of the Standing Rock land was effectively blocked, construction of the Oahe Dam was allowed to continue. Because of the federal court decision, the House of Representatives, which had been dragging its feet for nearly four years regarding the Oahe settlement, was pressed into action. New hearings on the bills introduced in 1957 were scheduled before the House Indian Subcommittee by late March. Led by Tribal Chairman Theodore E. Jamerson, the seven-member Standing Rock delegation that appeared in Washington was called on to defend proposals still in dispute.[7]

Points of disagreement centered on tribal requests for indirect damages. Tribal negotiators had by then agreed to accept a settlement for direct damages of $1,952,040, the amount of the latest MRBI valuation. They had also reached a separate agreement with the BIA to accept $3,805,832 for indirect damages. Army spokesmen as usual balked at this amount. Members of the Indian subcommittee, however, wanted the tribe to use at least one-half of the indirect damage payment to supplement the rehabilitation program. The Standing Rock negotiators, who constantly fought to have more direction and control of relocation and rehabilitation plans, resented having any restrictions placed on the use of these funds.[8]

Members of Congress wanted the Indians to drop their requests for separate compensation for the loss of the riverbed and the tax immunity on their land, since they felt these items were already adequately covered under either the direct or the indirect damage appraisals. Tribal delegates insisted that these losses had not previously been considered.[9]

The Standing Rock Sioux were eventually forced to drop the tax-immunity issue, but the debate on the riverbed touched off a heated controversy. The Cheyenne River tribe had received payment for their interest in the Missouri riverbed as part of their indirect damage settlement, but a precise value had never been determined. The Standing Rock negotiators had decided to ask for a specific amount for this property after discovering that the 22,230 acres under their ownership was worth $133,380. While debate on this request continued in Congress, Corps of Engineers officials decided that it was not necessary to acquire the tribe's interest after all. Assuming that its navigation rights on the Missouri would supercede any Indian rights over the property, the army reasoned that it could both save itself some money and end the entire controversy by simply allowing the tribe to keep the riverbed. In effect it was asking Congress to extinguish the Indian's property rights without purchasing their land.[10]

Tribal negotiators responded by proclaiming that, if they maintained ownership of the riverbed, they would continue to retain superior hunting and fishing rights within the reservoir area, which had been accorded to them by long-established treaties. Army spokesmen denied those rights, but House committee members upheld them, since the rights were reservationwide. The Standing Rock Sioux thus established a clear-cut argument for compensation for the relinquishment of either their rights or their title to the property. In the end the federal government decided to obtain full ownership of the riverbed and to extinguish all Indian rights. The Standing Rock Sioux never received the $133,380 that they had asked for this property because Congress held firm in maintaining that their loss was already included in the direct damage appraisal, although in truth it was not.[11]

New legislation for the Standing Rock tribe embodied the agreements and valuations reached during the March hearings. The bill was introduced by Congressman Berry on May 23 and asked $1,952,040 for direct damages, $3,937,832 for indirect damages, and $8.5 million for rehabilitation programs. In addition to previous demands, new language was added to include oil and gas among the mineral rights retained by the tribe and to exempt all settlement funds from taxation. The new legislation also increased the amount of reimbursement for negotiating expenses from $100,-000 to $135,000 without any restrictions on attorneys' fees.[12]

The new Berry bill was reported out of the Interior Committee without amendment on July 17, passed by the House on July 24, and referred to the Senate Interior Committee for consideration. Meanwhile, on August 3 at six o'clock in the morning, giant earth movers began dumping dirt into the Missouri River, and dignitaries gathered at the Oahe site for a public ceremony marking the closure of the dam. Realizing for the first time the urgency of a settlement, the Senate took just two more weeks to review the Standing Rock legislation before passing it on August 18 with only two amendments. Unfortunately, these two arbitrary changes cost the tribe $2,178,319. They reduced the indirect damage payment from $3,937,832 to $3,299,513 and the rehabilitation program funds from $8,500,000 to $6,960,000.[13]

A final agreement with the Standing Rock Sioux, as amended by the Senate and concurred with by the House, was signed into law by President Eisenhower on September 2, 1958. The act provided the tribe with a cash payment of $12,346,553. Although this was more than $14 million less than the Indians had originally demanded, it was considerably more than the Cheyenne River Sioux had received just four years earlier and was nearly as much as the total settlement granted the Fort Berthold Indians, even though both of the other tribes sustained far more extensive damages. Eight years of bickering with the government had caused tribal representatives to grow weary and upset about the Oahe experience. Now they could take some satisfaction that they had succeeded in negotiating the best overall settlement of any of the tribes affected by Pick-Sloan. Both the lessons learned from earlier settlements and their own dogged determination had made this possible.[14]

The Standing Rock Sioux received more money than the Cheyenne River Sioux for indirect damages and rehabilitation, even though the latter tribe lost nearly twice as much land and underwent a much more drastic relocation. The North Dakota-based Indians received only $297,960 less than their southern neighbors for direct property damages. The difference between the two settlements was due in part to an increase in land values between 1954 and 1958, but it reflected most clearly the federal government's arbitrariness in arriving at an agreement with the two tribes.[15]

Like any party seeking legal compensation, the Sioux tribes sought the most beneficial settlements possible. Their damage requests were based on generous, although not unreasonable, estimates of their potential damages. The precise cost of rehabilitation—an urgent need on all the reservations—was especially difficult to determine, and the value of their property was naturally greater to Indian owners than to outside appraisers. In considering the tribal requests, members of Congress, influenced by partisan and budgetary considerations, had to balance with them the recommendations of the Bureau of Indian Affairs, which was far more moderate in its damage estimates, and proposals offered by the army, which generally offered as little as possible. In seeking a middle ground, a few congressmen could chisel one or two million dollars from the Indian requests in the course of a single afternoon, to the great astonishment and chagrin of tribal negotiators.

Settlements could have been more uniform and equitable if all the tribes had been dealt with at the same time by a special court or commission established especially for that purpose. Ideally such a body would have been comprised of individuals more familiar with local land values and more willing to protect tribal interests. Such settlements would have been compatible with policies established under TVA, as well as those proposed by MVA advocates, but they were almost impossible under the disjointed, piecemeal procedures established by the Pick-Sloan Plan, dominated as it was by the federal water agencies. Of course, whether or not such a settlement would have granted millions of dollars to the tribes for rehabilitation, with the pressures generated by termination, can never be known.

Besides more money the Standing Rock Sioux received more favorable settlement terms than Congress had been willing to provide four years earlier. In addition to the same general rights, privileges, and benefits granted the Cheyenne River Sioux the tribe gained provisions that exempted settlement funds from all forms of taxation and protected their use from payment of any previous debts, liens, or claims except those owed the federal or tribal governments. The law held that all Standing Rock land not needed for the Oahe project was to be returned to tribal ownership, although none ever was. Oil and gas were specifically included under mineral rights, and the tribe was given a sixty-day period in which to salvage any property not previously disposed of by individual owners. The Interior Department was directed to give additional assistance to the Indians in purchasing and consolidating substitute lands and eliminating heirship interests. A formal request from 25 percent of the heirs was the only permission required for the BIA to sell an allotted tract.[16]

The Standing Rock Sioux received $135,000 without restriction for their negotiating expenses. The Cheyenne River tribe had been granted only $100,000, with the stipulation that not more than half of that amount could be used to pay attorneys' fees. When that tribe's total costs were added up, the amount was $119,802, of which $72,222 was for the expenses of their lawyer. Consequently, the Cheyenne River Sioux were compelled to make up the deficit of $22,222 out of their own funds. But the Standing Rock tribe managed to stay within its $135,000 limit, even though their expenses covered a much longer period. They also received more money in interest payments, since they were not required to spend all of their money within ten years as the Cheyenne River tribe had been. Congress saved them additional money by ruling that cash awards to individual property owners who had rejected their appraisals and had received higher settlements in court would be compensated from the army's project budget and not from the tribe's settlement compensation, as had been the case in the Cheyenne River legislation.[17]

Two important provisions found in the earlier settlement were eliminated from the Standing Rock legislation. Members of the House Indian Subcommittee succeeded in persuading tribal negotiators to drop their request to have the federal government take responsibility for livestock hazards created by the reservoir. Despite treaty provisions the legislation also held that tribal ratification of the final agreement was unnecessary because the receipt of just compensation in accordance with the Fifth Amendment was all that was required to make the transaction legal and binding.[18]

Unlike the Cheyenne River law, the Standing Rock settlement required the tribe to use at least one-half of its indirect damage payment for rehabilitation. It also prohibited distribution of any settlement funds on a per capita basis. Restrictions were placed on the funds that could be used to purchase land, and moving costs were limited to $726,146, the amount of the latest MRBI estimate. A schedule was established whereby the reservoir area would have to be evacuated within two years.[19]

On all of the Sioux reservations affected by Pick-Sloan there existed a very vocal faction who preferred to have their so-called "river money" distributed in equal cash payments to all tribal members rather than disbursed through a structured relocation and rehabilitation program. On Standing Rock, for example, this faction was led by John Gates and former chairperson Josephine Kelly. These Indians were skeptical of BIA and tribal-council intentions and dissatisfied with previous improvement programs and felt that they should be entitled to receive cash directly, to use as they saw fit. "Give me the money," said John Gates in summarizing their view, "and I will rehabilitate myself."[20] Some Lower Brulé tribal members had previously presented a petition that stated, "under no circumstances will we consent to the use of these funds for experimental reservation programs or projects instituted by either the Tribe or the Bureau of Indian Affairs."[21]

Most tribal leaders, together with most BIA officials and members of congress, were strongly opposed to per capita payments. Past experiences with that kind of settlement had convinced them that they seldom resulted in social and economic gains. Funds were too often spent foolishly, and tribal members were preyed upon by unscrupulous merchants. Although the Fort Berthold and Cheyenne River tribes were allowed to distribute part of their compensation in this way, the Standing Rock, Crow Creek, and Lower Brulé Indians were prohibited from doing so.

Legislation for the Crow Creek and Lower Brulé Sioux, pending since 1954, was also acted upon by the Eighty-fifth Congress and approved the same day as the Standing Rock settlement. The separate proposals followed a similar path through Congress, but provisions for the smaller tribes proved far less generous.[22]

In bills introduced in 1957 the Crow Creek Sioux had asked $685,138 for direct damages, $1,132,452 for indirect damages, and $5,686,036 for rehabilitation. The Lower Brulé Sioux, who were losing more acreage, requested $708,493, $788,904, and $6,348,316, respectively. Benefits similar to those demanded by the Standing Rock Sioux were also requested by both tribes. The House Indian Subcommittee, as with the Standing Rock legislation, held hearings on these proposals in 1957, but failed to file a report of its recommendations before Congress adjourned.[23]

During these hearings tribal members were called upon to justify all of their cash demands in minute detail. For example, when Lower Brulé representatives asked $6.00 per bushel for the value of their mouse beans, Richard LaRoche, Jr., recalled that the Congressmen "laughed like hell and said we never heard of such a damn thing."[24] Thus the Indians were required to gather samples of this food source and submit them to a University of Maryland botany professor, who finally verified their worth to Congress.

Another Congressman tried to convince his colleagues that cottonwood trees, which were plentiful in the reservoir area, were worthless. Consequently Lower Brulé negotiators were compelled to show newspaper clippings that documented the army's use of cottonwood lumber to crate overseas shipments. Signed statements that Indian women canned an average of twelve quarts of berries each year had to be presented, and a lengthy discussion took place in which the tribe tried to convince the solons of the value of "skunk oil."[25]

Army representatives at the hearings made their usual objections to tribal proposals, BIA spokesmen offered more moderate terms, and Congressmen probing the issue became totally confused. In the meantime the Lower Brulé tribe startled Washington officials by requesting a program of termination.[26]

By resorting to this desperate tactic, reservation leaders hoped to increase their bargaining power for generous compensation. They judged there was popular sentiment in Congress in favor of this measure and simply requested, through formal channels, that the amount of the Fort Randall settlement be doubled so that enough land and cattle could be purchased to make the tribe completely self-sufficient by 1975. Their proposal clearly challenged the legislators either to withdraw from the espoused policy of termination or vastly to expand the scope of compensation. When put on the spot, the legislators were unwilling to establish the precedent that the latter alternative represented, and somewhat embarrassed they chose the former. This, of course, did nothing to help the Lower Brulé cause. The tribe's proposal succeeded only in delaying negotiations further and may have hampered efforts for rehabilitation. Yet it did gain for them the dubious distinction of being the only tribe ever to initiate a program of termination.[27]

With the almost universal opposition of other tribal groups and a vigorous campaign waged by the National Congress of American Indians, termination was losing support on Capitol Hill and would later be totally repudiated. Although many Washington officials were at first delighted with the Lower Brulé request and the idea of a major tribal investment program, the BIA proved reluctant to take action on the proposal. Long after the political advantages of their tactic were lost, tribal leaders, more than a little embarrassed by the whole episode, were finally persuaded to withdraw their request.[28]

This incident serves well to illustrate both the plight of tribal negotiators and the limitations of the termination policy. It is unfortunate that the Lower Brulé representatives were so frustrated in their efforts to gain compensation for damages that had already disrupted the lives of tribal members that they were willing to gamble on a scheme that probably would have proven more disastrous. It is doubtful that even a settlement of $15,691,426 would have been enough to make them self-sufficient in any meaningful way. If, after federal services were abolished, the Lower Brulé Sioux failed in their bid for progress, they would have found themselves in an even worse predicament.

On the other hand, it was patently unfair of the federal government to pressure tribal leaders into a position where they felt that, to gain compensation, they had to endorse publicly a policy that was exceedingly unpopular among Indians and yet had already been declared and implemented by Congress. The absurdity of the situation was exceeded only by the underlying principle of termination itself, that is, the idea of first ending federal services and then making the tribes self-sufficient instead of the other way around.[29]

Following the 1957 hearings and the disruption caused by the Lower Brulé termination proposal, the tribes succeeded in reaching a compromise with army and BIA representatives on the issue of damages. The Crow Creek Sioux agreed to accept $555,787 for their direct damages and $1,463,433 for indirect damages, including $500,000 for the relocation of Fort Thompson. The Lower Brulé Indians settled on $536,327 for direct damages and $638,904 for indirect damages, including $150,000 for relocation expenses.[30]

Because of these agreements the tribes redrafted their settlement proposals. New legislation, which included previous BIA, army, and congressional recommendations, was subsequently introduced by Congressmen Berry and McGovern on May 23, 1958.[31]

The most dramatic change in these new bills was the complete elimination of all requests for rehabilitation. Because Indian land would soon be flooded again, this time by the Big Bend project, federal officials urged that consideration of the rehabilitation programs be postponed until after the army had completed all of its acquisitions on the reservations. South Dakota politicians were also afraid of the negative connotations that had become associated with the term "rehabilitation." Overly sensitive that this word had become synonymous with the idea of reparations in the minds of many congressmen, they decided that the Lower Brulé and Crow Creek tribes could wait a few more years to receive general improvement funds. After all, the damage had already been done and more was coming.[32]

Having streamlined tribal proposals, the South Dakota legislators did their best to push the new legislation through the House. "This bill is vitally needed at this time," Berry told his colleagues, "because of the fact that these lands have already been flooded, . . . and have already been taken by the government, probably without full authority. . . ."[33] McGovern also reminded House members that the tribes had been patiently waiting for many years for a settlement and were "fully entitled to the modest damage claims."[34]

The new bills, considered in tandem by the House Interior Committee, were reported without amendment and passed by the House on July 24. As it had with all previous Pick-Sloan settlement requests, the Senate Interior Committee made drastic cuts in the Indians' cash proposals. About $623,000 was slashed from the Crow Creek settlement and $199,000 from that of Lower Brulé. The legislation was then passed by the Senate on August 18 and signed into law by Eisenhower on September 2, along with the Standing Rock bill.[35]

The Crow Creek Sioux finally received $1,395,812 for their property, including their interest in the riverbed and all damages caused by the Fort Randall project. The Lower Brulé tribe was granted $976,523. Both tribes received settlement provisions similar to, but less generous than those granted the Standing Rock Sioux.[36] Unlike that tribe, neither was given rehabilitation money or the right to regain ownership of any former property found unnecessary for the project. Reimbursement for negotiating expenses was limited to $100,000, as it had been in the Cheyenne River settlement, with a similar restriction that not more than $50,000 could be used for attorneys' fees. Individual tribal members were given just twenty-eight days, or until the end of September, to salvage whatever property was left within the reservoir area. After that time the tribes were given until the first of the year to take whatever property private owners left behind. In effect these were false benefits because a great portion of the area was already underwater.[37]

Although no limit was placed on the tribes' moving costs, they were required to pay all relocation expenses out of settlement funds. The Standing Rock and Cheyenne River legislation had provided that such costs would be charged to the Corps of Engineers' project budget. Whereas the Standing Rock law provided that the BIA could, with the permission of 25 percent of the interest holders, sell heirship lands, these settlements required written approval from 51 percent of the owners.[38]

Unlike the Cheyenne River Sioux but like the Standing Rock Indians, the Crow Creek and Lower Brulé tribes received tax exemptions on all settlement funds and specific protection for their oil and gas rights. They were also granted more favorable conditions for the rejection of individual property appraisals, since their legislation did not require them to deposit money with the court or to cover the costs of petitioning for higher awards. They did not receive protection for livestock hazards as the Cheyenne River tribe had or the right to ratify the final agreement, nor were they permitted the same degree of autonomy over control and distribution of settlement funds, relocation of tribal members, or consolidation of their land.[39]

The Crow Creek and Lower Brulé tribes had fought against the same odds as the Cheyenne River and Standing Rock Sioux and were more disappointed with the results. Of those tribal groups only the Crow Creek and Lower Brulé had suffered the hardship and humiliation of having to move two years before receiving a settlement, and they alone had been denied funds for rehabilitating their reservations, although their poverty was relatively greater. They were also the only tribes that would face the same ordeal again.

Even as tribal negotiators were in Washington seeking compensation for Fort Randall damages, army crews were out surveying Crow Creek and Lower Brulé land for the Big Bend project. Construction of this dam was scheduled to begin in September 1960. This meant that the tribes had to negotiate a settlement by that time if they hoped to avoid losing more land without adequate compensation. The Corps of Engineers, however, worked ahead of schedule and groundbreaking ceremonies for the project, presided over by presidential hopeful Lyndon B. Johnson of Texas, took place on May 30.[40]

Legislation for the Crow Creek and Lower Brulé tribes was not introduced in Congress until March 2, 1960. A week later the Corps of Engineers again filed suit in federal district court to condemn the 867 acres of Indian land needed for the actual project site, despite the earlier decision handed down by the same court in regard to the Standing Rock suit in 1958. Congress had still not specifically delegated its powers of eminent domain to the army, yet the Corps of Engineers was allowed to take title to the reservation land.[41]

It was odd that neither the tribes themselves, their lawyers, the BIA, nor any of the Indian rights organizations protested the decision. Left unchallenged, the corps lived up to its fast-growing reputation as the "Bully of the Basin" and was permitted once again to skirt its legal obligations to the Indians.[42]

The army was no more generous when the time came to negotiate a settlement. Corps representatives would still not move from their previous positions on such items as salvage and shoreline rights, relocation costs, indirect damages, and rehabilitation.[43]

In contrast to the earlier settlements, however, Congress considered the tribal proposals in record time. They appeared to feel some guilt for what Senator Mundt described as their "shockingly dilatory" behavior in regard to the Fort Randall settlement. After expediently eliminating the requirement for a separate law to establish negotiation guidelines, the legislators took just two years and seven months to approve the Big Bend bills.[44]

In their original requests the Crow Creek Sioux asked for a settlement of $4,917,924. Of this sum $494,890 was for direct damages, $421,034 for indirect damages, and $4,002,000 for rehabilitation. The Lower Brulé tribe demanded $1,111,940, $783,998, and $2,670,300, respectively, plus $350,000 for a new high school, for a total of $4,916,238. In addition both tribes requested $123,000 for negotiating expenses.[45]

The Crow Creek and Lower Brulé proposals included several provisions not found in previous settlements. For example, each tribe asked that the federal government mark the boundary of the reservoir areas and provide fire protection for all adjoining Indian land. Each also proclaimed exclusive right to lease shoreline grazing areas to both tribal members and non-Indians. Preference for the leases would be given to former owners, and rents would be deposited with the United States Treasury and credited to the tribes. Both asked to have shoreline hunting and fishing rights exempted from state regulations.[46]

The Lower Brulé tribe requested that a new town be constructed on the reservation that would have paved streets, full utilities, an elementary and high school, a municipal building, and at least 61 new housing units. The Crow Creek Sioux also asked for a new townsite that would include a tribal office building, community center, and 100 new homes, but they did not ask for any new schools. In addition both tribes requested the right to purchase any land within fifty miles of the reservations for the purpose of industrial development or tribal housing projects. They stipulated that this land come under federal trust status.[47]

After these proposals were reviewed by the Indian subcommittees, made the subject of new legislation, and further reduced by the House and Senate, the tribes received a final settlement on October 3, 1962.[48] The Lower Brulé Sioux received $3,194,465, of which $825,000 was for direct damages, $400,715 for indirect damages, and $1,968,750 for rehabilitation. The direct damage payment included compensation for the tribe's interest in the riverbed, which the Corps of Engineers had finally decided to purchase, as well as its right to any gravel in the reservoir area. Moving expenses, covered by the indirect damage payment, were limited to no more than $247,325, the amount of an MRBI estimate of those costs, and the tribe was required to combine the remainder of this money with its rehabilitation funds. The tribe also received $75,000 for its negotiating expenses.[49]

The Crow Creek tribe was granted $355,000 for its direct damages (including the loss of the riverbed and gravel), $209,302 for for indirect damages, and $3,802,500 for rehabilitation: a total of $4,366,802. Its moving expenses were limited to $77,550, and its negotiating expenses to $75,000.[50]

Requests for shoreline boundary markers, fire protection, and unrestricted grazing, hunting, and fishing rights were systematically denied the tribes. They received the same salvage and shoreline rights provided in all previous settlements, subject to federal regulation, but with the additional right to lease shoreline grazing areas to non-Indians if they chose. No provision was given for special tribal funds to be developed from these revenues as the Indians had hoped, and the Corps of Engineers was given the authority to regulate the location, size, and nature of all lands so used.[51]

The Senate Interior Committee ruled that the army should be held responsible for construction of the new townsites on the reservations, but that replacement facilities needed only to be comparable to previously existing ones. If more elaborate structures were needed or desired, the senators maintained that they should be financed and constructed by the BIA out of its annual appropriations and not out of the Corps of Engineers' Big Bend project funds.[52]

Provisions for paved streets, sidewalks, gutters, and streetlights were dropped by the legislators. The provision for building facilities not already found on the reservations, such as a high school for the Lower Brulé, was also eliminated. The extent of new housing for the Lower Brule townsite was not specified in the law, but the Crow Creek housing project was reduced by fifty units. The latter tribe was also prohibited from spending more than $350,000 of its rehabilitation money for development of a new townsite for Fort Thompson.[53]

The tribes were granted permission to purchase property within fifty miles of the reservation for industrial development, but Congress ruled that federal trust status could not be extended outside the reservations. Each tribe was prohibited from spending more than $400,000 of its rehabilitation money for that purpose. They were permitted to pool their resources, if they chose, for the development of cooperative enterprises. Congress held that any industry attracted by the project would be required to give preferential employment rights to tribal members.[54]

Afraid that the Indians would squander their money, Congress restricted excessive land purchases and prohibited per capita payments, as it had done in the Standing Rock settlement. To appease the tribes, however, it granted their request to retain ownership of any former lands found unnecessary for the Big Bend project, although it was felt that there was little chance that the army would give up the property. Congress's other concessions included a tax exemption on all settlement funds.[55]

Several features of the Big Bend legislation made it unique. The Lower Brulé and Crow Creek Sioux were the only tribes to have their rehabilitation program extended to all enrolled tribal members rather than just those who resided on the reservation. This was done at the request of the tribes because of their large non-resident membership (over 50 percent). This factor also explains why these settlements were the only ones to permit tribal members to move family graves from old cemeteries within the reservoir area to new sites off the reservations.[56]

The Big Bend legislation established different procedures for settlement of contested property appraisals. Tribal members were given the same rights to have the value of their holdings determined in court at government expense, provided they filed suit within a year. Congress held that, while these cases were pending, an amount equal to 10 percent of the tribal member's Individual Indian Money (IIM) Account, or the money held and managed for them by the BIA, would be withheld from disbursement. This meant that the Indians were required as an act of good faith to forego some of their personal finances until their suits were decided. The provision had been included at the insistence of the army. Hoping to avoid the additional costs that resulted from higher court settlements, the Corps of Engineers obviously wanted to discourage further litigation.[57]

The Big Bend settlements were the only ones requiring the tribes to give up their gravel rights. These mineral resources, it seems, were needed for use in the construction of the dam. This legislation also stood alone in its consideration of non-Indian property interests. It was common for white ranchers to build improvements on land leased from the tribes. In previous settlements no provision had been made for these people or their property, and they had been forced to move what they owned at their own expense. The Big Bend acts, however, required the army to pay them the fair market value of their property.[58]

Crow Creek and Lower Brulé tribal members were given until July 1, 1963, to remain on their land and to make use of it free of charge. Although the BIA was directed to assist the tribes in their efforts to purchase and consolidate land, new and more elaborate procedures were established for the sale of heirship interests.

As in the Standing Rock legislation all settlement funds were exempted from the payment of previous liens, debts, or claims except those owed the federal or tribal government. Congress ruled that even these last two obligations could be exempted if it was found that such payment would create hardship for individual tribal members.[59]

With the passage of the Big Bend settlements in 1962 the federal government acquired the last tribal lands needed for the Pick-Sloan main-stem projects. Over the span of fourteen years and at a cost of over $34 million the United States had obtained title to approximately 204,124 acres of Sioux property, more Indian land than was taken for any other public works project in the United States. Because of the haphazard methods used to calculate compensation, the settlements with the five individual tribes differed considerably.

Although the Cheyenne River Sioux sustained the greatest damages, the Standing Rock tribe had the best settlement. The Yankton Sioux underwent the least disruption and also received the worst settlement. The Lower Brulé and Crow Creek tribes were most rudely dealt with in the Fort Randall negotiations, but they got the most generous rehabilitation provisions from the Big Bend legislation. None of the tribes considered their compensation adequate, but all suffered considerably less and received considerably more than the Fort Berthold Indians had.

As long and arduous as the process of negotiating final settlement was, it represented only the first stage of the Pick-Sloan ordeal for these tribal groups. Once compensation was received, and benefits and provisions were outlined by law (or even earlier in the case of the Fort Randall takings), plans had to be implemented for the relocation of tribal members and their property, the reconstruction and restoration of reservation facilities and services, and the rehabilitation of entire Indian communities. The disruption, chaos, and uncertainty generated by this experience made it a most painful one for all tribal members involved.

Chapter 10

RECONSTRUCTION

For the Sioux the period of reconstruction was the most distressing phase of the Pick-Sloan experience. Whereas problems encountered in settlement negotiations involved relatively few tribal members, the onerous task of relocation touched them all. Most drastically affected were those families who actually resided within the reservoir areas. Yet all suffered from the loss of their reservation's land and resources, the interruption of government services, and the disruption of the social, economic, and religious life of their tribe.

The difficult period of adjustment posed a challenge to both federal and tribal governments. Coordination and supervision of relocation and rebuilding activities demanded the most sensitive and sophisticated administrative talents. Unfortunately, neither party proved equal to the task. The federal government was ineffective in its role as protective steward. The tribes were ineffective because as semiautonomous victims, they were usually systematically removed from the actual decision-making process. Hapless chiefs and haphazard bureaucrats succeeded in creating nearly as many problems as the dam projects themselves.

From the moment when the first tribal member signed a settlement contract until the day when the final nail was driven into the last replacement house, the process of reconstruction was marked by confusion, delay, ruinous errors, and ill-fated incidents. The result was chaos, despair, and in many cases genuine hardship for the Sioux people involved.

The distribution and expenditure of settlement money was closely monitored in all cases by the Bureau of Indian Affairs. Based on the long-standing assumption that tribal members were not entirely competent to handle their own financial affairs, elaborate protective measures were established. These precautions seemed to be designed not so much to protect the Indians from monetary problems as to protect the settlement funds from Indians.

Except in the case of the Cheyenne River Sioux tribal leaders were given only a modicum of control over reconstruction transactions and were rarely permitted actually to handle any of the funds. Payments owed to property owners were deposited in their BIA-controlled Individual Indian Money accounts at local agencies. After determining the particular needs and desires of each individual family, expenditure of this money was carefully programmed by MRBI personnel in consultation with special tribal relocation committees created for the purpose. Once the expenditure schedules had been approved by the tribal council, the agency superintendent, the BIA area director, and the office of the Commissioner of Indian Affairs in Washington, tribal members were allowed to contract for the approved goods and services that had been programmed. Creditors were paid directly by the BIA, and inspections were conducted to guarantee both contract compliance and customer satisfaction. Payments due the tribe as a whole for land and improvements were credited to federally supervised accounts.[1]

MRBI personnel, who worked closely with the respective tribal councils, determined the amount of money to which each property owner was entitled. The final appraisal of the individual's damages, as arbitrated in the settlement negotiations, was the primary basis for these payments. In addition the BIA established a set formula to determine individual moving costs, which averaged approximately $1,000 per family. The primary role of tribal government in these matters was merely to correct any errors in the appraisal schedules or property descriptions. However, the Cheyenne River tribe again was given considerably more freedom and control over its own settlement funds.[2]

A combination of favorable circumstances explains the relative autonomy granted the Cheyenne River Sioux in these matters. The timing of their settlement was the most important factor. Cheyenne River delegates were fortunate enough to negotiate an agreement far in advance of the other tribes because the termination debate was at its height in Washington. Congressmen tended to be more easily swayed at that time by arguments for self-determination than they were just a few months later. They were also impressed by the tribe's strong leadership potential, as demonstrated by the Ducheneaux administration and its persistence in demanding additional rights of self-government. Consequently, Congress generously bestowed upon the Cheyenne River Sioux important concessions that they were either unable or unwilling to extend to the other tribes because of different circumstances, including an intervening shift in Indian policy goals. The valuable experience that tribal leaders on that reservation gained from having more control over reconstruction and rehabilitation programs can be considered one of the most important benefits that a native group received from the Pick-Sloan experience. It is unfortunate that it was a rare exception and not the rule.[3]

Sioux property owners who felt that their damages had received low appraisals were given the right to reject their settlement offers and to petition in the federal district court. They were usually given a year after the passage of their tribe's settlement act in which to file their rejections. According to law they had only to pay the costs of their own legal counsel, because the federal government was obliged to pay all other court costs.[4]

The amount of money, if any, that the tribe was required to deposit with the court in such cases varied with the tribe, as did the sources of additional funds for higher settlements awarded individual litigants. Thus the Cheyenne River Sioux had to put up the full amount of the individual's appraisal offer, whereas the Crow Creek and Lower Brulé tribes in the Big Bend settlement had to withhold only 10 percent of the money deposited for them in their IIM accounts. The Standing Rock Sioux and the tribes affected by the Fort Randall project were not required to make any deposit at all. With the exception of the Cheyenne River legislation all of the settlements provided that, if the court determined that a higher settlement was justified, the additional money would be

taken from the Corps of Engineers' project appropriations. The
Cheyenne River tribe was obliged to pay for higher awards out of
its own settlement funds.[5]

Based on the experience of non-Indian litigants affected by the
Pick-Sloan projects, tribal members knew that they could expect a
higher settlement from the court. White farmers who lost land to
the Fort Randall Dam had received an average of 40 percent more
money from the court than the army had been willing to pay them.[6]
Still, several factors worked to discourage Indians from taking this
course of action.

First, not many tribal members could afford even the minimal
legal fees involved, and even fewer could afford to wait any longer
for a settlement. Although the law provided that property owners
could receive up to 90 percent of their appraisal value while court
action was pending, most felt that they needed all the money they
could get when it came time to move. They were unwilling to wait
for the often lengthy litigation process. The five Standing Rock
tribal members who did reject their appraisals waited for five years
while the court decided their cases.[7]

Members of the Cheyenne River tribe were discouraged from
going to court by the excessive deposit requirement and by the
provision that additional payments for higher awards were to be
deducted from the tribe's own settlement funds. Peter Hiett, the
one tribal member who did reject his appraisal offer, learned that
a court settlement could prove less beneficial in the end. A comparatively wealthy member of the tribe, Hiett was offered $13,000
for his land and improvements and $8,000 for the value of his
timber. He rejected these valuations and, after two years of waiting,
received a court settlement of $22,000. Once legal fees and other
expenses were deducted, he was left with only $18,000, or $3,000
less than he was originally offered.[8]

In contrast to the Oahe and Fort Randall settlements the Big
Bend land takings produced a flurry of rejection cases. Tribal
members on the Crow Creek and Lower Brule reservations had
consistently held that their property had been valued too low. They
were also convinced by previous experience that those Indians who
pressed for litigation received better terms. Consequently, twenty-
nine of them, a record number for any of the settlements, decided

to seek a court decision. Because of a serious misunderstanding, however, most of these Indians failed to initiate court action within the one-year time limit stipulated by law.[9]

In an effort to avoid heavy legal expenses, some tribal members tried to consolidate their cases so that one lawyer could handle them all. This gave others the mistaken impression that the tribal attorney was assuming the responsibility of filing all rejection cases with the court. As a result only a few of those who had decided to reject their offers managed to meet the October 2, 1963, deadline. After learning of their error, these people made a desperate appeal to local congressmen for an extension of the time limit. Legislation introduced in 1964 to provide for the extension was not approved until June, 1969. After five additional years of waiting the Indian property owners finally succeeded in getting the time limit extended to September 1, 1969.[10]

Over the course of the next two years those Indians whose patience and determination had seen them through generally received more favorable settlements from the court. In the meantime they had placed themselves at an economic disadvantage during the relocation period because they were unable to receive the full cash value of their property at the crucial moment when they were forced to move and when the best replacement land was available.[11]

Big Bend litigation did not end here. In February 1971 eleven Indian plaintiffs, including four members of the Big Eagle family on Lower Brule, brought another suit before the federal district court of South Dakota. These tribal members, who had all previously gone to court for a property settlement, claimed that they were legally entitled to receive annual interest payments on the difference between the original appraised value of their property, as compensated in the Big Bend settlements of 1962, and the final judgments awarded by the courts about eight years later. In presenting this argument, their lawyer, John W. Larson of Kennebec, South Dakota, cited the precedent established in a 1938 decision involving the Klamath and Modoc tribes of Oregon. In that case the Supreme Court had ruled that just compensation for the federal taking of Indian property under the provisions of the Fifth Amendment must include the payment of interest.[12]

In the case of *Big Eagle* v. *United States* the district court upheld that ruling and also extended the rationale of a 1968 decision involving the Fort Berthold Indians. In that case the United States Court of Claims had held that, if the federal government made an effort in good faith to provide the full value of tribal property, including interest, as just compensation, then the taking of Indian property did not constitute "eminent domain" as commonly interpreted. If this decision had been rendered earlier, it might have been used to the great detriment of several of the tribes affected by Pick-Sloan, but it worked in this particular instance to the Indians' advantage. In determining the extent of the government's obligation to these tribal members, the court ruled that they were entitled to receive interest on the amount of the difference at a rate of 6 percent per annum between October 2, 1962, and the date of their final court judgment.[13]

Although the Big Eagle family and other litigants in the case thus received additional funds, the federal government did not volunteer to extend this decision to any of the other tribal members who had been forced for many months to await a court settlement. It was odd that none of the others ever stepped forward to press their claim.

Whether received from the court or directly through Congress, all of the funds granted Indian property owners were protected by law from certain debt payments. Each of the settlements provided that this money would be immune from any previous lien, debt, or claim except those owed the federal or tribal government. A large number of tribal members, however, were found to have delinquent accounts with these creditors. On the Crow Creek Reservation fourteen such individuals were found to have a total outstanding federal debt of $6,752. Some of the bills were for so-called "unpaid estate claims" incurred by deceased ancestors; others were for the repayment of relief loans extended during the Depression by the Farmers Home Administration. The tribal members directly involved realized that the payment of long-standing obligations out of their property settlement would restrict their efforts to buy new homesites and establish their families on new land. Consequently, the Crow Creek, Lower Brulé, and Standing Rock tribes petitioned Congress in 1959 to provide additional protection for their funds.[14]

The Indians asked to have all debts of more than six years standing automatically exempted. They also requested that the federal government drop all immediate payment requirements in those cases where demands would create a severe hardship for the Indian debtor. Congress balked at the six-year exemption but approved the hardship clause in a series of laws passed for the individual tribes on June 29, 1960. These acts gave the secretary of the interior, as the cabinet-level administrator of the Bureau of Indian Affairs, the sole authority to determine hardship cases. To avoid further complications, Congress also decided in 1962 to incorporate similar provisions in the Big Bend settlement acts.[15]

As the federal government attempted to supervise closely the distribution of settlement funds, it encountered other problems. Among the most difficult was the exact determination of heirship land interests. The Corps of Engineers and the Bureau of Indian Affairs found that the so-called "fractionization" of interests in allotted tracts required denominations of millionths, billionths, and trillionths in order to arrive at a common factor that would accurately express the size of an individual heir's interest. The army found that 54 billionths was the lowest whole-number common denominator for the varying interests held by 99 heirs to a 116-acre tract within the Fort Randall reservoir area. Expressed as a fraction the largest interest, held by Walking Many Arrows, was found to be 4,199,168,967,628/54,000,000,000,000. The smallest, belonging to Francis Hairy Chin, was 2,887,967,628/54,000,000,000,000. The former share was worth $586, and the latter $0.37. Three other heirs were found to have interests in the tract valued at $0.47, and the rest ranged from $0.64 to $384. A half-section tract in the Oahe reservoir area, worth only about $500, was similarly found to have 156 heirs, 29 of whom were found to be deceased, but whose interests in the estate had never been probated.[16]

Such complications caused federal bureaucrats to curse the ghost of Senator Dawes for the supposedly progressive legislation of 1887 that made this nightmare possible. Indian heirs, of course, had long realized that this absurd policy made it impossible for them effectively to use, sell, or lease their land. For many years they had received annual checks for fifty cents or less for their interest in leased allotments, or perhaps a few dollars if the land was sold. A Crow Creek resident, for example, once received a check for seven cents that cost him ten cents to cash. Many tribal members kept these tiny checks to display and joke about. As sad souvenirs they symbolized the ineptness of a government system that had allowed the Indian land problem to continue in chaos until tribal members received checks that cost more to process than they were worth. Although the Indian Reorganization Act forbade the further sale of inherited lands, Congress has yet to provide a solution for the heirship problem. The fragmentation of Indian interests continues and each year becomes more chaotic.[17]

In an effort to facilitate consolidation and sale of heirship lands, all of the settlements except those received by the Yankton and Cheyenne River tribes provided that the Bureau of Indian Affairs could sell allotted tracts upon the request of a certain number of heirs. The Standing Rock legislation required the permission of only 25 percent of the interest holders, whereas the Fort Randall settlements required the authorization of 51 percent of the heirs on the Crow Creek and Lower Brule reservations. The Big Bend settlements struck a compromise between these earlier provisions by requiring the consent of 25 percent of the owners where ten or more interests were involved, and 50 percent where there were less than ten heirs.[18]

It was ironic that the land consolidation program that received the least federal assistance turned out to be the most successful. The Cheyenne River Sioux were the only tribe given the freedom to implement their own methods, with only minor BIA supervision. These Indians established a land exchange policy whereby allotted interests were traded for individually held tribal lands. By 1970 they had managed to increase the amount of tribally owned land by 117,000 acres and their individual holdings by 107,000 acres. They succeeded at the same time in reducing the amount of land owned or used by non-Indians by 444,000 acres.[19]

The Cheyenne River land consolidation program soon became a model for other tribes across the nation. The National Congress of American Indians' Executive Director, Vine Deloria, Jr., praised the tribe's accomplishments and stated that, "if the other tribes would use their tribal land as the Cheyenne River Sioux have, we could solve our problems in a tribal way, and preserve our tribal way of life."[20]

In attempting to maintain government supervision over tribal life, federal officials were also plagued, in their efforts to distribute settlement funds, by the problems posed by nonresident and nontrust interest holders. Some Indians from other tribes or reservations were found to own land within the reservoir areas. An example of the complications presented by these cases is the experience of Myrtle Kitto, a resident of the Santee Sioux Reservation in Nebraska, who was discovered to have a 5/1,296 interest in an eighty-acre tract within the Fort Randall reservoir area on Crow Creek. After twenty-five acres of this land was condemned by the army in 1953, the BIA found it necessary to transfer a check for $6.04 from the Pierre Agency to Mrs. Kitto's IIM account at the Winnebago Agency, which administered the Santee reservation. After the final settlement was established in 1958, Mrs. Kitto was found to be entitled to an additional $1.91. Since she neglected to sign an acceptance form for this amount and did not indicate any intention to reject the offer before time limits elapsed, the Corps of Engineers had no choice but to turn her case over to the federal district court for final judgment. Consequently, in June 1963, after the government had compiled reams of paper work on this case and had undergone the complications involved in getting it before the court so that justice could be served, the additional money was finally credited to Mrs. Kitto's account.[21]

Although the Big Bend legislation provided compensation for improvements owed by non-Indians on tribal land, none of the settlements addressed the problem of those reservation lands that were held by non-Indians, Canadian natives, terminated tribal members, and others whose ownership did not come under federal trust status. A total of sixteen such persons were found to own interest in fifteen tracts of land in the Big Bend reservoir area worth approximately $9,300. The Bureau of Indian Affairs was reluctant to assist these people because the settlement acts had restricted compensation to trust land only. In the meantime the army resorted to its usual solution and filed condemnation suits against these owners in federal court. The presiding magistrate refused to hear these cases because, in his view, the issue of compensation had already been determined by the settlement acts.[22]

Completely frustrated by this runaround, the property owners finally decided to adopt the familiar approach of the tribes themselves and appealed to Senators Mundt and McGovern for a congressional solution. A bill was passed in 1968 that authorized these interests to be paid according to the same schedule used for the payment of trust land within the reservoir areas. The nontrust property owners were also given ninety days in which to reject the offers if they chose and to file for a court settlement. But Congress inappropriately ruled that these payments would also come out of the settlement funds already appropriated to the tribes. In effect, the Crow Creek and Lower Brulé Sioux were compelled to pay for the property held by nontrust owners of their reservation, while the federal government obtained title to the land without additional cost.[23]

The Sioux tribes affected by Pick-Sloan often experienced as much difficulty in obtaining their funds as the government did in distributing them. The army promised the Standing Rock tribe that their money would be available immediately following the passage of the settlement act in September 1958, but it was not until January 1959 that the Indians actually received their funds. While awaiting its so-called flood money, the already depressed reservation underwent a serious economic slump.[24]

In November, after the Corps of Engineers informed the tribe that it simply did not have funds available to pay them for their land damages, the Standing Rock Tribal Council appealed to Washington for assistance. Congressmen and BIA officials were asked to persuade the secretary of the army to disburse the money as soon as possible. A general meeting of all landowners was held at Fort Yates to discuss economic problems, and the North Dakota Welfare Department was called upon to lend assistance to the growing number of tribal members who needed relief.[25]

After investigating the situation, the state welfare office released a statement on November 25 claiming that the Standing Rock Indians were suffering as a result of army neglect. The national news media immediately picked up this story, and the "starving Indians of Standing Rock" were discovered for the first time by the general public. A team of government officials and investigative reporters were subsequently sent to inspect the reservation. Tribal leaders were immediately summoned to Washington, and a documentary on the tribe's living conditions was filmed by a Minneapolis television station.[26]

In response to this publicity generous people throughout America, particularly in Minnesota, took it upon themselves to donate food and clothing to needy tribal members, and Congress felt obliged to increase the tribe's annual assistance appropriation by $46,000.[27] Local white residents, however, preferred to downplay the Indians' plight and were generally unmoved. An editorial in the *Mobridge Tribune,* for example, insinuated that those tribal members who lacked "white folk's advantages" were merely lazy. "In most cases the Indian who has shown ambition and industry is doing all right," the editor observed, "some even have TV sets." As a solution to the problem he echoed his continued sentiments for termination: "They need to be removed from the yoke of government ownership—independence is the answer."[28]

In January 1960, when the Corps of Engineers finally delivered the funds, it also served the tribe with an immediate eviction order. In the midst of a fierce Dakota winter, with temperatures falling as low as thirty degrees below zero, Indian families who lived within the Oahe reservoir area were forced to gather all their possessions and to leave their land. Because the federal government had not yet made funds available for either the construction of new homes or the relocation of old dwellings, these people were crowded into cold and cheerless trailer houses, which they had to maintain at their own expense until permanent housing could be prepared.[29]

By this time the public no longer was concerned about the Standing Rock Sioux, and the new situation went completely unnoticed by the news media. Only later did the Indians learn that their hardship had been entirely unnecessary. The eviction date established by the corps had been an arbitrary one. Tribal members could have remained in their old homes until the more favorable months of summer without interfering with the completion of the Oahe project.[30]

The Standing Rock tribe was not alone in experiencing such

problems. Crow Creek and Lower Brulé Sioux had a particularly difficult time in relocating families from the Fort Randall reservoir area. Because the tribes only received money from the army's condemnation settlement at the time they were forced to move, their relocation program had to be tailored to fit the funds available rather than the goal of full reestablishment as contemplated by Congress. Aimed at immediate results rather than comprehensive rehabilitation, their programs failed to provide for such crucial items as development of satisfactory water supplies, construction of sufficient housing, or reestablishment of lost sources of income.[31]

Although the Fort Randall project had been announced a full decade earlier, neither the army nor the Bureau of Indian Affairs was prepared to implement an efficient relocation program when the time came for the Indians to move. Though it was clearly their responsibility to do so, neither agency had bothered to survey the reservations for new homesites or to investigate the actual cost of building materials. They failed to keep tribal members fully informed about the relocation plans affecting them. Kept in uncertainty until the last possible moment, the Indians were compelled to proceed in haste when the time came to evacuate their land. Consequently, this event was accompanied by a great deal of misery and confusion.[32]

Indian families were again crowded into temporary quarters until houses could be relocated and restored. In the chaos that followed, many were assigned to the wrong tracts of land and eventually had to move a second time. Shacks that should have qualified only for destruction had to be moved and repaired simply because there was not enough money for new housing. Nineteen of the Crow Creek families within the reservoir area were found to be ineligible for payment because they did not actually own property there. Tribal pleas for assistance for these Indians fell on deaf ears. The army ruled that these tribal members were not entitled to the usual payment for relocation (25 percent of the property value) until after their expenses had been incurred. As a result the Crow Creek Tribal Council found it necessary to create a special hardship fund for these people out of its own meager resources. The council also donated land within the tribal reserve for those who could not afford any other homesite.[33]

The Corps of Engineers was given the responsibility of moving or replacing most of the federal and tribal facilities on the reservations, including office buildings, schools, hospitals, and cemeteries, as well as reestablishing all bridges, roads, utilities, and water sources. Despite chronic unemployment problems on all of the reservations, the army was reluctant to hire tribal members to assist in clearing the reservation areas. Because the relocation activity so drastically affected their lives and property, the Sioux felt that qualified Indians should be given first preference for the jobs. In defense of its employment practices, the corps claimed that it had no authority to hire Indians because it was only authorized to enter into contracts with the lowest bidder on any approved project and could not dictate the policies of private contractors.[34]

The Standing Rock and Cheyenne River tribes responded by taking their protests to Washington, but Congress was slow to take action. Legislation requiring the army to enter into contracts with the tribes for completion of certain clearing and salvage operations was not introduced until 1961. By the time the Senate Committee on Public Works began to debate the bill, most of the Oahe reservoir area had already been cleared. Consequently, Congress took no further action, and the Sioux tribes were again denied one of the important benefits they had hoped to receive from Pick-Sloan.[35]

The relocation of government facilities generated controversy over the selection of new agency sites. In most cases the nearest most suitable upland area was designated as the new relocation site. But crucial BIA facilities serving the Crow Creek and Lower Brulé tribes were moved completely off the reservations; the Cheyenne River Sioux elected to move their facilities sixty miles inland; and the Standing Rock Indians had to go to Washington to end a dispute over the proposed site for a new hospital.

Despite tribal protests the BIA decided to move its administrative facilities at Fort Thompson, which served both the Crow Creek and Lower Brulé tribes, to Pierre, South Dakota. The Indian hospital also was moved from the reservation to Chamberlain. The BIA considered moving the Cheyenne River Agency to either Pierre or Mobridge and its boarding school to Gettysburg, or consolidating the agency with the Standing Rock Agency at some convenient location, but the tribe had other plans.[36]

Led by Chairman Frank Ducheneaux, the Cheyenne River Tribal Council was determined to keep all federal facilities on the reservation. After considering several possible new locations, it finally decided that the predominantly white town of Eagle Butte, located about sixty miles west of the existing agency, would best serve their purposes. The town was favored because of its central location and its convenient railroad and highway access and because the tribe already owned a large portion of land in the area.[37]

BIA officials opposed the Eagle Butte location. They felt that the town's water supply could not adequately serve the new Indian community. Anxious to boost the economy of their dusty little hamlet, the townspeople called a meeting and pledged to finance the construction of new utilities if the BIA approved a tribal petition favoring Eagle Butte. After months of negotiations, the Indian Bureau finally gave in to popular demand and officially designated the town as the new agency site on October 21, 1955.[38]

By the spring of 1960, 650 tribal members had been moved to Eagle Butte, and 81 new homes had been constructed. A new agency office building, a new hospital (named in memory of Ralph Hoyt Case, the tribal lawyer in the Oahe settlement, who died in 1957), and a new high school were in operation. With the opening of its new educational facility Eagle Butte became the first district in South Dakota to consolidate a public school with a BIA boarding facility. This precedent, which required specific authorization from the South Dakota legislature, was later followed in schools constructed at Fort Thompson and Lower Brule.[39]

Most of the new Eagle Butte Community School complex opened in time for the new school year in September 1959, but dormitories had not yet been completed. Many Indian students were required to stay in dormitories at the old Cheyenne River Agency site and had to be bussed from one location to the other. Each school day over 500 Indian children were given sack lunches in the morning and required to ride the 120-mile round trip to Eagle Butte. The *Sioux Falls Argus-Leader* called this "the biggest sack lunch pro-

The new Cheyenne River Agency, 1962. In the right center are the hospital, administration building, and high school. In the right center background is the tree-lined community of Eagle Butte, South Dakota. Courtesy of United States Army, Corps of Engineers.

gram in South Dakota," but it may also have been one of the earliest and longest public school busing programs in America.[40]

Most agency facilities at Standing Rock were left untouched by Oahe waters, but Indian families living in the area surrounding Fort Yates and in other communities (such as Cannonball, North Dakota, and Kenel, South Dakota) had to be moved from what one local BIA employee described as "some of the damndest squalor and shacks that you ever saw."[41] The Fort Yates families were moved to an area just west of the agency that became known as

Old Agency building, Standing Rock Sioux Reservation, Fort Yates, North Dakota. Courtesy of United States Bureau of Indian Affairs.

Ponderosa. Here several new houses, a community center, and an elementary school were constructed. New housing developments and community centers were built for the residents of the other communities who were moved to higher ground. In all 123 houses, 36 barns and garages, 44 corrals, and 78 miles of fencing were salvaged and moved to new sites.[42]

The most heated controversy arising from the Standing Rock relocation erupted over the selection of a site for the reservation's new hospital. It had been authorized by the Public Health Service in 1961 to supplement the tribe's general rehabilitation program. The majority of the Indians preferred to have the new building located near Fort Yates, where the old hospital had been, but Congressman Berry wanted it built in his hometown of McLaughlin, South Dakota, on the reservation's southern boundary. The tribe found it necessary to wage yet another battle in Washington to deal with this political meddling. A compromise was finally reached with the favorable influence of Senator Quentin L. Burdick of North Dakota and Abraham Ribicoff, secretary of health, education, and welfare, who argued the Indian's cause before the Senate Appropriations Committee. Fort Yates was chosen as the hospital site, but McLaughlin was designated as the location for a new Indian health clinic.[43]

The Standing Rock Indians eventually got what they wanted and were not opposed to having a new clinic as well as a hospital, but they resented the fact that an issue so important to their well-being had been soiled by pork-barrel politics. Nevertheless, to show their appreciation, they named the new hospital in honor of the senator's father, Usher L. Burdick, who as a congressman from North Dakota and long-time friend had served the tribe's interests in Washington for twelve years. He had also written a historical monograph about their most famous leader, Sitting Bull.[44]

Tribal facilities and individual residences on the Crow Creek and Lower Brule reservations were relocated from the Fort Thompson and Lower Brule townsites to the nearest convenient upland locations. Federal facilities were moved from these reservations completely. Replacement structures for the new Indian communities, carefully prescribed by Congress, included tribal offices, housing developments, community centers, schools, and a gymnasium-auditorium. Roads and utilities were also replaced, and a new Missouri River bridge constructed.[45]

Relocation on the Yankton Reservation was comparatively simple. The total number of improvements within the Fort Randall reservoir area included only fifteen houses, five shacks, four garages, and a windmill. Most of the families affected chose to move their property to Lake Andes, Greenwood, and other nearby communities. The army's condemnation settlement forced them to do so at their own expense. Although these tribal members were finally reimbursed by Congress in 1954, neither they as individuals nor the Yankton Sioux tribe as a whole ever received new facilities or general improvement funds as a result of the Fort Randall damages.[46]

Some tribes were treated more favorably than others, but the relocation experience was generally unpleasant for all. The receipt of "river money" created a seller's market on all of the reservations, and those who sought to buy land as well as goods and

The Sioux community of Lower Brule before completion of the Big Bend Dam, 1963. Courtesy of United States Army, Corps of Engineers.

services found themselves facing an obstacle that settlement legislation had not anticipated: rampant inflation. In many cases the Indians were placed at the mercy of unscrupulous white ranchers, merchants, and real estate agents, but in some instances they were taken advantage of by fellow tribal members.[47]

Knowing that they eventually would be reimbursed, merchants in the area of Standing Rock decided to extend credit to Indian families during the agonizing months while they awaited their settlement funds. Some were allowed to accumulate bills as high as $4,000 for groceries alone. Some older tribal members, who had previously established good credit and who were expected to

The relocated Lower Brule Agency, showing in the right background, buildings of the evacuated community and rising waters of Lake Sharpe, 1964. Courtesy of United States Army, Corps of Engineers.

receive large payments, were pressured by relatives and salesmen into buying furniture, appliances, and other goods beyond their individual needs. One fast-talking peddler, for example, reportedly enjoyed a great deal of success by selling $200 silverware sets. Consequently, the long delay in receiving settlement funds seriously hampered tribal and federal efforts to establish a successful rehabilitation program when money finally was disbursed. Indians were not legally obligated to pay off these kinds of debts with their settlement funds, but more than 80 percent of them did so.[48]

Only those Indians fortunate enough to buy land directly from their tribe or to find housing within the various tribally developed subdivisions were able to minimize the problems of inflation. Most found it difficult, if not impossible, to purchase the same quantity and quality of new land with the money they received for their old. On Cheyenne River, Chairman Frank Ducheneaux had previously owned 1,400 acres of choice ranch land. With money received from the Oahe settlement, he was able to purchase only 200 acres.[49]

There inevitably came for the Sioux families the most dreaded moment of all—the actual move. Once new homesites were found, and in many cases even earlier, they were forced to abandon the familiar surroundings of the bottomland environment that they loved. They lived in temporary quarters, sometimes for months, until old houses could be moved or new ones constructed on the treeless prairie of their new location. No matter how long it had been anticipated or how cleverly it had been rationalized, the injury and grief that these people felt as they walked across their riverside property for the last time would always remain their most vivid memory of the Pick-Sloan experience.

Tribal members were given the option of moving their own possessions or allowing a private contractor to do it for them. If they chose the latter, restrictions were placed on the distance of the move. If they chose the former, reimbursement was provided for time lost at regular jobs. In either case serious problems developed. Many houses suffered structural damage in the move, and several tribal members complained that their furniture and other household goods were destroyed or mysteriously lost in transit. Some families were assigned the wrong houses and tracts of land, and improvements were sometimes placed on the wrong sites.

A rancher on Cheyenne River Reservation built a house and barn and fenced a pasture on land that was later found to belong to another family. Another tribal member discovered that he had built a house on the wrong tract. He decided to buy the land from the rightful owner rather than go to the expense of moving the house himself, since the Corps of Engineers refused to authorize funds for a second move. Still another Indian had to remove a fence he had built around a quarter section of land that belonged to someone else. Later, this same man had his ranch divided into three widely separated sections as a result of yet another mistake in assignments.[50]

So shortsighted was the Corps of Engineers' planning at the Crow Creek Reservation that families forced to move by the Fort Randall project were relocated within the Big Bend reservoir area. Consequently, when the time came to open the second dam, these tribal members were compelled to move once again. The army also belatedly disclosed that its plans for the Big Bend project would eliminate two irrigation projects that the Bureau of Reclamation had planned for the reservation.[51]

Errors continued to be found in the appraisals and surveys serving as the basis for tribal settlements. Shortly after the Big Bend settlements were approved, a private realtor discovered that the government had inadvertently excluded eighty acres from the Lower Brule appraisal. The BIA corrected this error, and the tribe was eventually paid for the land. An island, which was surveyed by the BIA while the channel between it and the Crow Creek land was dry, was determined to belong to that reservation. Later inspection revealed Skunk Island to lie west of the Missouri's main channel, therefore it belonged to the Lower Brulé tribe.[52]

Land and possessions were not the only issues involved in relocation. Most distasteful to the Sioux, who strongly believed that the dead should be left undisturbed, was the necessity of moving their cemeteries and burial grounds. The majority of the graves on Standing Rock and Cheyenne River reservations and a large number on Crow Creek and Lower Brule had to be relocated. Even on the Yankton reservation, where a comparatively small amount of land was flooded and only a few families affected, a total of 509 burial plots had to be moved.[53]

Knowing that the Indians did not want to become directly involved in this grim activity, the BIA assigned the task to its MRBI staff. Tribal members were asked only to identify private or unmarked burial sites and to sign a form authorizing the government to reinter the remains of deceased relatives. The actual excavation of the graves as well as the transportation and reinterment of remains in new plots was carried out, in most cases, by local funeral directors under BIA contract. Later when the reservoirs were filled and the swirling waters began cutting away at the shores, tribal members and BIA employees discovered, to their horror, that human bones were found protruding out of the muddy soil because not all of the Indian burial sites had been identified.[54]

During many phases of reconstruction when the Sioux had to depend on the Corps of Engineers, they usually found that agency uncooperative or hostile. The tribes often had difficulty persuading the army to recognize their salvage rights. After the BIA denied the Standing Rock tribe's request to establish its own sawmill to assist timber salvage operations, the Indians hired a local lumber company to clear the reservoir area of its trees and to sell the rough timber back to the tribe. The Corps of Engineers filed an injunction to halt the activity, claiming that it interfered with its own clearing work. The tribe protested this action and a long period of litigation ensued.[55]

The court eventually upheld the Indians' salvage rights as declared by Congress and ruled against the army, but the hearing took so long that the tribe did not have sufficient time to salvage the remaining timber before it was flooded. As a result, the Standing Rock Sioux were denied lumber that could have been a valuable asset in their reconstruction program, and many acres of the Oahe reservoir were left cluttered with dead trees and perpetually filled with driftwood.[56]

Indian ranchers on the Standing Rock, Crow Creek, and Lower Brule reservations also claimed that the corps interfered with their shoreline grazing rights. Protesting to Congress in 1962, they pointed out that the army had taken complete control over these areas. Under army regulation only specifically designated areas could be used for grazing and all ranchers, including tribal members themselves, were required to obtain grazing permits. Some previous rangeland was opened to public access, and the proceeds from fees charged to non-Indian ranchers, which the tribes felt they were entitled to, were kept by the Corps of Engineers.[57]

The Indians asserted that all of this was illegal under the provisions of the 1958 settlement acts that gave them free shoreline access rights both for their grazing and for the leasing of lands to others. The congressmen quickly reminded tribal delegates that the laws had also clearly stated that these rights were subject "to all reasonable regulations which might be imposed by the Chief

Tribal members salvaging timber near Lake Oahe. Courtesy of United States Bureau of Indian Affairs.

of Engineers," and that the army was therefore entitled to issue permits, collect fees, restrict land use, and designate public access areas as it deemed necessary and proper.[58]

The Cheyenne River Sioux were also prevented by the corps from exercising full salvage rights to their timber, and, to a lesser extent, they experienced the same problems with the army. Because the corps, in its haste to fill the reservoir, refused to destroy some of the old buildings left standing at Cheyenne Agency, the water level of Lake Oahe barely cleared the structures. Consequently, clear navigation for even small craft was obstructed.[59]

Tribal salvage activities in the Fort Randall reservoir area were also restricted, principally because of the slow action by Congress to protect these rights. In the case of the Yankton Sioux, the situation was complicated because property owners mistakenly assumed that the army would salvage their timber and improvements for them, as it had in the Fort Berthold takings.[60]

In some cases the tribes had difficulty getting their facilities adequately replaced or restored. In the Moreau River district of Cheyenne River, Indians still await the replacement of their old school and bridge and the restoration of telephone service.[61]

In other instances the federal government was very generous to the Sioux. In 1958, Congress donated thirty-seven surplus buildings at the old Fort Thompson agency site for the use of the Crow Creek tribe in their Fort Randall relocation program. The BIA also gave the tribe free title to 1,276 acres of surplus federal school lands in 1961. These were to be used as homesites for families forced to move by the Big Bend project. Surplus school lands were also donated to the Cheyenne River, Standing Rock, and Yankton tribes during this period.[62]

Another serious effect of relocation was the disruption of federal and tribal services on the reservations. Administrative offices, law enforcement agencies, schools, hospitals, and health clinics could not effectively serve the Indians while they were being moved from one location to another. Social and religious activities were curtailed while churches, community centers, playgrounds, and recreation areas were relocated to higher ground.

Closure of the Fort Thompson hospital, for example, produced numerous complaints about the quality of health services on the Crow Creek and Lower Brule reservations. The BIA arranged to have biweekly clinics held by visiting Public Health Service physicians, and emergency ambulance service was also provided, but these stopgap measures proved inadequate. The clinics were underequipped, understaffed, and overcrowded; the ambulance driver was suspended for driving while drunk; and tribal members who sought treatment at other nearby hospitals were repeatedly turned away. When the new hospital was finally opened, the Indians still faced transportation problems. They also had to cope with the deep feelings of bigotry and hostility that they felt existed in the town of Chamberlain, where the new facility was located.[63]

The most serious effects of relocation were felt by the Indian economy. Ranchers, the most important economic group on the reservations, lost considerable income during the period needed to fence new lands, dig wells, and construct shelters to replace the natural features of bottomland pastures. Farmers also had difficulty finding fertile new plots and adequate water sources on the marginal reservation land that remained. Families that depended on their former land for game, wild fruit, and firewood had to search for alternative and usually more expensive sources of sustenance. All experienced higher living costs after moving because of inflated prices and the necessity of purchasing water, food, fuel, lumber, and other materials that previously had been easily accessible and free. Houses needed better weatherproofing on the open plains and warmer clothing was required. Those who now found themselves far from federal facilities also had to allow for increased transportation expenses.[64]

These problems led tribal members to bitterly regret they had not been more conscious of the consequences of relocation. "Like any other Indian," explained one Cheyenne River rancher who lost a half section of land, "I'd been hard up and I was waiting for my money, never realizing what we were losing. We look back now to see that we lost everything . . . we had the best part of our life in that area."[65]

Chapter 11

REHABILITATION

A sizeable portion of the compensation received by the Sioux
tribes, over $20 million after interest payments were added, was
allocated by Congress for the purpose of rehabilitation. The philo-
sophical basis for these awards and their relationship to the termination movement have been explained in previous chapters.
These funds were granted originally so that the tribes might establish social and economic programs that would move them toward self-sufficiency, allowing federal services and supervision eventually to be withdrawn. Because of this intent the Indians were
given far greater responsibility for the administration and use of
this money than they had had with any previous federal programs.
Congress placed few restrictions on the use of rehabilitation
money. It did require the Cheyenne River Sioux to spend all of
their money within ten years and did prohibit the other tribes
from distributing their money on a per capita basis. The Bureau
of Indian Affairs also took a laissez-faire position and permitted
tribal authorities to plan, implement, and administer their own
programs. Nevertheless, the BIA felt compelled to monitor closely
their activities and audit their accounts. BIA officials also volun-
teered to provide technical assistance and advice. Otherwise the
Indians were given a comparatively free rein.

With the exception of the Yankton Sioux, each of the tribes formed a planning committee that designed rehabilitation programs for its reservation before final settlement negotiations. The committees, which were usually dominated by elected tribal officials, had to estimate the cost of establishing the programs that would, in their view, best fit the immediate needs, long-range goals, and particular desires of their tribes. Although the moneys eventually requested appeared outlandish to many Washington officials, it is doubtful that even the maximum amounts requested would have been enough to allow the tribes to reach the elusive goal of self-sufficiency—an aim that the lawmakers on Capitol Hill supposedly shared with them. As it was, Congress saw fit to grant them only about half of what they requested and did not seem to realize or care that in so doing it was damaging the effectiveness of the Indian's rehabilitation efforts.

Once final settlements were negotiated, the tribes found it necessary to develop an administrative structure to oversee and implement their programs. The Standing Rock Sioux had the most elaborate organization, which consisted of a general program manager, a central rehabilitation committee, four special subcommittees under the tribal council, and local committees in each of the reservation's seven communities. The other tribes also hired general managers but preferred to work with fewer committees. The Cheyenne River Sioux, for example, chose to administer their program through a single rehabilitation committee under the close supervision of the tribal council.[1]

The separate programs that the tribal committees designed proved to be very similar in content, although the amounts designated for specific uses varied according to tribal priorities. The Cheyenne River and Lower Brulé tribes both established ranching programs, but the former tribe appropriated the greater part of its funds, $2,853,360, for this purpose while the latter set aside the smallest portion of its money, $120,000, for ranching. The other tribes also developed farm and ranching programs, and all established funds for family improvement, education, and business and industrial development. In addition the Cheyenne River Sioux initiated a general assistance housing program; the Crow Creek and

Standing Rock tribes developed a land improvement program; and all but the Cheyenne River tribe set aside money for community development.[2]

The largest portion of rehabilitation money, a total of nearly $8 million, was allocated for family improvement programs. These funds were designed to help tribal members make some improvement in their family living conditions. The Standing Rock program, which spent nearly $4 million for this purpose, provided a payment of $650 to every person on the tribal roll regardless of residence. The Crow Creek and Lower Brulé Sioux also granted $600 to every tribal member, but the Cheyenne River tribe restricted its funds to reservation residents and provided a per capita payment of only $489.[3]

On the Standing Rock, Crow Creek, and Lower Brule reservations tribal members were required to pool the total amount to which their family was entitled for allocation by the tribal rehabilitation committees. It was the job of these committees to ensure that funds were used to purchase goods and services that best suited family needs. In much the same manner as BIA authorities administered relocation funds, tribal officials closely scrutinized all fund requests, inspected all goods before approving payment, and established penalties for noncompliance with the family programs. The Cheyenne River tribe was unencumbered by prohibitions against per capita payments and distributed its family funds, a total of $2.3 million, in two installments without restriction or program requirements except in regard to outstanding debts owed the federal or tribal governments.[4]

Most of the family funds were used to make housing improvements. The remainder went for vehicles, livestock, farm and ranch equipment, and clothing and other personal items. Some funds were deposited into savings accounts. The amount of money available was usually not adequate to provide the most desirable housing for the Indians, but it was generally enough to make a dramatic improvement in their living conditions. Families who were previously forced to share a single dwelling were for the first time given an opportunity to purchase or lease their own home and, if they were truly fortunate, to experience the luxury of electricity and indoor plumbing. Others were able to buy their first car, purchase tools and equipment for a new trade, or enjoy the sense of freedom that came from paying off long-standing debts.[5]

In conjunction with the distribution of their family funds, the Cheyenne River Sioux also allocated $545,000 for a general assistance housing program. With this money the tribe built 132 housing units at a cost of about $2,500 each, to be used by elderly, disabled, or indigent tribal members. The tribe maintained ownership of these spartan structures and rented them for a minimal fee, usually between $8 and $30 per month. Funds were also provided to assist families to make home repairs. Both programs proved remarkably successful and a long waiting list soon developed for the low-rent housing. By 1970, however, many of these flimsy dwellings, constructed with an overriding concern for minimal costs, were no longer standing.[6]

The second largest rehabilitation expenditure went for establishment of ranching and farming programs on the four reservations. The Cheyenne River Sioux showed the importance that ranching had for them by investing over one-half of their total rehabilitation funds in a Repayment Cattle Program. The Standing Rock tribe also established a $1 million Farm and Livestock Program, and the Crow Creek and Lower Brulé people put $391,326 and $120,000, respectively, in farm and ranch programs.[7]

The Cheyenne River program aimed at establishing 100 new Indian ranchers, each with a starter herd of 150 head of cattle and $10,000 to cover initial operating expenses. Cattle loans were repayable to the tribe in kind at eleven head for each ten received and cash loans at 3 percent interest per annum. Outside consultants and supervisors were hired to assist the new ranchers, a sales pavilion was constructed for calf sales, and the tribe purchased seventy-five machinery units, including tractors with full attachments, and thirty pickup trucks. The tribal council established low rental rates for tribal members on all grazing land within the reservation as part of its successful land consolidation program, thereby saving the Indian ranchers more than $300,000 per year. A Rehabilitation Farm Program, originally established to provide

A buffalo herd grazing on the Standing Rock Sioux Reservation, 1971. Courtesy of United States Bureau of Indian Affairs.

twenty families with agricultural loans of up to $10,000 each, was discontinued because of lack of interest and the scarcity of suitable land.[8]

The Standing Rock Sioux envisioned a much less ambitious program. New ranchers on their reservation each received a maximum of only 90 head of cattle and $6,000 in cash. Repayment was required in cash rather than in kind, with the further stipulation that 20 percent of all calf sales be returned to the program. A limited amount of money also was made available to those families who wanted to enter or to expand farming operations.[9]

Because of the limited amounts of land and money available for new ranchers on the Crow Creek and Lower Brule reservations, even stiffer requirements were established for their tribal programs. By 1962, when the Big Bend rehabilitation funds were finally disbursed, the tribes had estimated that establishment of a basic

Indian cattle grazing near Lake Oahe. Courtesy of United States Bureau of Indian Affairs.

ranch unit of 15 breeding cows required an investment of over $44,000 and the consolidation of at least 3,000 acres. Applicants for tribal funds were obliged to make a security deposit equal to 10 percent of their loans. Few prospective Indian ranchers had both the funds and the acreage to make effective use of these loans, and most of the funds were allocated to established ranchers and farmers. Because the Crow Creek Sioux had a greater interest in horticulture, they used $20,000 of their money to establish a tribal irrigation farm.[10]

In 1970 the total number of cattle on the Cheyenne River reservation was over 46,000 head. Of the 230 new ranchers who had participated at one time or another in the Repayment Cattle Program, only 88 were still operating, and only 66 had managed to pay off their original loan. However, these figures may not be as dismal as they first appear. A BIA land-use expert assigned to the

Cheyenne River Reservation claimed that the success rate of the tribe's cattlemen was greater than that of local white ranchers who started operations during the same period.[11]

On Standing Rock Reservation thirty-four of the original fifty-one participants were still in operation in 1967. After nearly ten years of effort only three of these ranchers were able to realize an annual net income of more than $2,000, and only about one-half made any profit at all. The average profit was only $707 per year. At the same time the tribe lost $50,000 on the sixteen members whose ranches had to be liquidated.[12]

A significant amount of rehabilitation money, $3,131,703, was used to initiate education programs on the four reservations. All of the tribes were committed to providing scholarships and loans to deserving tribal members. It was hoped that these educated members would return and would add to the improvement of their communities. The Standing Rock Sioux were especially dedicated to this priority and allocated $2 million for the purpose.[13]

The Standing Rock program provided low-interest loans of up to $1,800 a year for college and vocational school enrollees. It also gave grants of $600 for each year of study successfully completed. By 1963 a total of 140 Indian tribal members had received assistance from the education fund, 11 had been graduated, and 63 were still enrolled. Moreover, the tribe had exhausted only about 10 percent of its money and was thus able to carry on the program for several more years. The continued dedication of the Standing Rock people to higher education was further demonstrated in 1972 when the reservation established its own community college at Fort Yates. This school, one of the first of its kind on the northern plains, offered several associate degree programs in conjunction with Bismarck Junior College.[14]

With the $500,000 that the Crow Creek Sioux had set aside for education, they financed a music education program on the reservation, including the purchase of new band instruments, and provided direct grants to high school and college students. During the 1970-71 school year this program helped 200 tribal members, 37 of whom were enrolled in colleges and universities throughout the nation. The Lower Brulé tribe established small grants for high school pupils to help curb a high dropout rate. They also granted college students as much as $1,000 to be apportioned over four years. By 1973, 149 tribal members were receiving benefits from this fund.[15]

The Cheyenne River education fund allocated a total of $449,953, including grants of up to $1,000 a year for college education and $2,500 a year for adult vocational education. The latter scholarship program was dropped in 1960 after a similar program was established by the BIA. (The existence of the BIA program also explains why the Crow Creek and Lower Brulé tribes did not designate funds for vocational training.) Although the Cheyenne River program suffered a 54 percent dropout rate during its first two years of operation, it later recovered and produced some significant results. In 1963 the tribe could boast of 79 members who had completed their course of study from among the 291 participants, and an even larger number were able to gain employment as a result of their training whether or not they had finished their programs. By 1970 the tribe's college money had been exhausted, and those who continued to take classes did so with the help of BIA scholarships.[16]

The four tribes set aside $1,827,536 for the development of local business and industry, another means of achieving economic progress. Because of the reluctance of most tribal members to leave their communities, Indian leaders hoped to use this money to create more job opportunities on the reservations. The Standing Rock Sioux allocated $770,000 for this program, the Crow Creek $700,000, the Lower Brulé $400,000, and the Cheyenne River tribe $257,536.[17]

The Standing Rock people used $253,885 of their money to construct a quilt factory in McLaughlin, South Dakota, which they leased to the Harn Corporation of Cleveland. The tribe anticipated that their investment would create 100 new jobs and even built a trailer park nearby, where Indian employees could live, but the company hired only half the expected number. The Standing Rock tribe also invested $92,000 in a cheese plant in Selfridge, North Dakota, which eventually employed only a handful of tribal members. Finally the tribe built a bowling alley in Fort Yates, the Sioux Lanes, which soon ran into financial difficulties.[18]

The Crow Creek Sioux used their money to establish an auto-

mobile muffler plant, a snowmobile factory, and an Indian artifact business. Grants were also provided to individual tribal members to establish a trucking firm and a landscaping service.[19]

The muffler manufacturer, who employed only six tribal members, was eventually forced to close, and the next two businesses
to occupy the plant also failed. By 1969 the snowmobile factory
had employed fifteen Indians. The tribe also had great hopes for
its booming artifact business. With a grant from the Economic
Development Administration, a 160-acre industrial park was constructed to house the artifact venture, known as Sioux Industries,
and the tribal labor force was soon increased to sixty. In 1971,
however, this company was also forced to close its doors.[20] The
Lower Brulé Sioux had better luck in maintaining an electronics
plant and a textile factory that they had attracted to their reservation, but these two industries together never employed more
than a dozen tribal members.[21]

A substantial portion of the Cheyenne River fund was used to
assist tribal members in establishing their own small private businesses. By 1963, however, all but three of the twenty-two Indians
who had participated in the program had been forced either into
repossession or liquidation. Three of the investments that collapsed
under individual control—a repair garage, a service station, and a
laundromat—were successful when taken over by the tribe. In
addition, a tribally owned supermarket was established in Eagle
Butte.[22]

The supermarket proved remarkably successful in restoring competitive grocery prices in the reservation area. To assist needy
tribal members and to keep food prices down for all, the market
operated at a minimal profit and extended long-term credit to
Sioux families. Despite these policies it managed not only to stay
in the black each year but also to provide employment for at least
ten tribal members. Between 1956 and 1958 the tribe also purchased two nearby rural telephone franchises and thus became
the first and only native group in America to control its own
telephone service. In 1972 the Cheyenne River Sioux Telephone
Authority, which claimed 2,000 hookups in a two-county area,
realized an annual profit of more than $25,000.[23]

Another important economic thrust on the reservations was

aimed toward development and consolidation of land resources. All of the tribes recognized the urgent need to reduce heirship interests in allotted tracts and to prevent the further alienation of trust holdings. In addition, all hoped to establish long-range policies for the efficient use, management, and development of existing lands as well as for the purchase of new acreage. To help achieve these goals, the Standing Rock and Crow Creek tribes allocated a total of $1,568,000. The Cheyenne River and Lower Brulé Sioux did not set aside any of their rehabilitation money for this use. They continued the successful land consolidation programs that they had previously started with money from the sale of certain tribal holdings within the reservoir areas. Furthermore, the four tribes were also able to receive supplementary financing for their land programs from other federal sources.[24]

In many ways the money that the tribes used to consolidate land resources became their best investment. Utilizing an initial fund of $1,268,000, the Standing Rock Sioux were able to consolidate 93,274 acres of reservation land by 1971. The Crow Creek tribe, with an investment of only $300,000, was able to purchase 7,000 additional acres to sell to its individual members. On Lower Brule, where a sound program was already underway, tribal officials were able to create a situation where in 1973 members of the tribe were for the first time making effective use of 90 percent of the reservation's land. The most dramatic results, however, were achieved by the Cheyenne River Sioux.[25]

Prior to the inundation caused by the Oahe reservoir, tribal members on Cheyenne River had only been able to make use of 41 percent of the reservation land base. Most of the remaining land was leased to white ranchers for as little as ten cents per acre. With the implementation of new land and livestock programs following the final settlement in 1954, tribal officials began cancelling those leases and consolidating ever larger areas of land through the use of exchange assignments. Despite the bitter attacks and angry cries of neighboring white cattlemen, the Indians were able to reclaim over 600,000 acres of grazing land for their own use within five years. Between 1957 and 1965 the tribe was able to purchase or consolidate an additional 170,000 acres. Consequently in 1972 tribal members were able to claim use of 87 per-

cent of their own land. Despite this progress the Cheyenne River
Sioux estimated that an additional $15 million investment would
be needed to eliminate heavily divided interests in the 96,000
allotted acres that remained.[26]

The Standing Rock, Crow Creek, and Lower Brulé tribes decided it was appropriate to use at least a small portion of their
rehabilitation money for community development. These funds
which totaled $1,256,837 for the three tribes, were used for the
general improvement of the reservations' primary population centers. The Standing Rock tribe provided $100,000 to each of its
seven major communities to improve community centers, public
playgrounds, recreation facilities, streets, sidewalks, and utilities.
The Crow Creek tribe similarly invested $341,326 to help develop
the new Fort Thompson townsite, and their tribal neighbors spent
$145,550 to improve the new Lower Brule community.[27]

The remaining rehabilitation money, a total of $1,225,760, was
used to administer other component programs, providing, for instance, for office space and equipment, salaries of program employees, and professional consultations. The Cheyenne River Sioux
used part of its $432,614 administrative budget to hire the former
state auditor of South Dakota to serve as their general rehabilitation manager. They also purchased a new fleet of vehicles for
the use of various program staff members. The Standing Rock
tribe set aside less money for administrative costs, $389,756, even
though it had more programs to administer and more total funds
to work with than the Cheyenne River tribe did. The Crow Creek
and Lower Brule programs were allocated $250,000 and $153,390
respectively.[28]

In attempting for the first time to administer their own multi-
million-dollar programs, the tribes encountered some thorny problems. Tribal officials found themselves responsible for controlling
more money than ever before, and they rapidly learned that it was
not enough to meet the objectives they had in mind. So meager
were the amounts that they received from Congress for their great
needs that their first and most difficult problem was to establish
funding priorities. Inevitably this issue, as well as all others related to the rehabilitation programs, became entangled in the web
of tribal politics. Thus, where the tribal council was dominated

by ranchers, as was the case at Cheyenne River, livestock programs received the major slice of the rehabilitation pie. A spoils system also operated on all of the reservations, and those on good terms with incumbent politicos were placed in key administrative posts. Similarly, no matter how expert or efficient the administrators proved to be in carrying out their duties, their policies were unanimously opposed by the political faction out of power.[29]

As a result of this political turmoil tribal council members and rehabilitation administrators constantly had to defend themselves against charges of abuse, misconduct, and fraud. These kinds of pressures eventually brought about the impeachment of Tribal Chairman Theodore E. Jamerson at Standing Rock in 1959, as well as the resignation of Cheyenne River Chairman Anthony Rivers in 1962. Although each of these men had serious personal problems and probably deserved to be turned out of office for such reasons, neither was ever found guilty of any wrongdoing in regard to the rehabilitation programs. BIA investigators, called on from time to time to look into the programs on all four reservations, were unable to find any evidence to substantiate criminal charges.[30]

Tribal administrators were more likely to be guilty of inexperience and lack of expertise, making them prone to error and vulnerable to the criticism of political opponents. The Cheyenne River program, for example, drew fire from local skeptics because of its failure to establish an adequate accounting system in its first years of operation. A later tribal chairman on the reservation voiced the opinion that the entire program would have been much better if it had not been run by "a bunch of amateurs" and that BIA supervision would have been preferred to that of the "dictatorial Ducheneaux."[31]

If tribal leaders often made costly and unnecessary mistakes, at the same time they gained practical experience in administering their own self-help programs for the first time. In doing so, they proved fully capable, for the most part, of making important decisions and establishing and implementing long-term plans and policies. This was, as Frank Ducheneaux maintains, perhaps the most significant and valuable result of the entire rehabilitation experience.[32] As a Lower Brulé tribal councilman so aptly put it at the time: "The government has been making programs for us for years, and all of them have failed. I think its time they gave us the right to fail."[33]

Among the rehabilitation programs, those designed for family improvement seemed to be organized with the most urgency and were therefore the most difficult to manage. Because tribal officials tried to coordinate the distribution of family improvement funds with relocation activities whenever possible, they often found that they had to proceed much too fast to allow for adequate planning and review. Consequently, the tribes were neither able to coordinate their efforts with existing welfare programs as closely as they would have liked, nor were they able to provide better counseling and advice for individual families. They came to regret the lack of socioeconomic data on which to base their plans and lack of personnel to supervise and enforce their programs properly.[34]

There were also the pressures generated by those tribal members who still demanded direct and unrestricted per capita payments. This was not a problem at Cheyenne River, where the funds were actually distributed in such a manner, but some families on the other three reservations persisted in trying to circumvent program requirements. Some refused even to draw up a family plan and therefore received no funds at all. Others applied great pressure on staff members to approve purchases that would have brought them no benefits whatsoever. Still others abused the program by immediately selling their approved goods. On Standing Rock, 16 percent of the families in the rehabilitation program sold some or all of their new goods at a fraction of their original cost to purchase liquor or enjoy a night in the city. One tribal member reportedly sold a pickup truck full of new furniture for $25 for drinking money. Another sold his new house for $600.[35]

Most tribal members managed to put their money to good use. Even on Cheyenne River, where there were no restrictions, Frank Ducheneaux praised and defended the actions of members of his tribe and their decision to distribute their money freely and equally: "Per capita payment has come and gone, and in some cases I rather imagine it has gone for no good purpose. But on the whole, I believe that most of our people got some good out of it if only in getting some of their debts paid off."[36]

Most complaints about the family rehabilitation programs and relocation plans had to do with housing. A MRBI-conducted poll on Standing Rock revealed that 80 percent of the families were dissatisfied with either the size, construction, or location of their new homes. Older Indians were particularly distraught about having to live in single- rather than extended-family dwellings. As a result some families on each of the reservations either refused to occupy their new houses or decided to divide their residence between the new house that had been provided for them and the homes of larger family groups. Many others lived in the new community subdivisions during the months when children had to be in school and then quickly retreated to the unimproved rural houses that they maintained in summer.[37]

Despite objections regarding housing, the vast majority of tribal members expressed general satisfaction with the family improvement programs and the manner in which they were carried out. The Cheyenne River tribe's only regret was that it had not designated more funds for this purpose instead of investing so much of its money in a cattle program that benefited relatively few of its people.[38]

Administration of the rehabilitation livestock funds was seriously hampered because the program goals were from the beginning exceedingly impractical. The long-standing Indian desire to establish small family ranches was simply out of step with recent economic and technological developments in the Great Plains cattle industry. Efficient and profitable operations demanded ever larger ranches and herds, corporate rather than individual management, and large-scale shelters and feedlots rather than open grazing. If tribal leaders had either been more cognizant of these changes or not given in so readily to popular demand, they would have realized the competitive advantage of incorporating one large tribally owned cattle enterprise instead of establishing several family-run units which were too small to be productive. As it was, their $4 million investment produced only a handful of tribal members who managed to earn a living as ranchers.[39]

Business and industrial programs were also crippled from the very beginning by preexisting handicaps. Among these were the relative isolation of the reservations, the lack of adequate resources and utilities, and the unstable work force. Outside employers had difficulty coping with native concepts of time and work, which from their point of view resulted in chronic tardiness, absenteeism, and shoddy production. Most tribal members who went into business for themselves also seemed to lack the skills, initiative, and personality necessary for success. A private consulting firm was hired by the Standing Rock tribe to look into these and other investment problems. The consultants concluded that the Sioux were "too shy, introverted, and reticent" to develop service businesses, especially catering to non-Indians, and that they definitely needed more training, experience, and outside exposure before they could do so successfully.[40]

Although the tribes could point with pride to many accomplishments of their business and industrial programs, their investments were certainly far less profitable than they had hoped. Because industry was not attracted to the reservations of the Missouri River Sioux, they lagged behind many of the other tribes in the Dakotas. By 1971, for example, the Rosebud Sioux had an electronics plant employing 77 tribal members, the Turtle Mountain Chippewas had a jewel bearing plant hiring 118 workers from the tribe, and the Pine Ridge Sioux had a moccasin factory providing work for 197 Indians.[41]

By the late 1960s tribal rehabilitation efforts had been supplemented by a series of new federal programs extended to reservations during the Kennedy and Johnson administrations. Chief among these was the Office of Economic Opportunity's (OEO) Community Action Program (CAP) and its various component projects: Head Start, Neighborhood Youth Corps, Senior Citizens, adult education, community health, housing, home improvement, and Legal Aid. VISTA (Volunteers in Service to America) and Job Corps workers were sent to assist the tribes in launching various new self-help programs, and Department of Agriculture officials distributed surplus food commodities. Health facilities were improved through the Department of Health, Education, and Welfare's Public Health Service. Housing projects were expanded under new BIA, OEO, and PHS programs, as well as those administered by the Department of Housing and Urban Development and the Farmers Home Administration. Federal and state welfare assistance were stepped up, and funds for economic development and vocational training were made available through the Economic Opportunity Act, the Manpower Development and Training Act, the Small Business Administration, and the Economic Development Administration of the Department of Commerce.[42]

These myriad programs pumped millions of dollars into the Sioux reservations. By 1970 the Standing Rock tribe had received more than $4 million in OEO funds alone. When compared with earlier rehabilitation efforts, these programs permitted the tribes to make giant strides in improving their living conditions. In the early 1970s, however, these Indians were still considered among the most underemployed and impoverished people in America.[43]

Although job opportunities and personal income had been greatly increased, and dependence on welfare assistance substantially reduced, unemployment remained high, and most family incomes still fell below the poverty level. In 1971, 70 percent of the available work force on Crow Creek was unemployed. Cheyenne River had the lowest unemployment rate among Sioux reservations at 32 percent with 85 percent of the families earning less than the established federal poverty level of $3,000 per annum. On Lower Brule the average per capita income in 1970 was $725, only 23 percent of the national average of $3,139, while 78 percent of the families on Standing Rock reported incomes below the poverty line.[44]

Despite vast improvements in housing, overcrowded and unsuitable living conditions remained common, and adequate utilities were still a novelty. On Standing Rock, where over 500 new houses had been constructed since 1960, 46 percent of the housing was still classified as substandard in 1972. Conditions were even worse on the Yankton, Lower Brule, Crow Creek, and Cheyenne River reservations. In 1969 only 3 percent of the houses on Cheyenne River could be classified as suitable for human occupancy. The majority of the families who lived in these dwellings were still dependent on unsafe water sources and unsatisfactory sewage and garbage disposal methods. Only 35 percent of the homes had electricity, 23 percent had satisfactory toilets, and 16 percent had running water. Even fewer had telephones, despite the tribe's own company, or the electrical appliances considered standard in most American homes.[45]

Although the number of Indian students who graduated from high school and went on to college or vocational training increased substantially, the average education level on the reservations remained at junior high school level. Health treatment facilities and services were rapidly updated and expanded, while disease prevention and health education programs lagged pitifully. The tribes continued to suffer from startling rates of alcoholism, tuberculosis, and infant mortality, as well as from a great variety of diseases related to improper diet and inadequate water and sanitary facilities.[46]

Conditions were generally worse on the Yankton reservation, which did not have the benefit of a rehabilitation program. Although the tribe attempted to provide more central authority over its own affairs in 1963 by establishing a new constitution and governing body, the Yankton Tribal Business and Claims Committee, the reforms were largely ineffective in providing more direction and control. Although denied rehabilitation funds as part of their Fort Randall settlement, the Yankton Sioux received a $1,250,000 award from the Indian Claims Commission in 1969 as additional compensation for lands previously forfeited by treaty, but this money, distributed as it was on a per capita basis, was soon dissipated.[47]

In the meantime problems on the reservation continued to multiply. The Yankton land base continued to erode. More than 62 percent of the land remained in heirship status, and over half continued to be leased to non-Indians at ridiculously low rates. Unemployment soared to 84 percent in 1974, the highest rate on any of the Sioux reservations, while 80 percent of the housing was classified as substandard. Educational, medical, and recreational facilities also remained sadly inadequate.[48]

On the four reservations that did receive rehabilitation funds, tribal members usually preferred the new federal programs over those previously established by the tribes themselves. A 1974 MRBI survey found this to be true at Lower Brule, although the Indians did admit that they liked their own programs better than those administered by the Bureau of Indian Affairs.[49]

The primary complaint most Indians had against the rehabilitation programs was that they became too intertwined with tribal politics. On Standing Rock, however, where the most money had been available, a vast majority of tribal members polled by MRBI expressed satisfaction with their program and the way it was carried out. They felt that it had been successful in improving their standard of living and had increased their community spirit, cooperation, and pride, even though it had not done much to enhance employment capabilities.[50]

On both Standing Rock and Cheyenne River a large number of residents were very disgruntled by the huge sums spent on livestock programs. By the mid-1960s it became painfully obvious to all the tribes that, even though they were naturally inclined toward agricultural occupations, the future of such pursuits was very limited and could no longer provide additional employment opportunities. It thus became incumbent upon tribal leaders to develop other sources of income, such as manufacturing or tourism. As a result new tribal development plans began to place more emphasis on those kinds of economic development, as well as on social and community improvement, and to deemphasize land consolidation and ranching.[51]

The overall impact of the Pick-Sloan rehabilitation funds is difficult to measure. Many of the tribal programs were more effective than previous federally sponsored projects, but most fell short of their intended goals. It was absurd to expect that the tribes could begin to solve their many social and economic problems with the limited sums made available to them. Even with the great proliferation of federal programs in the 1960s, progress towards the goals of economic self-sufficiency, community development, and family and individual improvement was excruciatingly slow on all of the reservations.

The great virtue of the rehabilitation programs was that they were administered by the tribes themselves. If the various component programs were not always very successful, or if the overall program sometimes suffered as a result of misplaced priorities, the Indian people involved generally learned from their mistakes. In this respect rehabilitation was a valuable educational experience, a praiseworthy experiment in self-determination, and altogether the most worthwhile aspect of the Pick-Sloan compensation.

President Kennedy and other dignitaries at the Oahe Dam dedication, August 17, 1962. Courtesy of United States Army, Corps of Engineers.

Chapter 12

CONCLUSION

On August 16, 1962, a crowd of over 10,000 people gathered at the Oahe Dam site to witness its formal dedication by President John F. Kennedy. Interior Secretary Stewart L. Udall, Army Secretary Cyrus R. Vance, and General Walter K. Wilson, Chief of Engineers, shared the platform with dignitaries from all ten basin states, as well as delegates from many of the river tribes. The president was introduced to the early-morning audience by George S. McGovern, who had recently left his post as director of the New Frontier's Food for Peace program to campaign as South Dakota's Democratic candidate for the United States Senate. Amid cheers and applause which echoed over the reservoir's rippling blue waters, Kennedy rose to speak. "This dam provides a striking illustration," he stated, "of how a free society can make the most of its God-given resources."[1]

The Pick-Sloan main-stem projects have now been completed for several years. The final structure, the Big Bend Dam, was officially opened in September 1966. If the benefits that the Sioux tribes received from these massive projects are to be gauged, they should first be measured in terms of the purposes for which these dams were originally constructed. Assuming that the government of a free society really did "make the most of its God-given resources," and that the multi-billion-dollar engineering wonder

Aerial view of Big Bend Dam and Lake Sharpe, looking north, near Fort Thompson, South Dakota, 1967. Courtesy of United States Army, Corps of Engineers.

known as the Pick-Sloan Plan was truly designed to be beneficial to the people of the Missouri Basin, then it should be of equal benefit to those people, both Indian and non-Indian, who suffered the most as a result of its implementation. But such is not the case.

The U.S. Army Corps of Engineers and the Interior Department's Bureau of Reclamation designed their integrated water development program to provide flood control, irrigation, hydroelectric power, navigation, recreation, and numerous other benefits. An evaluation of their efforts at this time reveals that their projects have not measurably improved the lives of the Sioux people in respect to these provisions.

Flood control has turned out to be a "legitimate offspring" of the Pick-Sloan shotgun wedding. The army and Interior Department have succeeded in making long stretches of the Missouri system safe from the catastrophe of high floods. This is particularly true in the populous region between Kansas City and Sioux City. In the basin as a whole, the Corps of Engineers claims that its dam and levee projects prevent more than $150 million in flood damages each year, yet the army's harness on "Big Muddy" is far from secure. Large areas of the lower basin are still vulnerable to destruction, as evidenced by the floods of 1967 and 1973, and annual losses still amount to about $95 million. Moreover, the flood damage is likely to increase if additional protective measures are not implemented.[2]

Floods on the Sioux reservations were never as serious or as frequent as those in the lower basin. Frank Ducheneaux could only recall two floods on Cheyenne River during his lifetime. Although the threat to tribal lands was substantially reduced by the main stem reservoirs, it was not completely eradicated. The Indians continued to be hampered by small tributary inundations such as the one that occurred on Cheyenne River in 1968 when the Moreau River left its banks. Whether or not the dams have improved flood control does not particularly impress the Indians. One Sioux woman said it is quite natural to assume that "if you flood the bottomlands you will then have flood control."[3]

The Indians are concerned that the rise in the maximum pool level of the reservoirs has caused water to infringe on Indian land never purchased by the federal government, and that the fluctuation of the water level has created a far greater hazard to the tribes than any of the infrequent floods of the past.[4]

The stream-bank erosion caused by undulating reservoir waters has become a serious problem. Shoreline conditions continually have been made unstable, and sediment deposits in the water have been much greater than expected. While Lake Sharpe, the Big Bend reservoir, is relatively stable, the waters impounded behind the Fort Randall and Oahe Dams (Lake Francis Case and Lake Oahe) fluctuate between ten and twenty feet each year. This

Preliminary shoreline work on Oahe reservoir, 1958. Courtesy of United States Army, Corps of Engineers.

has made it extremely difficult for the tribes to develop fully their shoreline land and resources. The cutting action of the water not only endangers tribal members and their livestock but also has, in at least one case, caused the exposure of skeletal remains from unmarked graves along the shore. Since the Corps of Engineers did not accurately project reservoir boundary lines prior to inundation, water now often infringes on Indian property when at maximum pool level. Because the army also refused tribal requests to build fences along the boundaries, Indian ranchers regularly suffer livestock losses, as their cattle either fall off the eroding banks or drift into the reservoirs in search of water.[5]

Damming the Missouri River. Shoreline work on Oahe Dam, near Pierre, South Dakota. Courtesy of United States Army, Corps of Engineers.

While the Pick-Sloan Plan has generally improved flood protection in the Missouri Basin, the advantage of this fact to the Sioux has been obscured by the present disadvantages of the reservoir projects. The benefits of flood control are outweighed by the damages that these people sustained in order to make these projects possible. The Indians did not have to forfeit their lives, but they certainly suffered greater losses from the human-caused inundations than they would have from any natural flood in their region.

Much the same can be said for hydroelectric power: the Pick-Sloan projects have enjoyed considerable success, but the Sioux have not yet seen any appreciable benefits. In 1972 the six main-stem dam projects on the Missouri were generating 13.2 billion kilowatt-hours of hydroelectric power, accounting for 28 percent of the basin's total generating capacity. Although the power plants have definitely helped make more electricity available to the Sioux, they have not been a factor in actually increasing the tribe's use of electrical power. The reservations lacked electrical power before the construction of the Pick-Sloan projects primarily because the residents could not afford it rather than because it was unavailable. To this extent the steady increase in the Indian's use of electric power over the past two decades is more a result of the rise in the general economic level of the reservations than of the increased availability of electrical power.[6]

Affordability remains the most important factor as far as the Sioux are concerned. Most areas of the reservations are still without electrical service because the Indians cannot afford it. There is no evidence to show that Pick-Sloan has provided the lower electrical rates its proponents promised. The tribes would have received more favorable hydroelectric benefits if blocks of power had been designated for their exclusive use or otherwise provided at low cost. Congress, however, refused to grant their demands, insisting that such action would violate the Rural Electrification Act of 1936, which with other federal statutes gave public bodies first preference in the use of public power. But the Indians were not the only ones who lost. Because South Dakota has no public power districts, most of the electric current generated by the giant power plants within its borders is sent to neighboring states, a situation that has long angered its citizenry.[7]

Within the next generation streamflow depletions on the Missouri are expected to substantially reduce the river's hydroelectric power capacity. During the same period, hydrogeneration is also expected to decline in importance as thermal generators, nuclear power plants, and fossil fuels become more expedient. Thus it appears that in the long run the people of the Dakotas, both Indian and non-Indian, would have had expanded energy sources even if the Pick-Sloan power plants had never been built.[8]

Dakota residents are still scratching their heads in bewilderment over the feasibility of irrigation in their region. The long and heated debate over the suitability and practicality of reclamation in this area has caused frustrating delays, serious cutbacks, and drastic revisions in the original Sloan Plan. Consequently, the Bureau of Reclamation has yet to begin substantial construction on its major projects: the Garrison and Oahe diversion units.

Once the Reclamation Bureau began to examine Sloan's plans more carefully, it discovered that much of the prairie land it had hoped to reclaim was simply not irrigable. Thus in North Dakota his grandiose Missouri-Souris Diversion project, found to be totally impractical, was scuttled in 1957 and replaced by the much smaller Garrison Diversion project. This latter unit was originally slated to cost $695 million but was completely redesigned in 1965 and eventually restricted to nonsurplus crops with a $248 million limitation established by Congress. But environmentalists and other opponents of the project managed to halt construction during the 1970s and managed to keep the issue of continued authorization in limbo into the 1980s.[9]

Although Sloan promised to irrigate a million acres in South Dakota, the bureau discovered that only about half that was actually feasible. Funds for the first phase of the largest project there, the Oahe Diversion Unit, were not authorized by Congress until 1968. Its total irrigation capacity was also cut from 450,000 to 190,000 acres, but like the Garrison project, construction of the Oahe unit, initiated in 1974, has been effectively tied up by controversy and public support for the project has gradually shifted to alternative water programs.[10]

The Reclamation Bureau has determined that approximately 125,000 acres of the Sioux reservations are potentially irrigable, yet it remains to be seen if the tribes will ever be able to develop this potential. First, there is the critical question of whether or not irrigated farming can ever be financially feasible for the Indians. On Standing Rock, for example, where the greatest possibility of irrigation exists, the BIA has determined that it would require an initial investment of at least $24,000 and an annual cost of over $4,000 to deliver water to 160 acres of farmland, based on 1973 prices. This investment requirement exceeds both the value of the reservation property itself and the financial capabilities of any Indian families.[11]

To make irrigation profitable, the Standing Rock tribe would have to develop it as a corporative venture. It would also have to concentrate on raising high gross crops, such as sugar beets or corn, neither of which has been grown extensively on the reservation before. Even then it would require extremely efficient management and higher-than-average yields to make the project financially feasible. It would entail a land base of at least two thousand acres to produce sufficient revenue to meet irrigation costs.[12]

Second, there is the question of how much of the Indian land is actually irrigable. On the Cheyenne River Reservation, where the Bureau of Reclamation had plans to irrigate seventeen thousand acres by diversion from the Moreau River, it has discovered that neither the water nor the soil was of sufficient quality to make the project worthwhile. Because of excessive amounts of dissolved sodium in the water, the potential is there for soil sterilization, so that the bureau was forced to cancel its plans. On the one thousand acres that it had already attempted to irrigate, the concentration of shale was found to be such that water would not soak into the soil but would merely stand on the land bringing up alkali to the surface.[13]

Conditions on the other reservations are similar. Tributary waters are generally of poor quality and soils are often impermeable and of a high saline and alkaline content. Shoreline beaches and fluctuating water levels on the main stem reservoirs also make it difficult and expensive to install adequate pumping facilities.[14]

Under the body of law that developed from the Winters decision of 1907, the Sioux have prior and paramount rights, for the purpose of irrigation, to all waters that flow either through or along the reservations. It has also been claimed that their rights include priority use of water for any other beneficial use, either at present or in the future. The actual extent of the Indians' reserved water rights beyond the purposes of irrigation, however, has never been judicially clarified.[15]

Despite the specific requirements of the law, the federal government has not made an effort to comply with the Winters Doctrine in regard to the Pick-Sloan Plan, and the Sioux tribes have not attempted to have their rights protected through the process of judicial appeal. Because no effort has ever been made to accurately determine and to quantify the precise water needs of the tribes, it is likely that their rights will continue to be ignored.

The Flood Control Act of 1944, which authorized the Pick-Sloan Plan, provided that the irrigation of tribal lands and repayment for such projects would be "in accordance with the laws relating to Indian lands."[16] The Leavitt Act of 1932 had established generous policies whereby payment of irrigation construction costs could be deferred by the tribes over a long period according to their repayment ability.[17] To comply with these laws and the provisions of the Winters Doctrine, the Bureau of Reclamation should have fully recognized the Indians' rights and made an effort to accurately quantify their water needs before committing any of the water under its control to other projects. Having guaranteed the priority of native rights, it should then have made plans to develop irrigation wherever feasible on the reservations, without regard to cost. Because this was not done, it is doubtful that the Sioux will ever realize the full benefits of irrigation.

Navigation on the Missouri, another of the byproducts of Pick-Sloan, has become the army's bad joke. Although 2.6 million tons of commercial freight was transported on the river in 1967, the amount of traffic has not been sufficient to justify the huge expense involved in keeping the river open. Having spent untold billions of dollars to establish a nine-foot channel from the Mississippi to Sioux City, the Corps of Engineers has finally admitted that the future of the project is very tenuous. In 1971 the Missouri Basin Inter-Agency Committee predicted that open navigation on the existing waterway would no longer be viable after the year 2000, and in 1973 the army admitted that there would not be sufficient water by then to maintain the channel unless drastic measures were taken. The drastic measure they proposed was the expenditure of an additional $60 billion to constantly dredge the river and extend navigation to Yankton, South Dakota. The unexpected response: Congress is still laughing.[18]

Residents of the Dakotas, including the Sioux tribes, did not actually expect many benefits from the lower basin's navigation channel, but they did anticipate clear sailing for small craft on the army's main stem reservoirs. To their dismay they have discovered that this was not provided. Because of the way clearing operations were conducted by the corps, clear navigation is obstructed in many parts of these man-made lakes. In some places the water level barely clears structures left standing at the old Indian agency sites. On Standing Rock and Cheyenne River where the tribes were not permitted to salvage all of their timber, and where the army made no attempt to do so, an entire forest was left standing, which projects above the water surface. As a result Lake Oahe is cluttered for many miles with dead trees and driftwood. These obstacles are a menace to boaters and interfere with recreational activities, one of the purposes for which Pick-Sloan was created.[19]

Of all the benefits promised by Pick-Sloan, the most immediate and successful results have been realized in the areas of outdoor recreation and tourism. Each year millions of vacationers are drawn to the hundreds of public access areas developed along the reservoirs for swimming, boating, camping, and picnicking, but the primary attraction is fishing. State and federal wildlife agents have gradually succeeded in increasing both the number and variety of species through constant restocking, and fishing has become exceptionally good. Lake Oahe, for example, is now widely recognized by anglers as one of the best areas in the country to catch walleye pike. Businesses catering to tourists and outdoor enthusiasts have thrived, and the Interior Department has considered making all six main stem reservoirs into a National Recreation Area.[20]

Although some of the Sioux tribes attempted to realize the economic potential of the sudden recreation boom, none have been able really to share in the new prosperity. Most determined to do so were the Standing Rock Sioux. Financed in large part by a grant from the Economic Development Administration, in 1972 the tribe constructed an elaborate tourist complex on the shores of Lake Oahe, across from Mobridge, South Dakota. This facility, known as the Chief Gall Resort, consisted of a restaurant and cocktail lounge, a fifty-six unit motel, a conference center, an amphitheater, campground, a golf course, an indoor pool, a museum, and a restored Indian village. In 1971 the Crow Creek tribe, also with the help of EDA funds, developed a similar al-

though somewhat smaller complex at Fort Thompson. Yet, both
units gradually fell victim to the strong anti-Indian economic bias
that exists in South Dakota and had eventually to be closed.[21]

Though these tribally owned businesses appeared to offer great
promise for the future, the other Sioux groups did not follow suit.
While all recognized the opportunity for profit in these kinds of
ventures, not all were able or willing to invest their capital in an
effort to lure more non-Indians into their reservation environment.
The trespassing of white sportsmen on Indian lands and the regulation of their activities within tribal boundaries has already become
a serious problem. In addition, relations between Indians and others
at the Chief Gall and Crow Creek tourist centers were not always
peaceful and friendly, particularly at Fort Thompson where several
unfortunate incidents and confrontations took place.[22]

Recreational development on the reservations is also limited by
natural conditions and the restrictive land policies of the Corps
of Engineers. Because the region is now devoid of trees, there is
no natural shelter for bathers from the hot summer sun, and boaters
have no protection from the strong prairie winds that often make
reservoir waters treacherous. Fluctuating shorelines make it difficult to develop good beaches and docks, and stumps and other obstructions create a menace to safe navigation. The large number of
limitations placed on the use of the reservoirs by the Corps of Engineers, which still maintains primary enforcement jurisdiction over
the waters and shoreline, makes it almost impossible for the tribes
to develop their own beaches. This is precisely the reason why the
Fort Thompson and Chief Gall complexes were not able to include
shoreline improvements.[23]

The recreational value of the reservoirs to Indians themselves is
very slight. Traditionally these Sioux people have seldom engaged
in fishing, boating, or swimming. While there is evidence to show
that they are gradually becoming more interested in these activities,
few can afford the luxury of a boat or camper. If anything, the
recreational activities of tribal members have declined as a result
of the Pick-Sloan projects. This is because the inundation of the
sheltered bottomlands drastically reduced the game population on
the reservations and led to the subsequent decline in hunting, which
had previously been the Indian's favorite sport. With the deer and

antelope nearly gone, Sioux hunters have had to content themselves with shooting game birds and rodents.[24]

Another of the benefits promised by Pick-Sloan was the development of adequate water sources for municipal, industrial, and domestic uses. While the main stem dams do provide an almost unlimited supply of good potable water, most of the farms, ranches, towns, and factories in the vicinity of the reservoirs are still dependent on groundwater sources of questionable quality. This situation is particularly acute in South Dakota, where satisfactory ground sources are difficult to find and where few pumping and treatment facilities have been developed on the Sioux reservations. Although the communities of Fort Yates, Fort Thompson, and Lower Brule do have plants that supply limited amounts of reservoir water, most Indian families are still forced to rely on water that is unfit for human use.

The community of Eagle Butte provides a good example of what most reservation water supplies are like. Having long exceeded federal standards for maximum impurities, the Eagle Butte water contains unacceptable amounts of iron, sulfate, fluoride, and dissolved solids. Iron in the water causes red and brown stains on bathroom fixtures and clothing and affects the color and taste of food and drink. The level of sulfates and dissolved solids is high enough to have a laxative effect on nearly everyone who drinks the water. Calcium deposits and sodium combine to form a hard scale on water heaters and boilers. Sodium mixed with chloride deposits produces an extremely salty taste. Although moderate amounts of fluoride can contribute to the prevention of tooth decay, the concentration in the Eagle Butte water supply is enough to mottle the enamel on children's teeth. Residents of the community claim that besides having a foul odor, terrible taste, and an extreme hardness factor that greatly reduces the lathering ability of soap their water "kills the grass and will rust door hinges five feet away."[25]

Not only is this mineralized water impossible to use, but it is also difficult to obtain. Wells must be drilled extremely deep through heavy deposits of shale. Consequently, a large number of Indian families still haul untreated water from streams and reservoirs, a practice that poses a constant threat to public health. Besides affecting health and living conditions on the reservations, the water problem also impedes economic growth. The lack of good water has contributed greatly to the high death rate of Indian livestock and has been a major factor in the tribe's inability to receive more federal housing assistance, as well as in their failure to attract more industry to the reservations.[26]

Although Pick-Sloan proponents made great claims about the development of industrial and mineral resources that would accrue from the army's main stem projects, the Sioux people have failed to see these benefits materialize. Industrial development on the reservations is almost nonexistent. Mineral development is also hampered because most tribal resources are now under water and subject therefore to the regulatory authority of the Corps of Engineers. While it is conceivable that the tribes could extract gas, oil, coal, sand, and gravel from the reservoirs, it is not likely that the army will ever let them do so, because it can easily prevent such activity by imposing its new pollution control standards. Thus, in one of the great ironies of this entire episode, the Corps of Engineers, which destroyed the environment of the Indians, is now in a position, having lately had its ecological consciousness raised, to prevent the tribes from "polluting" its own nature-destroying projects.[27]

In the wake of the national energy crisis of the 1970s, industrialists began to cast a covetous eye on the waters and mineral resources of the Missouri Basin. Hoping to cater to those interests and to encourage more rapid energy development, the Corps of Engineers and Reclamation Bureau launched a program in 1975 to market the water of the Missouri's main stem. Under the terms of the interagency agreement, the Interior Department calculated how much water was needed for its irrigation projects, the army estimated how much was needed to meet its own priorities, and the remainder was offered for sale to industrial bidders. What the federal agencies failed to protect, however, were the water rights of the Indians under the Winters Doctrine.[28]

In effect, the main stem water marketing effort was an extension of a program that the Bureau of Reclamation had established in the Yellowstone subbasin in 1967. At that time the bureau, without regard to the prior and paramount rights of the Wind River Indians in Wyoming and the Crow and Northern Cheyenne tribes in Montana, sold the "surplus" water of the Wind, Big Horn, and Yellowstone Rivers to twelve of the nation's largest energy corporations. As a result of these sales and the government's previous commitments under the Pick-Sloan Plan, the tribes were left with virtually no water for their own future development, despite the supposed superiority of their legal claim. At no time did the Interior Department attempt to acknowledge the Winters Doctrine, to quantify tribal needs, or to compensate the Indians for the loss of their water rights; and federal courts have failed as yet to redress the situation. Severely jeopardized by the extension of this marketing program to the main-stem reservoirs, the Sioux tribes cannot be very optimistic about the future of their own water rights.[29]

Among the minor benefits promised by the Pick-Sloan Plan were extensive land surveys, increased employment opportunities, and comprehensive historical and archaeological investigations in the Missouri Basin. Detailed land studies of the Sioux reservations were made by the Bureau of Indian Affairs as part of the main-stem dam projects, and they greatly aided the tribes in their land consolidation efforts. Through the Inter-Agency Archaeological Salvage Program, a project coordinated by the Smithsonian Institution and the National Park Service in cooperation with sixteen regional universities and museums, hundreds of archaeological, paleontological, and historical sites were located and investigated within the reservoir areas. Whether or not the tribes are willing to acknowledge the fact, several of these studies have contributed greatly to our knowledge of Plains Indian culture, and many were directly relevant to the history of the Sioux. By 1970 over ninety major sites, ranging from preceramic occupations before the Christian Era to rather recent Indian villages, were extensively excavated.[30]

The reservoir projects created many job opportunities for tribal members as government reports had predicted, but Indian employment was never as extensive as it could have been. Most of those who did get work were hired by their own tribes for temporary jobs related to reconstruction and rehabilitation activities. Federal contractors were extremely reluctant to hire tribal members and generally preferred to bring in white workers from outside the area to perform jobs that in many cases could have gone to Indians.

Sioux workers who were hired to work directly on the dam projects usually found that they were the last hired and first fired by both government contractors and the Corps of Engineers. Consequently unemployment remained high on the reservations throughout the entire construction period, and tribal leaders made desperate appeals in Washington to no avail for preferential employment rights within their own boundaries. Although the unemployment rate of the Sioux has steadily declined since the construction of the Pick-Sloan projects, this has been primarily because of the large number of federal manpower programs established on the reservations within the last decade, and it is neither a direct nor an indirect benefit of the army dams.[31]

The Missouri River Sioux tribes have received therefore almost none of the benefits that were supposed to be provided by the Pick-Sloan Plan, but they have suffered a great deal as a result of its implementation. Many federal officials feel strongly that the $20 million appropriated by Congress for tribal rehabilitation programs should be considered a direct benefit of the water development program, but that conclusion masks the truth.

The Sioux tribes were in dire need of federal aid prior to construction of the Pick-Sloan projects. That they could have received rehabilitation funds through separate legislation, as did the Navajos, Hopis, and numerous other tribes, is almost certain. It is also clear that rehabilitation programs were included in the Pick-Sloan settlements only as a matter of expediency, that is, as an appropriate way of making an initial step toward the espoused federal goal of termination.

Rather than being considered a benefactor, the Pick-Sloan Plan should more properly be viewed as a liability to tribal rehabilitation efforts. Federal funds could have achieved more effective results if the economic life of the reservations had not been so totally disrupted and if the money could have been used for the improvement rather than replacement of existing facilities and services. Had tribal leaders not had to devote so much of their time and energy to the problems of relocation and reconstruction, they might have enjoyed greater success in their efforts to bring the reservations up to an acceptable standard of living.

It is unlikely that the Corps of Engineers' mammoth Missouri

River dams would have been permitted in the 1970s. In response to a growing "ecology movement," Congress in 1969 passed an Environmental Policy Act, that required that impact studies be made prior to the construction of any and all federal projects affecting the environment.[32] Had these protective standards been in effect in 1944, the Pick-Sloan Plan would certainly not have passed muster. Ecology-conscious residents of the Missouri Basin have discovered, painfully, that their celebrated federal water development program is an environmental monster.

The army's main-stem dams and stream alteration projects have had a devastating effect on the Missouri's renewable natural resources. The ecological balance of the entire region, and that of the Dakotas in particular, has been permanently upset by the destruction of flora and fauna. The inundation of precious forests and bottomlands not only eliminated the natural wildlife habitat but also created serious erosion problems. Fluctuating reservoir waters cut into alluvial soils and soft loess plains when they rise and leave slick muddy beaches when they recede. The accumulation and disposition of sediment caused by this erosion destroys aquatic vegetation, making long stretches of the reservoirs unsuitable as nursing and spawning grounds for fish and greatly reducing the efficiency of the dams in regard to both flood control and power production.[33]

The marine environment has also been subjected to increased attacks from chemical and bacteriological agents introduced by the runoff or discharge of organic and solid waste materials from municipal and industrial sources, by animal waste from commercial feedlots, and by residues from agricultural chemicals. In 1973 the United States Fish and Wildlife Service reported that mercury concentration in Lake Oahe had reached a critical level. Because the Pick-Sloan Plan consistently failed to address the problems of soil conservation, reforestation, and water treatment, it stands in inevitable and almost irreconcilable conflict with natural conditions in the Missouri Basin.[34]

Long praised for the harmony that they traditionally established with their environment, the Sioux are agonizingly aware of these problems. Having suffered the most devastating effects of inundation, they fear that the reservoirs will continue to cut away at their land and to pollute their water sources. They are also apprehensive about the safety of the dams themselves. The Corps of Engineers admits their inspection methods have been less than circumspect, and numerous disasters indicate that even earth-fill dams are not indestructable. If, as the Indians fear, the Fort Peck Dam in Montana, first link in the Pick-Sloan chain, ever breaks or is bombarded by an enemy of this country, the resulting flash flood would sweep all of the other dams into the Gulf of Mexico, taking the entire midsection of America along with it.[35]

Another reason why it would have been more difficult for the army to build its projects even a score of years later than it did is the changing character of the Sioux themselves. Tribal leaders are no longer as docile, naive, or powerless as they were a generation ago. They are now more apt to be trained professionals, more sophisticated in their approach to tribal problems, more experienced in dealing with the federal government, while at the same time more skeptical of its intentions. Above all they are single-mindedly determined to give meaning to the concept of self-determination, sometimes to the point of advocating complete tribal sovereignty.

Having grown increasingly impatient with federal abuses, the seemingly unchanging status of reservation living conditions, and the inability of even the best tribal leaders to make significant changes, the Indian rank and file has also become more aggressive and outspoken. Combining the rhetoric of the early black civil rights movement and the tactics of the student movement of the 1960s, and adding a perspective that is distinctively Native American, this new spirit has found expression in both peaceful protests and violent confrontations. The leading role in this movement, at least in the Dakotas, has been assumed by the American Indian Movement (AIM), which was founded in Minneapolis in 1968 by a group of young, urban tribal members. To its credit, this organization has succeeded in publicizing the plight of Native Americans, the injustices and paternalism of the federal system as it applies to them, and the determination of tribal members finally to start making decisions according to their own goals and values. At the same time, because its demonstrations have too often resulted in death and destruction, AIM has been almost universally condemned by those outside the Indian community.[36]

In short, in the climate of the 1970s it would have been extremely difficult for either the army or Congress to overawe and bully tribal leaders into passively accepting the Pick-Sloan Plan. It seems unlikely that the same Indian people who occupied and destroyed the village of Wounded Knee in 1974 over a local political quarrel would have stood by idly while the federal government proceeded to destroy thousands of acres of tribal land.

In many respects the character of Pick-Sloan also changed by the 1970s. Having gradually grown disenchanted with the Missouri's water development program and its blanket project appropriations, Congress demanded in 1964 that all Pick-Sloan projects not already under construction would require reauthorization and extensive feasibility studies. This caused serious cutbacks for many of the Bureau of Reclamation's irrigation projects but came too late to affect the Corps of Engineers' main stem dams. The administrative structure of Pick-Sloan was also overhauled in 1964 when the Missouri Basin Inter-Agency Committee's parent commission, the Federal Inter-Agency Committee on Water Resources, was dismantled in favor of a new Water Resources Committee. In 1972 the MBIAC itself was replaced by the more representative Missouri River Basin Commission.[37] By this time even the Corps of Engineers, which was once described by Justice William O. Douglas as "public enemy number one" in regard to the environment, had been required by federal law to implement environmental protection policies.[38]

What then has been learned from the Pick-Sloan experience? The lessons for the Missouri River Sioux have been many and bitter, but for the federal government they appear to be few. In terms of recognizing Native Americans as human beings with legitimate property rights, the government has continued to demonstrate that it learned as little from Pick-Sloan as it did from the mistakes of the previous two centuries. In 1969, for example, the Interior Department proposed legislation that would make it possible to build dams, highways, and power lines on Indian land without tribal consent.[39] The very next year, the Bureau of Outdoor Recreation proposed establishment of a Great Prairie Lakes National Recreation Area to encompass all of the Missouri main stem reservoirs from Gavins Point to Garrison. This new plan called for the Corps of Engineers, which would have primary authority over the project, to condemn an additional 74,000 acres of private land, much of it on the Sioux reservations, to expand federal recreation facilities. Although neither of those proposals was ever implemented, the Sioux tribes found it disconcerting to think that federal agencies could continue even to suggest such ideas.[40]

In regard to the critical issue of water rights, the federal government also maintained the tradition of failing to abide by its own laws as far as the Sioux are concerned. The federal agencies involved in the Pick-Sloan program have never acknowledged the legal provisions of the Winters Doctrine. Because the possession of priority water rights is absolutely essential for the future economic development of the reservations, the Sioux need desperately to challenge the federal government on this issue. Judicial decisions or legislative acts are crucially necessary to settle the points of disagreement that continue to shroud the Indians' reserved water rights. If these legal questions are clarified, the federal agencies can be forced to quantify the tribe's future water needs and guarantee their reserved rights before committing any more of the Missouri's precious water resources to non-Indian users. But, given the ambiguity of Indian jurisprudence, the federal water agencies' head start in marketing Missouri water, the apathetic posture of the Bureau of Indian Affairs, and the impotence and naiveté of the tribes themselves, it does not seem likely that future water rights for the Sioux will fare any better than their land rights have in the past.

If nothing else, the Pick-Sloan program has demonstrated the sham of native rights and the hypocrisy of federal Indian policies in the twentieth century. Though their monstrous dams destroyed more Indian land than any previous public works, the Pick-Sloan administrators seemed not to have given more than an afterthought to the tribes of the Missouri Basin. Legislation was approved for the giant boondoggle and construction begun long before anyone thought about consulting tribal officials. Reservation lands were illegally condemned and even flooded in some cases before the issue of compensation was properly determined. Overwhelmed by the legal complexities of the ordeal, tribal representatives were finally forced to accept whatever alms Congress saw fit to bestow.

The Indian New Deal had established the goal of tribal self-determination, but Sioux leaders were either ignored or overruled during every phase of Pick-Sloan negotiations. Congress had espoused the goal of tribal self-sufficiency as part of its movement toward termination of the BIA, yet it was unwilling to grant settlements generous enough to help the tribes bring about that condition. The unfortunate state of the Bureau of Indian Affairs' tribal wardship, its timidity in confronting the federal water agencies, and its feeble status within the Interior Department were also painfully exposed.

Perhaps the only Indian policy goal that Pick-Sloan helped advance was that of acculturation. For over a century the federal government has implemented policies designed to integrate Indians into the mainstream of Anglo-American culture. For an even longer period tribes have fought to preserve their distinctive heritage. By seriously altering their traditional environment, natural resources, social patterns, and means of livelihood, Pick-Sloan has made sure that the Sioux tribes of the Missouri River have considerably less of their past to hang on to.

Many parties share the blame for the needless chaos and pathos caused by Pick-Sloan. The Corps of Engineers, with its impulse to bludgeon, was, of course, a primary culprit. The Bureau of Indian Affairs was as inert as Congress was lethargic in meeting its obligations to the Indians, and the Sioux themselves could have avoided many pitfalls if they had only managed to acquire a bit more political savvy. Nonetheless, responsibilty for many, if not most, of Pick-Sloan's failings must ultimately rest with the Truman administration and its inability to provide an adequate administrative structure for the Missouri Basin program.

In many respects the Sioux would have fared much better if a TVA-like Missouri Valley Authority could have been established. The Corps of Engineers' role would have been greatly reduced, local authorities would have attained more influence and control, and property settlements would have been far more equitable. It will never be known whether MVA would have destroyed less reservation land or paid any greater heed to Indian land and water rights. Because a valley authority might have had the power to circumvent Congress in negotiating settlements with the tribes, it might have provided even fewer rehabilitation benefits.

The simple truth is that no matter what form a federal public works project takes, the odds are heavily stacked against Indians from the beginning. When combined with long-established policies that make it impractical if not impossible for tribal members to leave their reservations, the federal power of eminent domain makes it inevitable that Indians will suffer injustice. The Sioux tribes of the Missouri River provide only the most dramatic example of the kind of developments that have taken place on dozens of reservations as a result of federal water projects.

The Crows of Montana fought for seventeen years to receive a settlement from the Bureau of Reclamation after 6,846 acres of their land were condemned for the Yellowtail Dam, another Pick-Sloan project on the Big Horn River. The tribe is still being deprived of its fair share of reservoir water. Meanwhile the economic development of the Fort Peck Reservation in the same state has been retarded by the Milk River Reclamation Project. In the Colorado River Basin the Corps of Engineers flooded the Papago village of Sil Murk and completed construction of the Painted Rock Dam long before displaced Indian families were even compensated.[41]

Reclamation Bureau dams built on the Truckee River in California have destroyed the primary economic resources of the Northern Paiutes' Pyramid Lake Reservation in western Nevada. The Pimas of Arizona, the Mission Indians of California, the Senecas of Pennsylvania, and the Salishes, Kootenais, and Yakimas of the Pacific Northwest are other tribes whose rights have been violated. In its own defense the federal government often points out the reclamation projects that have been specifically designed to benefit Indians, such as the San Carlos Indian Irrigation Project in Arizona and the Navajo Indian Irrigation Project in New Mexico, but the future of those projects is also clouded by water rights litigation, and construction has been allowed to fall far behind schedule.[42]

The rights of Native Americans as well as their land and resources continue to be eroded. Meanwhile many who call themselves Indian historians and profess a tribal affinity continue to dwell in the nineteenth century endlessly debating such issues as who killed Custer. If scholars are to be of service in this area of research, they urgently need to confront the realities of more recent Indian affairs and to place these important events in historical perspective.

The story of the Pick-Sloan Plan and its effects on the Sioux tribes of the Missouri River will continue well into the future. While it is impossible to ignore the abuse and suffering that have characterized this program, up to now, it is sincerely hoped that a more optimistic conclusion to the chronicle can someday be written.

NOTES

BIA: Bureau of Indian Affairs.
CIA: Commissioner of Indian Affairs.
CC: Crow Creek Sioux Tribe.
CE: Corps of Engineers, U.S. Army
CR: Cheyenne River Sioux Tribe.
DA: Department of the Army.
DI: Department of the Interior.
FRC-D: Federal Records Center, Denver, Colorado.
FRC-KC: Federal Records Center, Kansas City, Missouri.
HSTL: Harry S. Truman Presidential Library, Independence, Missouri.
LB: Lower Brulé Sioux Tribe.
MRBI: Missouri River Basin Investigations Project.
NA: National Archives, Washington, D.C.
RG 48: Record Group 48, Records of the Secretary of the Interior.
RG 75: Record Group 75, Records of the Bureau of Indian Affairs.
SI: Secretary of the Interior.
SR: Standing Rock Sioux Tribe.
WNRC: Washington National Records Center, Suitland, Maryland.
YS: Yankton Sioux Tribe.

CHAPTER 1

1. The word Missouri is derived from an Algonquian term in the Illinois dialect meaning "great muddy" or "big muddy." It was generally used to describe the river, but was also applied to the Chi subtribe of the Siouan linguistic group that settled in the lower Missouri Valley. For more information see U.S., Smithsonian Institution, Bureau of American Ethnology, Bulletin 30, Part I, *Handbook of American Indians North of Mexico,* ed. by Frederick Webb Hodge (Washington, D.C.; Government Printing Office, 1912), pp. 911-12.

2. The history and geography of the Missouri Basin are described in many works. Amusing episodes dealing primarily with the river itself are chronicled in Stanley Vestal, *The Missouri* (Lincoln: University of Nebraska Press, 1964). The best geographic description and discussion of modern problems is found in Henry C. Hart, *The Dark Missouri* (Madison: University of Wisconsin Press, 1957). Two other good works referred to here are Rufus Terral, *The Missouri Valley: Land of Drouth, Flood, and Promise* (New Haven: Yale University Press, 1947), and Richard G. Baumhoff, *The Dammed Missouri Valley: One-Sixth of Our Nation* (New York: Alfred A. Knopf, 1951). An important work treating the Upper Basin is Bruce Nelson, *Land of the Dacotahs* (Minneapolis: University of Minnesota Press, 1946).

3. In *The Great Plains* (Boston: Ginn and Company, 1931), Walter Prescott Webb developed the concept of the Great Plains as an environmentally hostile region that could be conquered only after the industrial revolution reached maturity. Another seminal work on the plains is James C. Malin, *The Grasslands of North America: Prolegomena to its History, with Addenda and Postscript* (Gloucester, Mass.: P. Smith, 1967).

4. Tree ring studies reveal that the series of wet and dry years have followed each other for at least the last six centuries with no discernible rhythm or predictable pattern. Hart, *Dark Missouri,* pp. 12-14.

5. Basin problems since 1930 are thoroughly discussed in U.S., Missouri Basin Inter-Agency Committee, *The Missouri River Basin Comprehensive Framework Study,* vol. 1, *The Report* (Washington, D.C.. Government Printing Office, 1971), pp. 24-29.

6. Ibid.

7. Ibid., p. 59; U.S., President's Water Resources Policy Commission, *Ten Rivers in America's Future,* vol. 2 (Washington, D.C.: Government Printing Office, 1950), pp. 171-72, 181; U.S., DA, CE, Missouri River Division, *The Development and Control of the Missouri River* (Omaha, 1947), p. 2.

CHAPTER 2

1. Nelson, *Land of Decotahs,* p. 318; Marian E. Ridgeway, *The Missouri Basin's Pick-Sloan Plan: A Case Study in Congressional Policy Determination,*

Illinois Studies in Social Science, vol. 35 (Urbana: University of Illinois Press, 1955), pp. 3-5.

2. Ridgeway, *Pick-Sloan Plan,* pp. 7-8; Hart, *Dark Missouri,* p. 120.

3. Hart, *Dark Missouri,* pp. 78-79, 83; CE, *Missouri Control and Development,* p. 14; Peter Briggs, *Rampage, The Story of Disastrous Floods, Broken Dams, and Human Fallibility* (New York: David McKay & Co., 1973), p. 74; *St. Louis Post-Dispatch,* 17 July 1951.

4. Ridgeway, *Pick-Sloan Plan,* pp. 22-23, 26, 32; *Federal Power Commission Act, Statutes at Large* 41 (1920): 1063; *Boulder Dam Act, Stat.* 45 (1928): 1011; *Tennessee Valley Authority Act, Stat.* 48 (1933): 58; *Flood Control Act of 1936, Stat.* 49 (1936): 1570.

5. Hart, *Dark Missouri,* pp. 12, 94-97; Arthur E. Morgan, *Dams and Other Disasters: A Century of the Army Corps of Engineers in Civil Works* (Boston: Porter Sargent Publishers, 1971), pp. 298-302.

6. *National Industrial Recovery Act, Stat.* 48, sec. 202 (b) (1933): 201.

7. When completed, Pakistan's Tarbela Dam will surpass Fort Peck as the world's largest dam structure based on total volume. *The World Almanac and Book of Facts, 1976* (New York: Newspaper Enterprise Association, Inc., 1976) p. 592.

8. Hart, *Dark Missouri,* pp. 94-97; Briggs, *Rampage,* p. 92.

9. *Stat.* 49, sec. 5 (1936): 1588; *Rivers and Harbors Act, Stat.* 52, sec. 4 (1938): 1218; *Rivers and Harbors Act, Stat.* 55, sec. 3 (1941): 646.

10. Hart, *Dark Missouri,* pp. 94-97.

11. Ridgeway, *Pick-Sloan Plan,* pp. 161-62; U.S., DA, Office of the Chief of Military History, *United States Army in World War II,* vol. 6, pt. 6: *The Technical Services;* and vol. 3: *The Corps of Engineers: Construction in the United States,* by Lenore Fine and Jesse D. Remington (Washington, D.C.: 1972), pp. 514, 603, 638.

12. U.S., Congress, House, Committee on Flood Control, *Missouri River Basin: Letter from the Secretary of War Transmitting a Letter from the Chief of Engineers, U.S. Army, Dated 31 December 1943, Submitting a Report, Together with Accompanying Papers and Illustrations, On a Review of Reports on the Missouri River, for Flood Control along the Main Stem from Sioux City, Iowa, to the Mouth, Requested by a Resolution of the Committee on Flood Control, House of Representatives, Adopted 13 May 1943,* Document no. 475, 78th Cong., 2d sess., 1944, pp. 1-31; Ridgeway, *Pick-Sloan Plan,* pp. 79-82; Hart, *Dark Missouri,* pp. 121-22.

13. Hart, *Dark Missouri,* pp. 123-24.

14. Terral, *Missouri Valley,* pp. 189-94.

15. Ridgeway, *Pick-Sloan Plan,* pp. 8, 79, 82; Hart, *Dark Missouri,* pp. 123-24.

16. U.S., Congress, Senate, *A Bill to Provide for Improvement and Development of Navigation, Irrigation, and Control of Floods on Missouri River and Its Tributaries, for Promotion of National Defense, and for Other Purposes,* S. 2100, 78th Cong., 2d sess., 1944.

17. U.S., Congress, Senate, Committee on Commerce, *Authorizing the*

Construction of Certain Public Works on Rivers and Harbors for Flood Control and Other Purposes, S. Rept. 1030, 78th Cong., 2d sess., 1944, pp. 30-31; Nelson, *Land of Dacotahs,* pp. 322-23; Hart, *Dark Missouri,* p. 124; Ridgeway, *Pick-Sloan Plan,* pp. 91-93.

18. Ibid.

19. Hart, *Dark Missouri,* p. 125; Ridgeway, *Pick-Sloan Plan,* p. 82.

20. Ridgeway, *Pick-Sloan Plan,* pp. 162-63; Terral, *Missouri Valley,* pp. 194-95.

21. Richard L. Berkman and W. Kip Viscusi, *Damming the West, Ralph Nader's Study Group Report on the Bureau of Reclamation* (New York: Grossman Publishers, 1973), pp. 2, 4; Ridgeway, *Pick-Sloan Plan,* pp. 143-44; Hart, *Dark Missouri,* pp. 110, 116; Briggs, *Rampage,* pp. 75-76.

22. U.S. Congress, Senate, Committee on Irrigation and Reclamation, *Conservation, Control, and Use of Water Resources of the Missouri Basin,* Document no. 191, 78th Cong., 2d sess., 1944, pp. 1-211; Hart, *Dark Missouri,* pp. 125-26; Ridgeway, *Pick-Sloan Plan,* pp. 82-88; Nelson, *Land of Dacotahs,* pp. 322-24; William E. Warne, *The Bureau of Reclamation* (New York: Praeger Publishers, 1973), pp. 163-64.

23. Ibid.

24. Ridgeway, *Pick-Sloan Plan,* pp. 212-15; Hart, *Dark Missouri,* p. 130; Terral, *Missouri Valley,* pp. 221-22.

25. *St. Louis Post-Dispatch,* 4 May 1944.

26. U.S., Congress, Senate, *A Bill to Improve the Navigability of the Missouri River; to Provide for the Flood Control of the Mississippi River and the Missouri River; to Provide for the Reforestation and the Use of Marginal Lands in the Missouri Valley; to Provide for the Restoration and Preservation of the Water Level in the Missouri Valley; to Provide for the Development of Electrical Power in the Missouri Valley; and for Other Purposes,* S. 1973, 73d Cong., 2d sess., 1934.

27. U.S., Congress, Senate, *A Bill Authorizing the Construction of Certain Public Works on Rivers and Harbors; Authorizing Investigations and Measures for Flood Control and Sediment Reduction on Watersheds, Through Runoff and Water Flow Retardation and Soil Erosion Prevention, Providing for Supervision by the Chief of Engineers of Dams Across Navigable Waters, and for Other Purposes,* S. 1812, 78th Cong., 2d sess., 1944.

28. Ridgeway, *Pick-Sloan Plan,* pp. 88-91, 93-96, 142; C. Frank Keyser, *Missouri Valley Authority: Background and Analysis of Proposal,* Public Affairs Bulletin 42 (Washington, D.C.: Library of Congress, Legislative Reference Service, 1946), pp. 29-36.

29. U.S., Congress, Senate, *A Bill to Establish a Missouri Valley Authority, to Provide for Unified Water Control and Reservoir Development on the Missouri River and Surrounding Region in the Interest of the Control and Prevention of Floods, the Promotion of Navigation and Reclamation of Public Lands, the Surrendering of the National Defense, and for Other Purposes,* S. 2089, 78th Cong., 2d sess., 1944.

30. U.S., Congress, Senate, Message from President Roosevelt Recommend-

ing Creation of Valley Authorities, *Congressional Record,* 78th Cong., 2d sess., 1944, 90: 8108.

31. Keyser, *Missouri Valley Authority,* pp. 16-17; Ridgeway, *Pick-Sloan Plan,* pp. 96-101.

32. Ridgeway, *Pick-Sloan Plan,* pp. 96-101; Hart, *Dark Missouri,* p. 126; Marvin Meade, *The Missouri River Proposals for Development,* Citizens Pamphlet 11 (Lawrence: University of Kansas, Bureau of Government Research, 1952), pp. 1-10; John W. Ball, "Midwest Flood Also Burst Political Dike," *Washington Post,* 29 July 1951; U.S., Congress, Senate, *Missouri River Basin, Report of a Committee of Two Representatives Each From the Corps of Engineers, U.S. Army, and the Bureau of Reclamation, Appointed to Review the Features of Plans Presented by the Corps of Engineers (H.R. Doc. 475) and the Bureau of Reclamation (S. Doc. 191) for the Comprehensive Development of the Missouri River Basin,* Document no. 247, 78th Cong., 2d sess., 1944, pp. 1-6.

33. Terral, *Missouri Valley,* p. 230.

34. Ibid.; Ridgeway, *Pick-Sloan Plan,* pp. 96-101.

35. For a detailed analysis of the Pick-Sloan legislation and its movement through Congress, see Ridgeway, *Pick-Sloan Plan,* pp. 99-132, and Hart, *Dark Missouri,* pp. 127-35.

36. *Flood Control Act, Stat.* 58 (1944): 827.

37. *Rivers and Harbors Act, Stat.* 59 (1945): 19.

38. *Stat.* 58 (1944): 827; Meade, *Missouri River Proposals,* pp. 10-14; Ridgeway, *Pick-Sloan Plan,* p. 126.

39. Ibid.

40. Nelson, *Land of Dacotahs,* p. 328.

41. Ibid.

42. U.S., Congress, Senate, *A Bill to Establish a Missouri Valley Authority, to Provide for Unified Water Control and Reservoir Development on the Missouri River and Surrounding Region in the Interest of the Control and Prevention of Floods, the Promotion of Navigation and Reclamation of Public Lands, the Promotion of Family Type Farming, the Development of Recreational Possibilities, and the Promotion of the General Welfare of the Area, the Strengthening of National Defense, and for Other Purposes,* S. 555, 79th Cong., 1st sess., 1945; U.S., Congress, House, H.R. 2203 (same title and session as above).

43. U.S., Congress, Senate, *A Resolution Providing for Reference and Report of Certain Committees on S. 555, the Missouri Valley Authority Act,* S. Res. 97, 79th Cong., 1st sess., 1945; Ridgeway, *Pick-Sloan Plan,* pp. 250-51; Meade, *Missouri River Proposals,* pp. 35-36.

44. U.S., Congress, Senate, *A Resolution to Change the Reference of Senate Bill 555, Establishing a Missouri Valley Authority, from the Committee on Commerce to the Committee on Agriculture and Forestry,* S. Res. 78, 79th Cong., 1st sess., 1945.

45. U.S., Congress, Senate, Committee on Commerce, *Missouri Valley Authority Act,* S. Rept. 246, 79th Cong., 1st sess., 1945, pp. 1-13; and

Committee on Irrigation and Reclamation, S. Rept. 639 (same title and session as above), pp. 1-23; Senator Overton to President Truman, 1 September 1945, Papers of Samuel I. Rosenman, HSTL.

46. Barton J. Bernstein and Allen T. Matusow, eds. *The Truman Administration: A Documentary History,* (Harper & Row, 1966), pp. 86-87; Cabell Phillips, *The Truman Presidency* (New York: The Macmillan Company, 1966), p. 27; Louis W. Koenig, ed., *The Truman Administration: Its Principles and Practices* (New York: New York University Press, 1956), p. 138; Senator Murray to President Truman, 19 April 1945, Papers of Harry S Truman, Official File, HSTL; *St. Louis Post-Dispatch,* 13 October 1944.

47. Announcement of Missouri Conference on MVA, St. Louis Committee on MVA, 16 April 1945, Truman Papers, Official File, HSTL; Baumhoff, *Dammed Missouri Valley,* pp. 261-72; Terral, *Missouri Valley,* pp. 209-26; Nelson, *Land of Dacotahs,* pp. 325-38; Meade, *Missouri River Proposals,* pp. 40-42.

48. Announcement of Missouri Valley Development Association, 19 April 1945, Undated Resolution of Minnesota Farm Bureau Federation on MVA Proposal, Truman Papers, Official File, HSTL; Statement of Missouri River States Committee, 15 August 1945, Rosenman Papers, HSTL; Ridgeway, *Pick-Sloan Plan,* pp. 173, 180, 182, 184, 189-90, 192-207; Keyser, *Missouri Valley Authority,* pp. 64-72.

49. Keyser, *Missouri Valley Authority,* pp. 40-44, 49; Meade, *Missouri River Proposals,* pp. 35-36; David E. Lilienthal, *TVA-Democracy on the March* (New York: Harper & Bros., 1944), p. 154.

50. Keyser, *Missouri Valley Authority,* pp. 29-36; Meade, *Missouri River Proposals,* pp. 37-39.

51. Ibid.

52. Keyser, *Missouri Valley Authority,* pp. 75-78; Ridgeway, *Pick-Sloan Plan,* pp. 207, 306-307.

53. U.S., Congress, Senate, S. 1156, 80th Cong., 1st sess., 1947; S. 1160, 81st Cong., 1st sess., 1949; S. 1883, 82d Cong., 1st sess., 1951 (all with same title as S. 555, 79th Cong., 1st sess., note 42 above); Meade, *Missouri River Proposals,* pp. 32-33.

54. U.S., Missouri Basin Inter-Agency Committee and the Missouri River States Committee, *The Missouri River Basin Development Program* (Washington, D.C.: Government Printing Office, 1952), p. 11; Meade, *Missouri River Proposals,* pp. 15-16, 28-29; Ridgeway, *Pick-Sloan Plan,* pp. 282-83; Baumhoff, *Dammed Missouri Valley,* 169-79; Terral, *Missouri Valley,* p. 236; Warne, *Bureau of Reclamation,* pp. 165-66.

55. Ibid.; John R. Ferrell, "Water in the Missouri Valley: The Inter-Agency River Committee at Mid-Century," *Journal of the West* 7 (January, 1968): 97-98.

56. William B. Arthur, "MVA—Its Backgrounds and Issues," *Congressional Digest,* 29: 14; Baumhoff, *Dammed Missouri Valley,* pp. 261-72; Terral, *Missouri Valley,* pp. 209-26; Nelson, *Land of Dacotahs,* pp. 325-38.

CHAPTER 3

1. U.S., DI, BIA, MRBI, *Listings of Missouri River Basin Investigation Reports,* MRBI Rept. 108 (Billings, 1970), pp. 1-14.

2. For the early history of the Sioux see Doane Robinson, *A History of the Dakota or Sioux Indians,* 2d ed. (Minneapolis: Ross & Haines Inc., 1967); George E. Hyde, *Spotted Tail's Folk: A History of the Brulé Sioux* (Norman: University of Oklahoma Press, 1961), chaps. 1-2, and *Red Cloud's Folk: A History of the Oglala Sioux,* 2d ed. (Norman: University of Oklahoma Press, 1956); Ernest L. Schusky, *The Forgotten Sioux: An Ethnohistory of Lower Brule Reservation* (Chicago: Nelson-Hall, 1975), chaps. 1-2; Roy W. Meyer, *History of the Santee Sioux: United States Indian Policy on Trial* (Lincoln: University of Nebraska Press, 1967), chaps. 1-2; and U.S., DI, National Park Service, Western Museums Laboratory, *Teton Dakota Ethnology and History,* by John C. Ewers (Berkeley: 1938). The Sioux are classified in U.S., Smithsonian Institution, Bureau of American Ethnology, *The Indian Tribes of North America,* by John R. Swanton, Bulletin 145 (Washington, D.C.: Government Printing Office, 1952), pp. 280-84.

3. James H. Howard, *The Dakota or Sioux Indians: A Study in Human Ecology,* Dakota Museum, Anthropological Papers, no. 2, pt. 3 (Vermillion: University of South Dakota, 1966), pp. 1-9.

4. For an analysis of federal Indian policy during this period, see Robert A. Trennert, Jr., *Alternative to Extinction: Federal Indian Policy and the Beginning of the Reservation System, 1846-1851* (Philadelphia: Temple University Press, 1975); Loring B. Priest, *Uncle Sam's Stepchildren: The Reformation of United States Indian Policy, 1865-1887* (New Brunswick: Rutgers University Press, 1942); Henry E. Fritz, *The Movement for Indian Assimilation, 1860-1890* (Philadelphia: University of Pennsylvania Press, 1963); and Robert W. Mardock, *The Reformers and the American Indian* (Columbia: University of Missouri Press, 1971). Sioux military resistance has been best described by Robert M. Utley in three outstanding volumes: *The Last Days of the Sioux Nation* (New Haven: Yale University Press, 1963); *Frontiersmen in Blue: The United States Army and the Indian, 1848-1865* (New York: The Macmillan Co., 1967); and *Frontier Regulars: The United States Army and the Indian, 1866-1891* (New York: The Macmillan Co., 1974). The Sioux War of 1865 to 1867 is also detailed in James C. Olson, *Red Cloud and the Sioux Problem* (Lincoln: University of Nebraska Press, 1965).

5. Utley, *Last Days of the Sioux,* pp. 44-45; Howard, *Dakota or Sioux Indians,* pt. 1, p. 9, pt. 3, p. 6; Meyer, *History of the Santee Sioux,* pp. 155-57.

6. Baumhoff, *Dammed Missouri Valley,* p. 23; Herbert S. Schell, *History of South Dakota,* 3d ed. (Lincoln: University of Nebraska Press, 1975), pp. 4, 8-12.

7. Ibid.

8. Utley, *Last Days of the Sioux,* pp. 18-39; George E. Hyde, *A Sioux*

Chronicle (Norman: University of Oklahoma Press, 1956), pp. 3-25.

9. *Dawes Severalty Act, Stat.* 24 (1887): 338. For a full discussion of the implications of the Dawes Act, see D. S. Otis, *The Dawes Act and the Allotment of Indian Lands,* ed. by Francis Paul Prucha (Norman: University of Oklahoma Press, 1973), and Wilcomb E. Washburn, *The Assault on Indian Tribalism: The General Allotment (Dawes Act) of 1887* (Philadelphia: Lippincott, 1975).

10. *Act of 2 March 1889, Stat.* 25 (1889): 888; Utley, *Last Days of the Sioux,* pp. 40-59.

11. Utley, *Last Days of the Sioux,* pp. 40-59; Schell, *History of South Dakota,* pp. 335-38.

12. Ibid.

13. Ibid.

14. Utley, *Last Days of the Sioux,* p. 25; Schell, *History of South Dakota,* p. 335-36.

15. *Act of 2 June 1924, Stat.* 43 (1924): 253; U.S., DI, BIA, *A History of Indian Policy,* by S. Lyman Tyler (Washington, D.C.: Government Printing Office, 1973), p. 110.

16. Tyler, *History of Indian Policy,* pp. 112-15; Lewis Merriam, *The Problem of Indian Administration* (Baltimore: Johns Hopkins Press, 1928); Richard N. Ellis, ed., *The Western American Indian: Case Studies in Tribal History* (Lincoln: University of Nebraska Press, 1972), pp. 144-45.

17. Tyler, *History of Indian Policy,* pp. 125-36; Ellis, *Western American Indian,* pp. 144-45, 173-74.

18. Ibid. Historians have just begun to assess the successes and failures of John Collier's Indian New Deal reforms. The best studies thus far have been Graham D. Taylor, *The New Deal and American Indian Tribalism: The Administration of the Indian Reorganization Act, 1935-45* (Lincoln: University of Nebraska Press, 1980); Kenneth R. Philp, *John Collier's Crusade for Indian Reform, 1920-1954* (Tucson: University of Arizona Press, 1977); and Donald L. Parman, *The Navajos and the New Deal* (New Haven: Yale University Press, 1976).

19. Harry R. Stephens, *The Government of the Indians of South Dakota,* The Government Research Bureau, University of South Dakota, Report No. 8 (Vermillion, 1952), pp. 28-29, 34, 41-43; Schell, *History of South Dakota,* pp. 338-39; U.S., Congress, House, Committee on Interior and Insular Affairs, *Report with Respect to the House Resolution Authorizing the Committee on Interior and Insular Affairs to Conduct an Investigation of the Bureau of Indian Affairs,* H. Rept. 2503, 82d Cong., 1st sess., 1953, pp. 346-47.

20. Stephens, *Indians of South Dakota,* pp. 52-53.

21. Tyler, *History of Indian Policy,* pp. 134-36; Vine Deloria, Jr., "This Country Was A Lot Better Off When the Indians Were Running It," *New York Times,* 8 March 1970, 6:32.

22. Deloria, "This Country," p. 32.

23. Michael Harrington, *The Other America: Poverty in the United States* (New York: Macmillan, 1962), p. 4.

24. In the introduction to the second edition of *The Other America* Harrington apologized for omitting Native Americans from his original analysis, though he made no mention of their economic plight other than to state that they were "probably the poorest of all" (Baltimore: Penguin Books Inc., 1971, p. x). *Poverty in America* was another study which served as a source book for the War on Poverty. Edited by Louis Fermin, Joyce L. Kornbluth, and Alan Haber with an introduction by Harrington, this work identified Indians as the "hardest hit of the country's poverty stricken," but then devoted only two more sentences to the nature of their poverty (Ann Arbor: University of Michigan Press, 1965), p. 132. Vine Deloria, Jr., suggested in *Custer Died for Your Sins: An Indian Manifesto* (New York: Avon Books, 1969), p. 20, that Indians are also culturally invisible because of the great amount of misinformation about them that exists in the minds of most white Americans.

25. H. Rept. 2503 (1953), pp. 88, 1317-18, 1323-24, 1329, 1580-84; U.S., DI, BIA, MRBI, *Progress Report on the Standing Rock Planning Survey*, MRBI Rept. 97 (Billings, 1949), p. 3; *Socio-Economic Report and Costs of Removal from Oahe Taking Area, Cheyenne River Reservation, South Dakota*, MRBI Rept. 117 (Billings, 1951), pp. 12-14; *Report of Socio-Economic Survey, 1951, Standing Rock Indian Reservation, North Dakota and South Dakota*, MRBI Rept. 124 (Billings, 1951) pp. 6, 10, 12; *Problems of Indian Removal and Rehabilitation Growing Out of the Fort Randall Reservoir Taking on Crow Creek and Lower Brule Reservations, South Dakota*, MRBI Rept. 136 (Billings, 1953), p. 7; *Social and Economic Conditions of Resident Families on Yankton Sioux Reservation, South Dakota*, MRBI Rept. 141 (Billings, 1954), pp. 25-27; *Cultural and Economic Status of Sioux People, 1955, Standing Rock Reservation, North and South Dakota*, MRBI Rept. 151 (Billings, 1957), p. 1.

26. MRBI Rept. 141, p. 1.

27. H. Rept. 2503 (1953), pp. 1318, 1322, 1324, 1330, 1333-34, 1580-81. See also John Cassel, Etra Page, and Gaynelle Hogan, *Economic and Social Resources Available for Indian Health Purposes: A Study of Selected Reservations in the Aberdeen Area* (Chapel Hill: University of North Carolina, Institute for Research in Social Sciences, 1956).

28. H. Rept. 2503 (1953) pp. 1318, 1322, 1324, 1330, 1333-34, 1580-81; Cassell, Page, and Hogan, *Indian Health Resources*, pp. 38-41.

29. H. Rept. 2503 (1953), pp. 1318, 1322, 1324, 1330, 1333-34, 1580-81.

30. H. Rept. 2503 (1953), pp. 1324, 1583; MRBI Rept. 136, pp. 8-11; MRBI Rept. 151, pp. 2, 45; U.S., Department of Commerce, Bureau of Census, *United States Census of Population: 1950*, vol. 1, *Characteristics of Population*, pt. 1, *United States Summary*, and pt. 41, *South Dakota*.

31. H. Rept. 2503 (1953), pp. 1319, 1321, 1323, 1329, 1333; MRBI Rept. 136, pp. 12-15; MRBI Rept. 151, p. 2; Cassel, Page, and Hogan, *Indian Health Resources*, F-4.

32. MRBI Rept. 136, p. 7; Ernest Schusky, *Politics and Planning in a Dakota Indian Community* (Vermillion: Institute of Indian Studies, University of South Dakota, 1959), pp. 34, 41 n.

33. U.S., Congress, House, Committee on Interior and Insular Affairs, *Acquisition of Lands for Reservoir Created by Construction of Oahe Dam on the Missouri River and the Rehabilitation of the Standing Rock Indians, South Dakota and North Dakota,* H. Rept. 1888, 85th Cong., 2d sess., 1958, p. 7; H. Rept. 2503 (1953), pp. 361-62; MRBI Rept. 141, p. 33.

34. MRBI Rept. 97, pp. 9-10; MRBI Rept. 117, pp. 32-36; MRBI Rept. 124, pp. 22-25.

CHAPTER 4

1. *Winters* v. *U.S.,* 207 U.S. 564, 575-77 (1907); *Conrad Investment Company* v. *U.S.,* 161 Fed. 829 (CA9, 1908); *Arizona* v. *California,* 373 U.S. 546, 598-600 (1963).

2. U.S., DI, BIA, MRBI, *Annual Report, Fiscal Year 1948* (Billings, 1948), pp. 6-8; "Programs and Accomplishments of Interior Agencies Using Missouri Basin Project Transfer Funds," DI Rept., 7 January 1958, 50745-44-074, Missouri Basin Project, 1955-58, RG 75, NA; "Statement of Responsibilities and Relationships for the Administration of the Oahe-Cheyenne River Act, P.L. 776, 83d Cong." 16822-074.1, Missouri River Basin, Oahe Dam, Cheyenne River-Standing Rock, 1951-55, RG 75, WNRC.

3. U.S., DA, CE, *Annual Report of the Chief of Engineers, U.S. Army, 1948,* pt. 1, vol. 2 (Washington, D.C.; Government Printing Office, 1949), pp. 1718, 1720, 1723, 1754; *Annual Report of Chief of Engineers, U.S. Army, 1949,* pt. 1, vol. 2, (Washington, D.C.: Government Printing Office, 1950), pp. 1557, 1559, 1561, 1593; MRBI Rept. 108, pp. 15-22.

4. U.S., DA, CE, Missouri River Division, *Fort Randall Reservoir: Lake Francis Case* (Omaha, 1972), pp. 1-4; *Annual Report of the Chief of Engineers, U.S. Army, 1973,* pt. 2, vol. 1 (Washington, D.C.; Government Printing Office, 1974) sec. 21, pp. 12-14; U.S., DA, CE, Missouri River Division, *The Development and Control of the Missouri River* (Omaha, 1947), p. 7.

5. U.S., DI, BIA, MRBI, *Damages to Indians of Five Reservations from Three Missouri River Reservoirs in North and South Dakota,* MRBI Rept. 138 (Billings, 1954), pp. 1, 18-19, 47; "Summary and Evaluation of Experiences of Six Indian Reservations Affected by Large Dam and Reservoir Projects on Missouri River, 1960," 1766-074.1, MRBI, pt. 1-A, General Programs, 1960, RG 75, WNRC, pp. 5-10, 44-45; U.S., DI, BIA, MRBI, *Appraisal of Indian Property on the Fort Randall Reservoir Site Within the Lower Brule and Crow Creek Indian Reservations, South Dakota,* MRBI Rept. 135 (Billings, 1953), pp. 1-7; *Problems of Indian Removal and Rehabilitation Growing Out of the Fort Randall Taking on Crow Creek and Lower Brule Reservations, South Dakota,* MRBI Rept. 136 (Billings, 1953), pp. 1-6, 17-20; *Report of Ownership Status of Restricted, Alloted, and Tribal Indian Lands on the Crow Creek,*

Notes

211

Lower Brule, and Rosebud Reservations, South Dakota, Affected by Fort Randall Dam and Reservoir Project, MRBI Rept. 83 (Billings, 1949), pp. 1-4.

6. Ibid.

7. MRBI Rept. 138, pp. 1, 18-19, 47; MRBI, "Experiences of Six Reservations Affected by Large Dams," pp. 5-10; "Brief in Justification of a Bill to Authorize the Appropriation of $85,000 for Benefit of Certain Yankton Sioux Families Whose Homes are within the Taking Line of Fort Randall Reservoir Site, 1948," Box A-1, Rosebud Agency, file 869, Yankton Flood Papers, RG 75, FRC-KC.

8. U.S., DA, CE, Missouri River Division, *Oahe Dam: Lake Oahe* (Omaha: 1972), pp. 1-4.

9. Ibid.; *Annual Report of Chief of Engineers, 1973,* pt. 2, vol. 2, sec. 21, p. 14.

10. MRBI Rept. 138, pp. 1, 18-19, 47; MRBI, "Experiences of Six Reservations Affected by Large Dams," pp. 5-10, 44-45; U.S., DI, BIA, MRBI, *Problems on the Cheyenne River and Standing Rock Reservations Arising from the Oahe Project,* MRBI Rept. 100 (Billings, 1950), pp. 1-8.

11. Ibid.

12. Ibid.

13. U.S., DA, CE, Missouri River Division, *Big Bend Dam: Lake Sharpe* (Omaha, 1972), pp. 1-4; *Annual Report of the Chief of Engineers, 1973,* pt. 2, vol. 2, sec. 21, p. 12.

14. MRBI Rept. 138, pp. 1, 18-19, 47; MRBI, "Experiences of Six Reservations Affected by Large Dams," pp. 5-10, 44-45; U.S., DI, BIA, MRBI, *Damages to Indians on Crow Creek and Lower Brule Reservations from Big Bend Dam and Reservoir Project, South Dakota,* MRBI Rept. 165 (Billings, 1960), pp. 1-10.

15. Ibid.

16. MRBI Rept. 138, pp. 12-14, 18-19; "Experiences of Six Reservations Affected by Large Dams," pp. 5-10, 44-45.

17. Ibid.

18. MRBI Rept. 138, p. 79; Ethel Nurge, "Dakota Diet: Traditional and Contemporary," in *The Modern Sioux: Social Systems and Reservation Culture,* ed. Ethel Nurge (Lincoln: University of Nebraska Press, 1970), pp. 39, 75-89. For a full discussion of traditional plant uses, see Melvin Randolph Gilmore, "Use of Plants by the Indians of the Missouri River Region," in *Thirty-third Annual Report of the American Bureau of Ethnology* (Washington, D.C.: Government Printing Office, 1919), pp. 43-154.

19. MRBI Rept. 138, pp. 12-14.

20. Ibid., pp. 77; Nurge, "Dakota Diet," p. 39.

21. "Experiences of Six Reservations Affected by Large Dams," pp. 8-9, 49-53.

22. MRBI Rept. 138, pp. 9-11, 61-67.

23. Ibid., pp. 8-9, 11-12, 51, 56-60; MRBI Rept. 165, pp. 2, 10; MRBI Rept. 136, p. 2.

24. MRBI, Rept. 138, pp. 15-16.

25. Ibid.

26. Resolution of the CC Tribal Council, 2 May 1947; Owl to Ashley, 25 May 1947, Box 55, CC Agency, Decimal File 064, Tribal Council Minutes, 1939-49, RG 75, FRC-KC.

27. For a detailed analysis of the Fort Berthold experience, see Roy W. Meyer, "Fort Berthold and the Garrison Dam," *North Dakota History* 35 (Summer and Fall, 1968): 220-355. MRBI Rept. 138, pp. 1, 18-19, 47; MRBI, "Experiences of Six Reservations Affected by Large Dams," pp. 5-10, 44-45.

28. U.S., DA, CE, Missouri River Division, *Garrison Dam: Lake Sakakawea* (Omaha, 1972), pp. 1-4; *Annual Report of the Chief of Engineers, 1973,* pt. 2. vol. 2, sec. 21, p. 13.

29. U.S. Congress, House, *Congressional Record,* "Remarks of Representative Burdick on Due Process of Law and the Fifth Amendment," 83d Cong., 1st sess., 1953, 99: 3394; *War Department Civil Appropriations Act of 1946, Stat.* 60 (1946): 163; Meyer, "Fort Berthold," pp. 242-43.

30. Meyer, "Fort Berthold," pp. 245-55; MRBI, "Experiences of Six Reservations Affected by Large Dams," p. 8.

31. Morgan, *Dams and Other Disasters,* p. 46.

32. *War Department Civil Appropriation Act of 1947, Stat.* 61 (1947): 690; Meyer, "Fort Berthold," pp. 256-61; U.S., Congress, House, Committee on Interior and Insular Affairs, *Fort Berthold Indian Reservation, North Dakota, Hearings before the Subcommittee on Indian Affairs, Committee on Interior and Insular Affairs, House of Representatives, on H.J. Res. 33,* 81st Cong., 1st sess., 1949, pp. 47-59; *Act of 29 October 1949, Stat.* 63 (1949): 1026-49.

33. *Stat.* 63 (1949): 1026-49; Meyer, "Fort Berthold," pp. 262-64; Morgan, *Dams and Disasters,* pp. 49-50.

34. Meyer, "Fort Berthold," pp. 329-55; Morgan, *Dams and Other Disasters,* pp. 51-55; MRBI Rept. 138, pp. 2-3, 12-15, 18-19, 45-46; MRBI, "Experiences of Six Reservations Affected by Large Dams," pp. 5-10, 44-45, 49-53.

35. Minutes of Joint Council, CR and SR, Regarding Oahe Dam, 1 November 1949, Box 518796, CR Agency, Decimal File 060-064, CR Council Minutes, 1946-49, RG 75, FRC-KC; Frank Ducheneaux, interviews held on CR Reservation, S. Dak., 30-31 July 1972; Minutes of CR Tribal Council, Regular Session, 5-9 December 1950, File 2226-47-341.3, Oahe Dam Legislation, RG 75, NA.

36. Cassel, et al., *Indian Health Resources,* F20-21; H. Rept. 2503 (1953), pp. 50, 346-47.

37. "Brief in Justification of Appropriation for Certain Yankton Sioux Families," pp. 4-8; Pick to Zimmerman, 28 February 1948, File 5491-48-308, Fort Randall Legislation, RG 75, NA.

38. *Stat.* 11 (1858): 743; *Cherokee Nation* v. *Southern Kansas Railroad Company,* 135 U.S. 641 (1890); *Thomas* v. *Gay,* 169 U.S. 264 (1898);

Chaote v. *Trapp,* 224 U.S. 665 (1912); *U.S.* v. *North American Transportation and Trading Company,* 253 U.S. 330 (1920).

39. "Brief in Justification of Appropriation to Certain Yankton Sioux Families," pp. 4-8.

40. Ibid.; U.S., Congress, Senate, *A Bill Authorizing an Appropriation for the Removal and Reestablishment of Indians on Yankton Indian Reservation, South Dakota, to be Removed from the Taking Area of Fort Randall Dam and Reservoir, Missouri River Development, and for Related Purposes,* S. 2171, 81st Cong., 1st sess., 1949.

41. Zimmerman to Pick, 10 May 1948, 5491-48-308, RG 75, NA; U.S., Congress, House, *A Bill to Authorize the Negotiation and Ratification of Separate Settlement Contracts with Sioux Indians of the Cheyenne River Reservation, South Dakota, and the Standing Rock Reservation, North and South Dakota, for Indian Lands and Rights Acquired by the United States for the Oahe Dam and Reservoir, Missouri River Development, and for Related Purposes,* H.R. 3582, H.R. 5372, 81st Cong., 1st sess., 1949; U.S., Congress, Senate, *A Bill Authorizing the Negotiation of Contracts with Indians in Connection with the Construction of the Oahe Dam, S. Dak.,* S. 1488, 81st Cong., 1st sess., 1949.

42. U.S., Congress, House, Committee on Public Lands, *To Authorize the Negotiation, Approval, and Ratification of Settlement Contracts with Sioux Indians of the Cheyenne River Reservation, South Dakota, and the Standing Rock Reservation, North and South Dakota, for Indian Lands and Rights Acquired by the United States for the Oahe Dam and Reservoir, Missouri River Development, and for Related Purposes,* H. Rept. 1047, 81st Cong., 1st sess., 1949, p. 2.

43. *Act of 30 September 1950, Stat.* 64 (1950):1093-95.

44. Draft of Statement by the President Announcing Approval of H.R. 5372, 30 September 1950, File 40716-45-074, Missouri Basin Project, 1950-54, RG 75, NA.

45. *Stat.* 64 (1950):1093-95.

46. Ibid.; Ralph Hoyt Case to Frank Ducheneaux, 26 October 1950, 2226-47-341.3, RG 75, NA.

47. *Stat.* 64 (1950):1093-95; H. Rept. 1047 (1950), p. 7. U.S. Congress, House, *Congressional Record,* Remarks of Representative Case on Oahe Settlement Provisions, 81st Cong., 2d sess., 1950, 96:15609.

48. G. Warren Spaulding, Aberdeen Area Director, BIA, to Commissioner of Indian Affairs, 22 November 1950, 2226-47-341.3, RG 75, NA.

CHAPTER 5

1. Reinhold Brust, Acting Aberdeen Area Director, BIA, to General Don G. Shingler, Missouri Division Engineer, CE, 27 September 1951, File 14499-304, SR Agency, 1951, RG 75, WNRC; Minutes of the Negotiators for the

Federal Government and for SR, Fort Yates, North Dakota, 31 July-1 August 1951, File 17889-074.1, SR Agency, Oahe Project, Missouri River Basin, pt. 1-A, Contract Negotiations, 1951-55, RG 75, WNRC; Frank Ducheneaux, interviews.

2. Brust to Singler, 27 September 1951, RG 75, WNRC.

3. Frank Ducheneaux, interviews.

4. Minutes, CC Tribal Council, 10 May 1952, Box 56, CC Agency, Decimal File 064, CC Tribal Council Minutes, 1950-52, RG 75, FRC-KC; LB Resolution 52-12, 7 May 1952, File 7115-056, Aberdeen Area Office, Legislation, 1952-56, RG 75, WNRC; Myer to Senator Case, 2 October 1952, File 48776-054. CC Agency, CC Tribal Relations, 1951-52, RG 75, WNRC; U.S., Congress, House, *A Bill to Authorize the Negotiation and Ratification of Separate Settlement Contracts with the Sioux Tribes of the Lower Brule and Crow Creek Reservations in South Dakota for Indian Land and Rights Acquired by the United States for the Fort Randall Dam and Reservoir, Missouri River Development, and to Authorize an Appropriation for the Removal from the Taking Area of the Fort Randall Dam and Reservoir, Missouri River Development, and the Reestablishment of the Yankton Sioux Reservation in South Dakota,* H.R. 8293, 82d Cong., 2d sess., 1952.

5. Frank Ducheneaux, interviews; Dale Doty, Assistant SI, to Kelly, 21 February 1951, Central Classified Files, 1937-53, 5-1, Missouri River Basin, RG 48, NA.

6. Appendix to Letter, Curry to SR Negotiating Committee, 1 November 1952, 5-1, RG 48, NA.

7. Ibid.; *New York Times,* 4 January 1952, 4 January 1953.

8. Ibid.; Senator Mundt to Chapman, 3 May 1951, Congressman Burdick to Chapman, 7 May 1951, Congressman Berry to Chapman, 16 May 1951, Congressman Lovre to Chapman, 14 May 1951, 5-1, RG 48, NA.

9. Weltfish to Chapman, 16 May 1951, Chapman to Mrs. James B. Patton, 16 May 1951, 5-1, RG 48, NA; *New York Times,* 5 January 1952, 20 March 1952.

10. Appendix to Letter, Curry to SR Negotiating Committee, 1 November 1952, 5-1, RG 48, NA.

11. Curry to Negotiating Committee, 13 August 1951, 17899-074-1, pt. 1-A, RG 75, WNRC; *New York Times,* 20 March 1953.

12. Mastin G. White, Acting SI, to Alexander Lesser, Executive Director, Association on American Indian Affairs, 22 July 1952; Roger Baldwin, National Chairman, American Civil Liberties Union, to Chapman, 26 July 1952; Chapman to Jonathan M. Steere, President, Indian Rights Association, 30 July 1952; McKay, SI, to Curry, 29 April 1953; 5-1, RG 48, NA; Minutes, LB Tribal Council, 19 March 1953, Box 58, CC Agency, Decimal File 064, LB Tribal Council Minutes, 1948-55, RG 75, FRC-KC.

13. SR Delegation to Chapman, 26 September 1951; Myer to Chapman, 26 September 1951; Memorandum of Protest Filed by CR, 22 September 1951; Josel D. Wolfson, Assistant SI, to DI Solicitors Office, 6 November 1952; 5-1, RG 48, NA.

14. Ibid.

15. Tyler, *History of Indian Policy*, pp. 161-81; Ellis, *Western American Indian*, 188-89; William T. Hagan, *American Indians* (Chicago: University of Chicago Press, 1961), pp. 161-62; Ernest Schusky, "Political and Religious Systems in Dakota Culture," in Ethel Nurge, *The Modern Sioux: Social Systems and Reservation Culture* (Lincoln: University of Nebraska, 1970). p. 141; Schusky, *Politics and Planning in a Dakota Indian Community*, p. 68-69.

16. SR Delegation to Chapman, 26 September 1951, 5-1, RG 48, NA.

17. Gerald T. Hart and Associates, *Basic Data Report, Oahe Reservoir Valuation Project, Sioux Indian Lands* (Denver, 1951), pp. 3-4; U.S., DI, BIA, MRBI, *The Timber Resources of the Cheyenne River and Standing Rock Reservations Within the Oahe Reservoir in North and South Dakota*, MRBI Rept. 131 (Billings, 1952), pp. 1-2.

18. Minutes of Meetings, Federal Representatives and SR Negotiating Committee, Fort Yates, North Dakota, 31 July-1 August 1951, 17899-074.1, pt. 1-A, RG 75, WNRC.

19. Ibid.

20. Ibid.

21. Ibid.

22. Ibid.

23. These agencies defined it as "the highest price fairly determined in terms of money which could be commanded for property by a seller who is fully informed as to the rights and benefits inherent in or attributable to the property and as to the highest and best use to which it is adaptable, from a buyer who is also well informed as to said rights, benefits, and uses inherent in or attributable to the property, if the property should be exposed for sale in the open market for a reasonable length of time." U.S., DI, BIA, MRBI, *Appraisal of Indian Property of the Oahe Reservoir Site within the Cheyenne River Indian Reservation, South Dakota*, MRBI Rept. 132 (Billings, 1952), p. 20. Hart and Associates, *Basic Data Report, Oahe Valuations*, p. 9.

24. Minutes of Conference, between Gerald T. Hart and BIA Representatives, Aberdeen, South Dakota, 9 February 1951, File 5603-074.1, MRBI, Oahe Project, 1952, RG 75, WNRC.

25. Frank Ducheneaux, interviews; MRBI Rept. 132, p. 4.

26. U.S. Congress, House, *Congressional Record,* CR Tribal Council Report on H.R. 2233, 83d Cong., 1st sess., 29 January 1953, 99: 647.

27. Bigelow Neal, "Valley of the Dammed," reprinted in *Congressional Record*, 81st Cong., 1st sess. (1949), 95:A5957.

28. Kris Kristjanson, *TVA Land Acquisition Experience Applied to Dams in the Missouri Basin* (Brookings, 1953).

29. Ibid., pp. 25-27; Neal, "Valley of the Dammed," A4229-4321, A4983; "Some Local Impacts of Reservoirs in South Dakota," Agricultural Economics Pamphlet 46, Agricultural Economics Department, Agricultural Experiment Station, South Dakota State College (June, 1953), pp. 6-12.

30. Ibid.; U.S., Congress, House, *Congressional Record,* Remarks of Repre-

sentative Usher L. Burdick, 83d Cong., 2d sess., 1954, 100: 3680-81.

31. Ibid.

32. Ibid.; U.S., Congress, House, *Congressional Record,* Remarks of Representative Burdick, 83d Cong., 1st sess., 1953, 99: 3394; Act of 14 July 1952, *Stat.* 66 (1952): 624, sec. 401 (b).

33. Kristjanson, *TVA Land Acquisition,* pp. 9-15; Charles J. McCarthy, "Land Acquisition Policies and Proceedings in TVA—A Study of the Role of Land Acquisition in a Regional Agency," *Ohio State Law Journal* 10 (Winter, 1948): 48-51.

34. Ibid.

35. Kristjanson, *TVA Land Acquisition,* pp. 39-41; McCarthy, "Land Acquisition Policies," pp. 60-63; President's Water Resources Policy Commission, *Ten Rivers in America's Future;* vol. 2; *The Missouri,* pp. 228-30.

36. Kristjanson, *TVA Land Acquisition,* pp. 28-30.

CHAPTER 6

1. Telephone files of G. Warren Spaulding, MRBI Director, 1-2 May 1952, 17899-074.1, pt. 1-A, RG 75, WNRC.

2. *Act of April 8, 1952, Stat.* 66 (1952): 46.

3. Minutes, Meetings of Representatives of CR, CE, BIA, Cheyenne Agency, South Dakota, 13-14 May 1952, 16822-074.1, RG 75, WNRC.

4. Ibid.

5. *Stat.* 64 (1950): 1093-95.

6. Statement of Legality of Hart Appraisal Schedule, 23 June 1952, Accession 74A390, FRC 223836, MRBI, RG 75, FRC-D; Minutes, Meetings of Representatives of CR, CE, BIA, 13-14 May 1952, 16822-074.1, RG 75, WNRC; J. M. Cooper, MRBI Director, to Spaulding, Aberdeen Area Director, BIA, 28 February 1951, 5603-074.1, RG 75, WNRC.

7. Minutes, Meetings of Representatives of CR, CE, BIA, 13-14 May, 1952, 16822-074.1, RG 75, WNRC.

8. Pick to SI, 13 June 1952, Walter Y. Fuhriman, MRBI Director, to Pick, 23 June 1952, 16822-074.1, RG 75, WNRC.

9. Telephone Memo, Lloyd Atchley, CE, to Spaulding, 7 August 1952, A. B. Melzner, MRBI, to Cooper, 29 September 1952, 16822-074.1, RG 75, WNRC.

10. Frank Ducheneaux, interviews; CR Tribal Council Report on H.R. 2233, p. 648; Agenda for CR Negotiating Conference, Washington, D.C., 10 November 1952, CR Tribal Records, Eagle Butte, South Dakota.

11. Ibid.

12. Criteria for Negotiations, CR Negotiating Committee, Washington, D.C., 14 November 1952, CR Tribal Records; U.S., Congress, House, Committee on Interior and Insular Affairs, *Providing for the Acquisition of Lands by the United States Required for the Reservoir Created by the Construction of Oahe Dam on the Missouri River and for the Rehabilitation of the Indians*

of the Cheyenne River Sioux Reservation, S. Dak., H. Rept. 2484, 83d Cong., 2d sess., 1954, pp. 3-8.

13. Ibid.

14. *Stat.* 64 (1950): 1095, sec. 2 (b).

15. Institute of Indian Studies, University of South Dakota, *Tribal Rehabilitation Programs: Programs and Proceedings, Fifth Annual Conference on Indian Affairs* (Vermillion, 1959), pp. 5-6; U.S., Congress, House, *Congressional Record,* Remarks of Representative D'Evart on Costs of Foreign Aid Compared to Costs of Aid to Indians, 82d Cong., 1st sess., 1951, 97: 9993; *Act of 19 April 1950, Stat.* 64 (1950): 44-47; Tyler, *History of Indian Policy,* pp. 161-81.

16. Criteria for Negotiations, CR Negotiating Committee, 14 November 1952; H. Rept. 2484 (1954), pp. 3-8; U.S., DI, BIA, MRBI, *Socio-Economic Report and Costs of Removal from Oahe Taking Area, Cheyenne River Reservation, South Dakota,* MRBI Rept. 117 (Billings, 1951), pp. 1-52.

17. Criteria for Negotiations, CR Negotiating Committee, 14 November 1952; H. Rept. 2484 (1954) pp. 3-8.

18. Ibid.

19. Ibid.

20. Ibid.

21. Ibid.

22. Frank Ducheneaux, interviews; CR Tribal Council Report on H.R. 2233, p. 648; "Statement of Representatives of the Chief of Engineers Submitted to Chairman of the Tribal Negotiating Committee of the Sioux Indians of the Cheyenne River Reservation and the Representatives of the Secretary of the Interior at a Meeting on 24 November 1952 at Washington, D.C.," CR Tribal Records.

23. "Statement of the Tribal Negotiating Committee of the Cheyenne River Sioux Tribal Council Submitted to the Negotiators under Public Law 870, 26 November 1952, Washington, D.C.," CR Tribal Records.

24. Lloyd LeBeau, interview held at Eagle Butte, South Dakota, 31 July 1972; CR Tribal Council Report on H.R. 2233, p. 649.

25. Frank Ducheneaux, interviews; H. Rept. 2484 (1950), pp. 1-2, 6-8.

26. Ibid.; U.S., Congress, House, H.R. 2233 (same title as H. Rept. 2484, note 12, above), 83d Cong., 1st sess., 1953.

27. Curry to SR Negotiating Committee, 1 November 1952, Brust to Myer, 21 November 1952, 5-1, RG 48, NA.

28. Brust to Myer, 21 November 1952, 5-1, RG 48, NA.

29. "Summary of Negotiations for Settlement of Oahe Taking held at Standing Rock Indian Agency, 13-14 January 1953," 17899-074.1, pt. 1-A, RG 75, WNRC.

30. Ibid.

31. Ibid.

32. Melzner to Spaulding, 16 January, 12 March, 1953, Summary of Meetings of SR Negotiators, 10 February, 6, 7, 24 March 1953, Melzner to SI, 8 May 1953, 17899-074.1, pt. 1-A, RG 75, WNRC.

33. U.S., Congress, House, *A Bill to Promote the Rehabilitation of the Standing Rock Sioux Indians and Better Utilization of the Resources of the Standing Rock Indian Reservation, and for Other Purposes,* H.R. 3974, 81st Cong., 1st sess., 1949.

34. "Final Report on Contract Negotiations with the Standing Rock Tribe," 17899-074.1, pt. 1-A, RG 75, WNRC.

35. Cooper to Spaulding, 22 September 1953, SR Tribal Council Resolution, 3 February 1954, Telephone Memo, Senator Mundt's Office to Homer B. Jenkins, BIA, 5 February 1954, Fuhriman to H. Rex Lee, Associate CIA, 7 February 1954, 17899-074.1, pt. 1-A, RG 75, WNRC.

36. U.S., Congress, House, *A Bill to Provide for the Acquisition of Lands by the United States Required for the Reservoir Created by the Construction of the Oahe Dam on the Missouri River and the Rehabilitation of the Standing Rock Sioux Reservation in North Dakota and South Dakota, and for Other Purposes,* H.R. 9533, 83d Cong., 2d sess., 1954.

37. Minutes, General Meetings, CC Tribe, 4 May, 6 July, 15, 23 November 1951, 56, 064, RG 75, FRC-KC; *Congressional Record,* 82d Cong., 1st sess., 31 August 1951, 97:10874; U.S., DI, BIA, MRBI, *Report on Negotiations Between the United States and the Sioux Indians of the Crow Creek and Lower Brule Reservations Regarding the Acquisition of Indian Lands and Rights Needed for the Fort Randall Reservoir, South Dakota,* MRBI Rept. 143 (Billings, 1955), pp. 1-2.

38. Minutes, Special Meeting, CC Tribal Council, 31 August 1951, 48776-054, RG 75, WNRC.

39. Herbert Wounded Knee to McNickle, 27 August 1951, 48776-054, RG 75, WNRC; William E. Warne, Assistant SI, to Don Stansky, State Senator, South Dakota, 13 April 1950, 5-1, RG 48, NA.

40. Myer to Wounded Knee, 5 October 1951, 48776-054, RG 75, WNRC; Cooper to Myer, 4 February 1952, 3811-01.1, Aberdeen Area Office, Relocation Plans, 1952, RG 75, WNRC; Minutes, Special Meeting, CC Tribal Council, 11 October 1954, Box 57, CC Agency, Decimal File 064, CC Tribal Council Minutes, 1953-54, RG 75, FRC-KC.

41. Minutes, Special Joint Meetings, LB and CC Tribal Councils, 6, 30 July 1951, 48776-054, RG 75, WNRC; U.S., DA, CE, *Annual Report of the Chief of Engineers, U.S. Army, 1953,* vol. 2, pt. 1 (Washington, D.C.: Government Printing Office, 1954), pp. 59-62; MRBI Rept. 143, p. 4.

42. MRBI Rept. 143, p. 4.

43. Ibid.; Eva J. Nichols to McKay, 25 April 1953, Jerry McBride, CC Indian Rights Association, to Congressman Lovre, 31 March 1953, and Orme Lewis, Assistant SI, to Lovre, 6 May 1953, 5-1, RG 48, NA; Telephone Memo, Atchley to Spaulding, 7 August 1952, 17899-074.1, pt. 1-A, RG 75, WNRC.

44. MRBI Rept. 143, pp. 5-6.

45. MRBI Rept. 143, pp. 7-10.

46. U.S., Department of Justice, District Court, South Dakota District, Central Division, *U.S. v. 9,148 Acres of Land, et al., and the Crow Creek*

Tribe of Sioux Indians, Civil No. 184; U.S. v. *7,996 Acres of Land, et al., and the Lower Brule Tribe of Sioux Indians,* Civil No. 186, 4 August 1953.

47. *New York Times,* 20 March 1953; *Congressional Record,* 83d Cong., 1st sess., 25 February 1953, 99: A887.

CHAPTER 7

1. Frank Ducheneaux, interviews. The Cheyenne River negotiations are more fully described in Michael L. Lawson, "Reservoir and Reservation: The Oahe Dam and the Cheyenne River Sioux" (Master's thesis, University of Nebraska at Omaha, 1973), pp. 90-123.

2. Ibid.

3. Ibid.; Ellen Ducheneaux, former member, CR Tribal Negotiating Committee, interviews held at Eagle Butte, S.Dak., 31 July, 1 August 1972; Ellis, *Western American Indian,* p. 188.

4. U.S., Congress, House, Remarks of Representative Berry on Oahe Dam and the Rehabilitation of the Cheyenne River Sioux Indians, 83d Cong., 2d sess., 3 August 1954, *Congressional Record* 100: 13160.

5. H. Rept. 2484 (1954), pp. 12-14.

6. H. Rept. 2484 (1954), pp. 9-10.

7. H. Rept. 2484 (1954), pp. 6-8.

8. Ibid.

9. Ibid.

10. Nancy Lee Lamport, "Francis Case: His Pioneer Background, Indian Legislation, and Missouri River Conservation" (Master's thesis, University of South Dakota, 1972), pp. 2-3, 29, 35-36, 39-40, 45.

11. U.S., Congress, Senate, Remarks of Senators Watkins and Case on Land Acquisition for Oahe Dam, S.Dak., 83d Cong., 2d sess., 1954, *Congressional Record* 100: 14979-80.

12. U.S., Congress, Senate, Committee on Interior and Insular Affairs, S. Rept. 2489 (same title as H. Rept. 2484, Chap. 6, note 12 [1954]), 83d Cong., 2d sess., 1954, pp. 1-6.

13. U.S., Congress, Senate and House, "Senate approves H.R. 2233 as Amended, House concurs," 83d Cong., 2d sess., 1954, *Congressional Record* 100: 14972, 15229; *Act of 3 September 1954, Stat.* 68 (1954): 1191.

14. *Stat.* 68 (1954): 1191; Frank Ducheneaux, Ellen Ducheneaux, Lloyd LeBeau, interviews.

15. Ibid.

16. *Stat.* 68 (1954): 1191.

17. Ibid.

18. Ibid.

19. Ibid.

20. Ibid.

21. Ibid.

22. Ibid.

23. *Eagle Butte* (S.Dak.) *News,* 24 December 1954, 14 January 1955; U.S., Congress, House, Committee on the Judiciary, *Providing Reimbursement to the Tribal Council of the Cheyenne River Sioux Reservation In Accordance with the Act of 3 September 1954,* H. Rept. 602, 85th Cong., 1st sess., 1957, p. 2.

24. U.S., Congress, House and Senate, H.R. 5608, S. 1712 (same title as H.R. 9533, chap. 6, note 36 [1954]), 84th Cong., 1st sess., 1955; U.S., Congress, House, Committee on Interior and Insular Affairs. *Acquisition of Lands for Reservoir Created by Construction of Oahe Dam on the Missouri River and Rehabilitation of the Standing Rock Sioux Indians, South Dakota and North Dakota,* H. Rept. 1888, 85th Cong., 2d sess., 1958, p. 4.

25. H. Rept. 1888, 85th Cong., 2d sess., 1958, p. 23; U.S., Congress, House, Committee on Interior and Insular Affairs, H. Rept. 2498 (same title as H. Rept. 1888, chap. 3, note 33), 84th Cong., 2d sess., 1956, p. 7.

26. H. Rept. 2498, 84th Cong., 2d sess., 1956, p. 7; U.S., DI, BIA, MRBI, *Range and Soil Survey, Standing Rock Reservation, North and South Dakota,* MRBI Rept., 146 (Billings, 1955), p. 1.

27. Ibid.

28. H. Rept. 2498, 84th Cong., 2d sess., 1956, p. 8.

29. Ibid., pp. 13-15.

30. U.S., Congress, Senate, Resolution of Standing Rock General Council, 84th Cong., 2d sess., 1956, *Congressional Record* 103: 2023.

31. U.S., Congress, House, H.R. 6075, H.R. 6256 (same title as H.R. 9533 [1954]), 85th Cong., 1st sess., 1957.

32. U.S., DA, CE, *Annual Report of the Chief of Engineers, U.S. Army, 1957,* vol. 2 (Washington, D.C.: Government Printing Office, 1958), pp. 914-16; Aljoe Agard, former SR Tribal Chairman, interview held at Fort Yates, North Dakota, 8 August 1972.

33. U.S., DA, CE, *Annual Report of the Chief of Engineers, U.S. Army, 1954,* vol. 2 (Washington, D.C.: Government Printing Office, 1955), pp. 834-37; *Act of 6 July 1954, Stat.* 68 (1954): 452-54.

34. *Stat.* 68 (1954): 452.

35. Ibid.

36. Ibid.

37. MRBI Rept. 143, p. 11; U.S., DI, BIA, MRBI, *Progress Report on Removal of Families from Fort Randall Reservoir Area, Crow Creek and Lower Brule Reservations, South Dakota,* MRBI Rept. 145 (Billings, 1955), p. 1; U.S., Congress, House and Senate, *A Bill to Provide for Acquisition by the United States of Lands Required for the Reservoir to be Created by the Fort Randall Dam on the Missouri River, and to Provide for the Rehabilitation of Sioux Indians of the Crow Creek Reservation in South Dakota,* H.R. 9833, S. 3747 (H.R. 9832, S. 3748, same title as above except for Lower Brule Sioux), 83d Cong., 2d sess., 1954.

38. MRBI Rept. 143, p. 18; LB Tribal Council Resolution, 54-42, 27 May 1954, 58, 064, RG 75, FRC-KC.

39. Minutes, Special Meetings, CC Tribal Council, 7 May, 23 July, 9

August, 11 October 1954, 57, 064, RG 75, FRC-KC.

40. MRBI Rept. 143, p. 10; MRBI Rept. 145, pp. 1-2; U.S., Congress, House, Committee on Interior and Insular Affairs, *Providing Additional Payments to Indians of the Lower Brule Reservation, South Dakota, Whose Lands Have Been Acquired for the Fort Randall Dam and Reservoir Project,* H. Rept. 2054, 85th Cong., 2d sess., 1958, pp. 1-3.

41. MRBI Rept. 145, pp. 2, 16.

42. Ibid.; Minutes, CC Tribal Council Meeting, 9 March 1955, 57, 064, RG 75, FRC-KC.

43. U.S., Congress, House and Senate, H.R. 3602, S. 952 (same title as H.R. 9833 [1954]), H.R. 3544, S. 953 (same title as H.R. 9832 [1954]), 84th Cong., 1st sess., 1955; H.R. 6125, H.R. 7758, S. 2152 (same title as H.R. 9833 [1954]), H.R. 6074, H.R. 6569 (same title as H.R. 9832 [1954]), 85th Cong., 1st sess., 1957; H.R. 12670, H.R. 10786, S. 3225 (same title as H.R. 9833 [1954]), H.R. 12663 (same title as H.R. 9832 [1954]), 85th Cong., 2d sess., 1958.

44. C. H. Beitzel, Pierre Agency, BIA, to CIA, 6 May 1957, file 7115-1952-056, Pierre Agency, RG 75, WNRC; U.S., DA, CE, *Annual Report of the Chief of Engineers, U.S. Army, 1956,* vol. 2 (Washington, D.C.: Government Printing Office, 1957), pp. 937-39; *New York Times,* 12 August 1956.

45. Richard LaRoche, former LB Chairman, interview held at Lower Brule, South Dakota, 1 September 1971, American Indian Research Project, South Dakota Oral History Center, University of South Dakota, Tape 789, p. 30.

CHAPTER 8

1. John W. Ball, "Midwest Flood Also Burst a Political Dike," *Washington Post,* 29 July 1951; Otto G. Hoiberg, *Its Your Business and Mine: Missouri River Basin Development Program, A Study Guide,* University of Nebraska, Extension Division, Booklet No. 175 (May 1950), pp. 39, 60; Meade, *Missouri River Proposals,* p. 22.

2. Ridgeway, *Pick-Sloan Plan,* pp. 288-92; Ferrell, "Water in the Missouri Valley," p. 98; *Water Pollution Act of 1948, Stat.* 62 (1948): 1155.

3. Ibid.

4. The last MVA bill was introduced in the 84th Congress by Representative Wier of Minnesota (see H.R. 2687, 84th Cong., 1st sess., 1955).

5. Ball, "Midwest Flood Burst Political Dike."

6. Remarks of Congressman Ben F. Jensen of Iowa, *Omaha World-Herald,* 14 August 1949.

7. Public Affairs Institute, Washington, D.C., *The Big Missouri: Hope of Our West,* Rept. No. 2 (June 1948), pp. i-ii; Commission on Organization of Executive Branch of Government, *Task Force Report on Natural Resources* (January 1949), Appendix L, pp. 108-32, 135.

8. Ibid.

9. Ibid.

10. Ibid.; Roscoe Fleming, "Blasting Pick-Sloan: Hoover Commission Heaps Criticism," *Nebraska State Journal,* 6 April 1949.

11. U.S., Congress, House, *Missouri River Agricultural Program,* Document no. 373, 81st Cong., 1st sess., 1949, pp. 1-176; Hoiberg, *Your Business and Mine,* pp. 52-57; Meade, *Missouri River Proposals,* pp. 43-50; Baumhoff, *Dammed Missouri Valley,* p. 170.

12. Ibid.

13. Ball, "Midwest Flood Burst Political Dike."

14. Baumhoff, *Dammed Missouri Valley,* p. 170.

15. *Ten Rivers in America's Future,* vol. 2: *The Missouri,* p. 239.

16. Water Policy Panel, Engineering Joint Council, *National Water Policy,* 2 vols. (Washington, D.C., 1950); Ridgeway, *Pick-Sloan Plan,* pp. 299-302.

17. *St. Louis Post-Dispatch,* 17 July 1951; U.S., Congress, Senate, Remarks of Senator Murray on Floods in Middle West, 82d Cong., 2d sess., 1952, *Congressional Record* 98: 4360-61.

18. Statement of Policy and Resolutions Adopted by Associated Missouri Basin Conservationists, Sioux City, Iowa, 13-14 August 1951; Phillip Murray, President, CIO, to Truman, n.d.; Truman to Murray, 6 August 1951; William E. Kavan, Nebraska MVA Committee, to Truman, 6 January 1952; Statement of President on Appointment of Members to Missouri Basin Survey Commission, 9 February 1952; Truman Papers, HSTL.

19. Ridgeway, *Pick-Sloan Plan,* pp. 302-305; M. B. Donald, publisher, *Daily Republic,* Mitchell, S.Dak., to Truman, 23 August 1951, Truman Papers, HSTL.

20. Ibid.; *Kansas City Star,* 28 March, 12 April 1952; *St. Louis Globe-Democrat,* 5 April 1952; *Pierre* (S.Dak.) *Capitol-Journal,* 6 April 1952; *Aberdeen* (S.Dak.) *American News,* 5 April 1952.

21. Ridgeway, *Pick-Sloan Plan,* pp. 302-305.

22. *Overbrook* (Kans.) *Citizen,* 26 July 1951.

23. U.S., Missouri Basin Survey Commission, *Missouri: Land and Water, The Report of the Missouri Basin Survey Commission* (Washington, D.C.: Government Printing Office, 1953), pp. 8-20, 25-26.

24. Ibid.

25. Ibid.

26. Ferrell, "Water in the Missouri Valley," pp. 102-104.

27. *Annual Report of the Chief of Engineers, 1973,* vol. 2, sec. 21, p. 19.

CHAPTER 9

1. *Sioux County* (N.Dak.) *Pioneer-Arrow,* 16 January, 1958.

2. Ibid.

3. *Sioux County* (N.Dak.) *Pioneer-Arrow,* 13 February 1958.

4. U.S., Department of Justice, District Court, South Dakota District, Northern Division, *U.S.* v. *2005.32 Acres of Land, et al., and Standing*

Rock Tribe of Sioux Indians, Civil No. 722, N.D. Tract R. 18251, 10 March 1958; H. Rept. 1888 (1958), pp. 35-43.

5. *Stat.* 15 (1868): 635; *Stat.* 21 (1877): 254; *Stat.* 35 (1889): 888; *U.S.* v. *North American Transportation and Trading Company,* 253 U.S. 330 (1920); *Youngstown Sheet and Tube Company* v. *Sawyer,* 343 U.S. 579 (1952).

6. H. Rept. 1888 (1958), p. 43.

7. Ibid., p. 22; *McLaughlin* (S.Dak.) *Messenger,* 20 March 1958; *Sioux County* (N.Dak.) *Pioneer-Arrow,* 7 April 1958.

8. H. Rept. 1888 (1958), pp. 25-26.

9. Ibid.

10. Ibid., pp. 29-32.

11. Ibid.; *Act of 2 September 1958, Stat.* 72 (1958): 1762-68.

12. U.S., Congress, House, H.R. 12662 (same title as H.R. 9533 [1954]), 85th Cong., 2d sess., 1958.

13. U.S., Congress, House and Senate, Daily Digest, 85th Cong., 2d sess., 1958, *Congressional Record* 104: D646; *New York Times,* 3 August 1958; *Pierre* (S.Dak.) *Capitol-Journal,* 2-3 August 1958; U.S., Congress, Senate, Committee on Interior and Insular Affairs, S. Rept. 2374 (same title as H. Rept. 1888, chap. 7, note 24 [1958]), 85th Cong., 2d sess., 1958, p. 1.

14. *Stat.* 72 (1958): 1762-68; Agard, interview.

15. Ibid.; *Stat.* 68 (1954): 1191.

16. Ibid.

17. Ibid., H. Rept. 602 (1957), 364; *Act of 2 September 1957, Stat.* 71 (1957): 598-99.

18. H. Rept. 1888 (1958), p. 25.

19. *Stat.* 72 (1958): 1762; *Stat.* 68 (1954): 1191.

20. *Sioux County* (N.Dak.) *Pioneer-Arrow,* 16 January 1958.

21. Minutes, LB Tribal Council Meetings, 3 February 1954, 58, 064, RG 75, FRC-KC.

22. *Act of 2 September 1958, Stat.* 72 (1958): 1766-68 (Crow Creek), 1773-75 (Lower Brule).

23. H. Rept. 2054 (1958), p. 6; U.S., Congress, House, Committee on Interior and Insular Affairs, H. Rept. 2086 (same title as H. Rept. 2054, chap. 7, note 40, except for Crow Creek), 85th Cong., 2d sess., 1958, p. 6.

24. LaRoche, interview held at Lower Brule, S.Dak. 25 August 1971, South Dakota Oral History Project, Tape 784, p. 30.

25. LaRoche, interview, 1 September 1971, South Dakota Oral History Project, Tape 789, pp. 28-29; George C. Estes and Richard R. Loder, *Kul-Wicasa-Oyate: Lower Brule Sioux Tribe* (Lower Brule, S.Dak.: Lower Brule Sioux Tribe, 1971), p. 70.

26. Ibid.

27. Schusky, *The Forgotten Sioux,* pp. 209, 226-27; Schusky, *Politics and Planning in a Dakota Community,* p. 58; Schusky, "Political and Religious Systems in Dakota Culture," pp. 146-47.

28. Schusky, *The Forgotten Sioux,* pp. 226-27.

29. Schusky, *Politics and Planning in a Dakota Community,* p. 63 n.

30. H. Rept. 2086 (1958), pp. 3-6; H. Rept. 2054 (1958), pp. 3-5.

31. H. Rept. 2054, pp. 11-14; H. Rept. 2086, pp. 15-21; H.R. 12663, H.R. 12670 (1958).

32. Schusky, *Politics and Planning in a Dakota Community,* p. 58; U.S., Congress, House, Committee on Interior and Insular Affairs, *Providing for the Payment for Individual and Tribal Lands of the Lower Brule Sioux Reservation in South Dakota, Required by the United States for the Big Bend Dam and Reservoir Project on the Missouri River, and for the Development of the Members of the Tribe,* H. Rept. 852, 87th Cong., 1st sess., 1961, p. 11.

33. U.S., Congress, House, Remarks of Representatives Berry and Mc-Govern on Crow Creek and Lower Brule Settlements, 85th Cong., 2d sess., 1958, *Congressional Record* 104: 15014-16.

34. Ibid.

35. U.S., Congress, Daily Digest, 85th Cong., 2d sess., 1958, *Congressional Record* 104: D646; *Stat.* 72 (1958): 1766; *Stat.* 72 (1958): 1773.

36. *Stat.* 72 (1958): 1762, 1766, 1773; *Stat.* 68 (1954): 1191.

37. Ibid.

38. Ibid.

39. Ibid.

40. LaRoche, interview, Tape 784, pp. 31-32; U.S., DA, CE, *Annual Report of the Chief of Engineers, U.S. Army, 1960,* vol. 2 (Washington, D.C.: Government Printing Office, 1961), pp. 939-41; *New York Times,* 30 May 1960.

41. U.S., Department of Justice, District Court, South Dakota District, Northern Division, *U.S. v. 867.5 Acres of Land, et al., and Crow Creek and Lower Brule Tribes of Sioux Indians,* Civil No. 335, 9 March 1960.

42. Ibid.

43. H. Rept. 852 (1958), pp. 25-34; U.S., Congress, House, Committee on Interior and Insular Affairs, H. Rept. 853 (same title as H. Rept. 852, note 32, except for Crow Creek), 87th Cong., 1st sess., 1961, pp. 25-33; Summary of Joint Negotiations by Representatives of CE, BIA, CC, and LB on Big Bend Project, 3-4 January 1961, 74A390, 223836, RG 75, FRC-D, pp. 1-16; Memorandum of Understandings Between CE, LB, and CC, 23 May 1961, Washington, D.C., 5-1, RG 58, NA.

44. U.S., Congress, Senate, Remarks of Senator Mundt on Payment of Certain Individual and Tribal Lands in South Dakota, 86th Cong., 2d sess., 1960, *Congressional Record* 106: 5697.

45. U.S., Congress, House, *A Bill to Provide for the Payment for Individual and Tribal Lands of the Lower Brule Sioux Reservation in South Dakota, Required by the United States for the Big Bend Dam and Reservoir Project on the Missouri River, and for the Rehabilitation, Social and Economic Development of the Members of the Lower Brule Sioux Tribe, and for Other Purposes,* H.R. 11214 (H.R. 11237, same for Crow Creek), 86th Cong., 2d sess., 1960.

46. H. Rept. 852 (1961), p. 20; H. Rept. 853 (1958), p. 20.

47. Ibid.

48. U.S., Congress, House and Senate, H.R. 5144, S. 1251 (same title as H.R. 11214, note 45, above, [1960]), H.R. 5165, S. 1252 (same title as H.R. 11237, note 45, above [1960]), 87th Cong., 1st sess., 1961; U.S., Congress, Senate, Committee on Interior and Insular Affairs, S. Rept. 1636 (same title as H. Rept. 852 [1961]), S. Rept. 1637 (same title as H. Rept. 853 [1961]), 87th Cong., 2d sess., 1962; *Acts of 3 October 1962, Stat.* 76 (1962): 698-703 (Lower Brule), 704-10 (Crow Creek).

49. *Stat.* 76 (1962): 698.

50. *Stat.* 76 (1962): 704.

51. Ibid.; *Stat.* 76 (1962): 698.

52. S. Rept. 1636 (1962), pp. 10-13.

53. *Stat.* 76 (1962): 698, 704.

54. Ibid.

55. Ibid.

56. Ibid.

57. Ibid.; H. Rept. 852 (1961), pp. 30-34.

58. *Stat.* 76 (1962): 698, 704.

59. Ibid.

CHAPTER 10

1. Special Report on the Use of Missouri River Dam and Reservoir Project Settlement Funds, 16 December 1963, CC, Big Bend Dam, p. 14, CR, Oahe Dam, pp. 9-10, LB, Fort Randall Dam, p. 3, 74A390, 223836, RG 75, FRC-D; Report Prepared for CIA's Trip to North and South Dakota, April 1962, Papers of Philleo Nash, HSTL; MRBI Rept. 145, p. 4; Big Bend Relocation Program, CC, 1962, Box 6, Pierre Indian Agency, Decimal File 060, CC Tribal Relations, 1962-66, RG 75, FRC-KC; Billy Bolin, Administrative Assistant, Yankton Subagency, BIA, to Fuhriman, MRBI, 27 November 1956, A-1, 870, RG 75, FRC-KC.

2. MRBI Rept. 165, p. 3.

3. CR Use of Oahe Funds, MRBI Rept. 165, pp. 21-22; Frank Ducheneaux, interviews; W. O. Roberts, Aberdeen Area Director, BIA, to Jenkens, CIA Office, 1 April 1955, 16822-074-1, RG 75, WNRC. The Cheyenne River Reconstruction is described in fuller detail in Lawson, "Reservoir and Reservation," pp. 124-45, 161-74.

4. *Stat.* 68 (1954): 1191; *Stat.* 72 (1958): 1762, 1766, 1773; *Stat.* 76 (1962): 698, 704.

5. Ibid.

6. Kristjanson, *TVA Land Acquisition Experience Applies to Missouri Basin*, p. 40.

7. U.S., Congress, Senate, Committee on Interior and Insular Affairs, *Amending Sections of the Acts of 3 October 1962, and for Other Purposes,* S. Rept. 1146, 90th Cong., 2d sess., 1968, p. 4.

226   *Dammed Indians*

8. Frank Ducheneaux, interviews.

9. Martin N. B. Holm, Aberdeen Area Director, BIA, to CIA, 5 May 1969, Box 81632, Aberdeen Area Office, Decimal File 001, Correspondence, 1950-65, RG 75, FRC-D; S. Rept. 1146 (1968), p. 1.

10. Ibid.; U.S., Congress, Senate, *A Bill to Amend Sections 13(b) of the Acts of 3 October 1962 (72 Stat. 698, 704), and for Other Purposes,* S. 2044, 88th Cong., 2d sess., 1964, and S. 203, 90th Cong., 1st sess., 1967; *Act of 11 July 1968, Stat.* 82 (1968): 337.

11. Robert J. Philbrick, Chairman, CC Tribal Council, to author, 24 August 1972.

12. *Big Eagle* v. *United States,* 323 F. Supp. 60 (D.S.D., 1971); Monroe E. Price, *Law and the American Indian, Readings, Notes, Cases* (Indianapolis: Bobbs-Merrill Co., 1973), pp. 487-89; *United States* v. *Klamath and Modoc Tribe of Indians,* 304 U.S. 119 (1938).

13. Ibid., *Fort Berthold Reservation* v. *United States,* 390 F. 2d 686, 691, 182 Ct. Cl. 543 (1968).

14. U.S., Congress, House, Committee on Interior and Insular Affairs, *Concerning Payment of Debts out of Compensation for Trust Land on the Crow Creek Sioux Reservation Taken by the United States,* H. Rept. 1716, 86th Cong., 2d sess., 1960, p. 2; *Sioux County* (N.Dak.) *Pioneer-Arrow,* 30 April 1959; U.S., Congress, House, *A Bill Concerning Payment of Debts out of Compensation for Trust Land on Lower Brule Reservation taken by the United States,* H.R. 6465, H.R. 6498 (same for Standing Rock), H.R. 6529 (same for Crow Creek), 86th Cong., 2d sess., 1960.

15. H.R. 6456, H.R. 6498, H.R. 6529, 86th Cong., 2d sess., 1960; *Acts of 29 June 1960, Stat.* 74 (1960): 252 (Lower Brule), 254 (Standing Rock), 254 (Crow Creek).

16. U.S., Congress, Senate, "Indian Lands, Indian Rights, and the Stockgrower," by Senator Francis Case, 85th Cong., 1st sess., 1957, *Congressional Record* 103: 12393-94 (reprinted from July, 1957 issue of *South Dakota Stockgrower*); U.S., DI, BIA, Aberdeen Area Office, "The Missouri River Program—Its Impact on the Indian People" (Aberdeen, n.d.).

17. MRBI Rept. 145, p. 4; Angie Debo, *A History of the Indians in the United States* (Norman: University of Oklahoma Press, 1970), p. 294.

18. *Stat.* 72 (1958): 1762, 1766, 1773; *Stat.* 68 (1954): 452, 1191; *Stat.* 76 (1962): 698, 704.

19. U.S., DI, BIA, Aberdeen Area Office, *Aberdeen Area Statistical Data, 1971* (Aberdeen, 1971), pp. 21, 24; Henry W. Hough, *Development of Indian Resources,* Indian Community Action Program (Denver: World Press, 1967), p. 39.

20. Stan Steiner, *The New Indians* (New York: Harper & Row, 1968), p. 172.

21. Rex H. Barnes, Aberdeen Area Realty Officer, BIA, to Alfred Dubray, Superintendent, Winnebago Agency, BIA, 5 August 1964, 81632, 001, RG 75, FRC-D.

22. U.S., Congress, Senate, Remarks of Senator Mundt on Indian Justice, 90th Cong., 2d sess., 1968, *Congressional Record* 114: 15306-15307.

23. *Acts of 21 July 1968, Stat.* 82 (1968): 396-97.

24. Morgan, *Dams and Other Disasters,* pp. 55-56; *Sioux County* (N. Dak.) *Pioneer-Arrow,* 15 January 1959.

25. *Sioux County* (N. Dak.) *Pioneer-Arrow,* 15 January 1959.

26. Ibid.

27. Ibid.; "Experience of Six Reservations Affected by Large Dams," pp. 5-10, 44-45.

28. *Mobridge* (S. Dak.) *Tribune,* 4 December 1958.

29. Agard, interview; Morgan, *Dams and Other Disasters,* pp. 55-56.

30. Ibid.

31. MRBI Rept. 145, p. 16.

32. Ibid.

33. Ibid., pp. 2, 10, 16.

34. *Sioux County* (N. Dak.) *Pioneer-Arrow,* 17 August 1961; CR Reloca-ation Plans (n.d.), Box 528577, CR Relocation, 1954-60, FRC-KC; Memoran-dum of Understanding Between CE, BIA, and Public Health Service (n.d.), 16822-074.1, RG 75, WNRC.

35. Ibid.; U.S., Congress, Senate, *A Bill Authorizing the Standing Rock and Cheyenne River Indian Tribes to Participate in Clearing Oahe Reservoir,* S. 340, 87th Cong., 1st sess., 1961.

36. Roberts to Glenn L. Emmons, CIA, 27 April 1955, 81632, 001, RG 75, FRC-D; Robert J. Murray, retired Aberdeen Area Director of Education, BIA, interview held at Aberdeen, S. Dak., 10 March 1977, American Indian History Research Project, Oral History Center, Northern State College, Aberdeen. S. Dak., Accession no. 22.

37. Frank Ducheneaux, Ellen Ducheneaux, interviews; *Eagle Butte* (S. Dak.) *News,* 25 February, 2 April, 21 October 1955, 30 November 1956; Wolfgang Mueller, *Community Background Reports: Cheyenne River Sioux Reservation, South Dakota* (Chicago: National Study of American Indian Education, 1959), p. 17.

38. Ibid.

39. Murray, interview; *Eagle Butte* (S. Dak.) *News,* 4 January, 15 February, 17 May 1957; U.S., DI, BIA, Aberdeen Area Office, *Fact Sheet on Cheyenne River Indian Reservation, South Dakota* (Aberdeen, 1970), p. 5; U.S. Depart-ment of Health, Education, and Welfare, Indian Health Service, *Summary of Indian Health Service Reports in South Dakota* (Aberdeen, 1968), p. 10.

40. *Sioux Falls* (S. Dak.) *Argus-Leader,* 23 October 1959.

41. Wilfred S. Parrow, Engineering Technician, Aberdeen Area Office, BIA, interview held at Aberdeen, S. Dak., 28 April 1976, Northern State Indian Oral History Project, Accession no. 7.

42. U.S., DI, BIA, MRBI, *Family Plan and Rehabilitation Program, Standing Rock Reservation,* MRBI Rept. 177 (Billings, 1964), pp. 1, 33-34; Standing Rock Tribal Council, *Programs for Progress* (Fort Yates, N.Dak., 1963), pp.

5-11, 14; Special Report on the Use of Missouri River Dam and Reservoir Project Settlement Funds, 16 December 1963, SR, Oahe Dam, p. 11, 74A390, 223836, RG 75, FRC-D.

43. *Mobridge* (S. Dak.) *Tribune,* 27 April, 4, 11, 18 May, 1 June 1961; *Sioux County* (N. Dak.) *Pioneer-Arrow,* 3 October 1960, 13, 20 April, 4 May, 1, 21, 29 June 1961.

44. Elwyn B. Robinson, *History of North Dakota* (Lincoln: University of Nebraska Press, 1966), pp. 194, 383, 467-68, 473; Usher L. Burdick, *The Last Days of Sitting Bull, Sioux Medicine Man* (Baltimore: Wirth Brothers, 1941).

45. Big Bend Redevelopment Commission, *Big Bend Overall Economic Development Plans,* 2d Annual Report (Pierre, S. Dak.: 1964), p. 7; U.S., DI, BIA, Aberdeen Area Office, *Preliminary Comprehensive Development Plan for Lower Brule Indian Reservation, Lower Brule, South Dakota* (Aberdeen, 1963), p. 4.

46. MRBI Rept. 141, p. 6; "Brief in Justification of Appropriation to Certain Yankton Sioux Families," pp. 1-4.

47. MRBI Rept. 151, p. 7.

48. LaRoche, interview, Tape 784, p. 6; SR Use of Oahe Funds, pp. 41-42.

49. Frank Ducheneaux, interviews.

50. George Shubert, CR Agency, BIA, to Harry Johnson, Jobbers Warehouse, Aberdeen, S. Dak., 25 April 1960, 528577, RG 75, FRC-KC; CR Relocation Plans; U.S., DI, BIA, MRBI, *Present Status and Projected Future Needs of the Cheyenne River Rehabilitation Program as of 15 April 1958,* MRBI Rept. 157 (Billings, 1958), p. 25; SR Use of Oahe Funds, p. 10; MRBI Rept. 165, p. 3; Report for CIA Trip, 1962; Big Bend Relocation Program, CC, 1962.

51. MRBI Rept. 165, pp. 1-5; H. Rept. 853 (1961), p. 6.

52. Fuhriman to Roderick H. Riley, Assistant to CIA, 20 February 1963; Earl Sonnenschein, Sunshine Realty, to Richard LaRoche, LB Tribal Chairman, 29 December 1962; George E. Schmidt, Assistant Aberdeen Area Director, BIA, to Fuhriman, 20 September 1962, 74A390, 223836, RG 75, FRC-D.

53. U.S., DI, BIA, MRBI, *Location and Census of Indian Cemeteries, Standing Rock Reservation, North and South Dakota,* MRBI Rept. 119 (Billings, 1951), pp. 1-4, *Location and Census of Indian Cemeteries, Cheyenne River Reservation, South Dakota,* MRBI Rept. 120 (Billings, 1951), pp. 1-4, *Removal of Indian Burials Located Within and Adjacent to the Yankton Reservation from the Taking Area of the Fort Randall Dam and Reservoir, South Dakota,* MRBI Rept. 75 (Billings, 1949), pp. 1-6.

54. Ibid., *Mobridge* (S. Dak.) *Tribune,* 19 June 1958; Donald Kritzsinger, Oahe Area Manager, CE, interview held at Pierre, S. Dak., 27 July 1972.

55. Agard, interview; Morgan, *Dams and Other Disasters,* pp. 56-57; Resolution Adopted by State Commission of Indian Affairs, Pierre, S. Dak., 10 December 1954; Assistant Commissioner for Resources, BIA, to George E. Hendrix, Program Coordination Staff, BIA, 8 February 1955; Emmons, CIA,

to F. R. Wanek, South Dakota Indian Commissioner, 18 February 1955, 16822-074-1, RG 75, WNRC.

56. Ibid.

57. Frank Ducheneaux, Lloyd LeBeau, interviews.

58. MRBI Rept. 141, p. 5.

59. U.S., Congress, Senate, Elvis J. Stahr Jr., Secretary of the Army, to Clinton P. Anderson, Chairman, Committee on Interior and Insular Affairs, U.S. Senate, 24 August 1962, in *Providing for the Use of Lands in Garrison Dam Project by the Three Affiliated Tribes of the Fort Berthold Reservation,* S. Rept. 1723, 87th Cong., 2d sess., 1962, p. 6.

60. Ibid.

61. Frank Ducheneaux, Lloyd LeBeau, interviews.

62. *Act of 2 September 1958, Stat.* 72 (1958): 1436; *Act of 24 October 1961, Stat.* 75 (1961): 802; *Acts of 30 October 1969, Stat.* 83 (1969): 168 (Cheyenne River), 169 (Standing Rock); *Act of 21 October 1970, Stat.* 84 (1970): 1039.

63. Minutes of Special Meeting, CC Tribal Council, 9 August 1954, 57, 064, RG 75, FRC-KC; Philbrick to author, 24 August 1972.

64. "Experience of Six Reservations Affected by Large Dams."

65. Gib LeBeau, Tribal Judge, CR, interview held at Eagle Butte, S. Dak., 19 May 1977, Northern State Indian Oral History Project, Non-Accessioned Tape.

CHAPTER 11

1. CR Use of Oahe Funds, pp. 4-5; SR Use of Oahe Funds, p. 5; CC Use of Big Bend Funds, p. 5; LB Use of Big Bend Funds, p. 3; Report for CIA Trip, 1962.

2. Ibid.

3. CR Use of Oahe Funds, p. 2; SR Use of the Oahe Funds, pp. 13-15; CC Use of Big Bend Funds, pp. 5, 7, 10; LB Use of Big Bend Funds, p. 3; Report for CIA Trip, 1962.

4. Ibid.; U.S., DI, BIA, MRBI, *Family Plan and Rehabilitation Program, Standing Rock Reservation,* MRBI Rept. 177 (Billings, 1964), pp. 6-9, 16-18.

5. Ibid.

6. CR Use of Oahe Funds, pp. 4-5; U.S., CI, BIA, MRBI, *Progress Report on Individual and Tribal Rehabilitation Programs of Cheyenne River Sioux People to 31 December 1956,* MRBI Rept. 152 (Billings, 1957), pp. 27-28; MRBI Rept. 157, p. 13; CR Tribal Council, *Tribal Rehabilitation Program,* rev. ed., CR Tribal Council Files, Eagle Butte, S. Dak., pp. 44-46; U.S., Congress, Senate, Extension of Remarks by Senator Karl E. Mundt on rehabilitation of Cheyenne River Sioux Indians, 86th Cong., 2d sess., 1960 *Congressional Record* 106: A3299-A3300; U.S., Congress, House, Committee on Interior and Insular Affairs, *Providing for the Distribution of Judgment Funds*

to the Cheyenne River Sioux Tribe, H. Rept. 92-1372, 92d Cong., 2d sess., 1972, pp. 16-17. The Cheyenne River Rehabilitation Programs are more fully described in Lawson, "Reservoir and Reservation," pp. 124-45, 161-74.

7. CR Use of Oahe Funds, pp. 4-5; SR Use of Oahe Funds, p. 23; CC Use of Big Bend Funds, p. 3; LB Use of Big Bend Funds, p. 2; Report for CIA Trip, 1962.

8. CR Use of Oahe Funds, pp. 4-5; CR Tribal Rehabilitation Program, pp. 15-30; MRBI Rept. 157, p. 3; CR Tribal Council Resolution 9-61, 31 January 1961, CR Tribal Council Files, H. Rept. 92-1372 (1972), pp. 8-9.

9. SR Use of Oahe Funds, pp. 23-26; MRBI Rept. 177, p. 44.

10. Leo A. Daly and Associates, *Comprehensive Plan for Crow Creek Reservation, South Dakota* (Omaha, 1967), p. 20; LB Use of Big Bend Funds, p.3 .

11. H. Rept. 92-1372 (1972), pp. 16-17; *CR Fact Sheet,* p. 4; Donald Pennington, BIA Land Operations Officer, CR Agency, interview held at Eagle Butte, S. Dak., 3 August 1972.

12. U.S., DI, BIA, MRBI, *Evaluation of Livestock Phase of Standing Rock Rehabilitation Program, North Dakota and South Dakota,* MRBI Rept. 188 (Billings, 1967), pp. 1-1A.

13. CR Use of Oahe Funds, pp. 4-5; SR Use of Oahe Funds, p. 36; CC Use of Big Bend Funds, p. 2; LB Use of Big Bend Funds, p. 3; Report for CIA Trip, 1962.

14. SR Use of Oahe Funds, p. 36; MRBI Rept. 177, pp. 30-32; U.S., DI, BIA, Planning Support Group, *The Standing Rock Reservation, Its Resources and Development Potential,* PGS Rept. 202 (Billings, 1973), p. 68. The functions of MRBI were taken over and enlarged by the BIA's Planning Support Group in 1972.

15. Big Bend Redevelopment Commission, *Big Bend Overall Economic Development Plan,* 4th Annual Rept. (Pierre, S. Dak.: 1966), pp. 10-11; U.S., CI, BIA, Aberdeen Area Office, *Fact Sheet on Crow Creek Sioux Reservation, South Dakota* (Aberdeen, 1971), p. 4; Estes and Loder, *Kul-Wicasa-Oyate,* p. 73; U.S., DI, BIA, Aberdeen Area Office, *Fact Sheet on Lower Brule Sioux Reservation, South Dakota* (Aberdeen, 1973), p. 3.

16. CR Use of Oahe Funds, pp. 4-6, 16; H. Rept. 92-1372 (1972), pp. 11-13, 16-17; MRBI Rept. 152, p. 26; *CR Tribal Rehabilitation Program,* pp. 38-43.

17. CR Use of Oahe Funds, p. 4; SR Use of Oahe Funds, p. 5; CC Use of Big Bend Funds, p. 5; LB Use of Big Bend Funds, p. 3; Report for CIA Trip, 1962.

18. SR Use of Oahe Funds, pp. 31-33; *Corson County* (S. Dak.) *News,* 21 December 1961, 26 April 1962; *Mobridge* (S. Dak.) *Tribune,* 6 July 1961, 27 December 1962; SR Redevelopment Committee, *Provisional Overall Development Plan* (Fort Yates, N. Dak.: 1966), pp. 24-25.

19. Daly and Associates, *CC Comprehensive Plan,* p. 21; Big Bend Redevelopment Commission, *Big Bend Overall Economic Development Plan,* 3d Annual Rept. (Pierre, S. Dak.: 1964), p. 4; Status Report for CIA on CC, 16 October 1969, Box 511118, Pierre Agency, Decimal File 060, Tribal Rela-

tions, 1950-70, RG 75, FRC-KC; *CC Fact Sheet,* p. 3; *LB Fact Sheet,* p. 2; LB Use of Big Bend Funds, p. 3.

20. Ibid.

21. *LB Fact Sheet,* p. 2; LB Use of Big Bend Funds, p. 3.

22. CR Use of Oahe Funds, pp. 4-6, 13, 15; H. Rept. 92-1372 (1972), pp.7-8; *CR Fact Sheet,* p. 4; MRBI Rept. 157, pp. 4-5.

23. Ibid.

24. SR Use of Oahe Funds, pp. 39-40; CC Use of Big Bend Funds, p. 2; H. Rept. 92-1372 (1972), pp. 8-9.

25. SR Use of Oahe Funds, pp. 39-40; SR Tribal Council and Planning Staff, *Developmental Plan, Phase II* (Fort Yates, N. Dak.: 1971), p. 31; CC Use of Big Bend Funds, p. 2; Big Bend Development Plan (1966), Status Report for CIA on CC (1969); *LB Fact Sheet,* p. 3.

26. *Time,* December 12, 1959; H. Rept. 92-1372 (1972), pp. 8-9; U.S., DI, BIA, Aberdeen Area Office, CR Agency, *Preliminary Comprehensive Development Program for Cheyenne River Indian Reservation* (Eagle Butte, S. Dak.: 1965), pp. 5-6; Hough, *Development of Indian Resources,* pp. 38, 41; *Eagle Butte* (S. Dak.) *News,* 3 November 1956.

27. SR Use of Oahe Funds, pp. 21-22; MRBI Rept. 177, pp. 32-33; CC Use of Big Bend Funds, p. 2; LB Use of Big Bend Funds, p. 3.

28. CR Use of Oahe Funds, pp. 4-5; MRBI Rept. 152, p. 22; *CR Tribal Rehabilitation Program,* pp. 53-55; *Eagle Butte* (S. Dak.) *News,* 23 December 1955; SR Use of Oahe Funds, pp. 37-38; CC Use of Big Bend Funds, p. 5; LB Use of Big Bend Funds, p. 3.

29. MRBI Rept. 177, p. 54; U.S., DI, BIA, Planning Support Group, *The Lower Brule Reservation: Its History, Population, and Economy,* PSG Rept. 219 (Billings, 1974), pp. 46-47; Frank Ducheneaux, interviews; Theodophile L. Traversie, CR Tribal Chairman, interview held at Eagle Butte, S. Dak., 31 July 1972.

30. *McLaughlin* (S. Dak.) *Messenger,* 20 March 1959; *Eagle Butte* (S. Dak.) *News,* 10 February 1961, 5 April 1962; Holm to CIA, 31 May 1966, 15 January 1964, Philbrick, CC Tribal Chairman, to Stewart L. Udall, SI, 31 January 1965, E. Reeseman Fryer, Assistant Commissioner for Economic Development, BIA, to Holm, 7 April 1966, 81632,001, RG 75, FRC-D.

31. Traversie, interview.

32. Frank Ducheneaux, interviews.

33. Schusky, *Forgotten Sioux,* p. 69.

34. SR Use of Oahe Funds, pp. 18-20; MRBI Rept. 177, pp. 8-9; PSG Rept. 219, pp. 46-47.

35. CC Use of Big Bend Funds, pp. 14-15; MRBI Rept. 177, pp. 65-69.

36. Ducheneaux to Ben Reifel, Aberdeen Area Director, BIA, 15 November 1956, 81632, 001, RG 75, FRC-D. In 1969 the Cheyenne River Sioux Tribe was awarded $1.3 million by the Indian Claims Commission, most of which was distributed on a per capita basis.

37. MRBI Rept. 177, p. 20; *Cong. Rec.* 106: A3300; Lloyd LeBeau, interview.

38. MRBI Rept. 177, p. 55; PSG Rept. 202, pp. 46-47; Traversie, Ellen Ducheneaux, Lloyd LeBeau, interviews.

39. SR Use of Oahe Funds, pp. 27-28; MRBI Rept. 188, pp. 1-1A; Mueller, *CR Community Background Report,* pp. 7-9.

40. MRBI Rept. 177, pp. 35-36; *Aberdeen Area Statistical Data (1971),* pp. 30-31; Corwine and Doell, Consultants, *The Fort Yates Land Use and Recreation Planning Report* (Minneapolis, 1964), pp. 55-56.

41. *Aberdeen Area Statistical Data (1971),* pp. 30-31.

42. Calvin A. Kent and Jerry W. Johnson, *Indian Poverty in South Dakota,* Bulletin No. 99, Business Research Bureau, University of South Dakota (Vermillion: University of South Dakota School of Business, 1969), pp. 93-94, 112; Mueller, *CR Community Background Report,* pp. 10, 13-15.

43. Ibid.; *Aberdeen Area Statistical Data (1971),* pp. 10-11; H. Rept. 92-1372 (1972), pp. 9-10; PSG Rept. 202, pp. 26-27; U.S., DI, BIA, Aberdeen Area Office, *Fact Sheet on Standing Rock Indian Reservation, North and South Dakota* (Aberdeen, 1970), pp. 1-2.

44. *SR Fact Sheet,* pp. 1-2; PSG Rept. 202, pp. 42-43; Kent and Johnson, *Indian Poverty in South Dakota,* pp. 40-41; *Aberdeen Area Statistical Data (1971),* pp. 10-11; H. Rept. 92-1372 (1972), pp. 13-14.

45. U.S., Department of Commerce, *Federal and State Indian Reservations and Indian Trust Areas* (Washington, D.C.: Government Printing Office, 1974), pp. 433-44, 489-93, 496-97, 505-507; Mueller, *CR Community Background Report,* pp. 13-14; H. Rept. 92-1372 (1972), pp. 13-15.

46. Ibid.

47. Yankton Redevelopment Committee, *Yankton Redevelopment Area* (Wagner, S. Dak.: 1964), pp. 2-4; *Act of 6 October 1972, Stat.* 86 (1972): 782; U.S., Congress, House, Committee on Interior and Insular Affairs, *Providing for Disposition of Judgment Funds for the Yankton Sioux Tribe,* H. Rept. 639, 92d Cong., 1st sess., 1971, pp. 3, 7-10; *Aberdeen Area Statistical Data (1971),* pp. 10-11; *Federal and State Indian Reservations,* pp. 505-507; U.S., Congress, House, "Indian Unemployment, Sioux Reservations, 1973," 93d Cong., 1st sess., 22 December 1973, *Congressional Record* 119: 43336-41.

48. Ibid.

49. PSG Rept. 219, p. 46.

50. MRBI Rept. 177, pp. 55-56.

51. Report of SR Economics Committee, 1 March 1966, 74A390, 223836, RG 75, FRC-D; Mueller, *CR Community Background Report,* pp. 8-9; *CR Comprehensive Development Program (1965),* pp. 57-58; *Aberdeen Area Statistical Data (1971),* pp. 30-31; MRBI Rept. 177, p. 46; *SR Developmental Plan, II (1971),* pp. 18-19.

CHAPTER 12

1. *Pierre* (S. Dak.) *Daily Capitol-Journal, New York Times,* 17 August 1962.

2. Hart, *Dark Missouri,* pp. 154-55; U.S., DA, CE, Missouri River Division, *Water Resources Development: South Dakota, 1973* (Omaha, 1973), p. 13. Floods in the region below Kansas City caused an estimated $23.6 million in damages in 1967 (*Kansas City Times,* 21 June 1967). In 1973 serious flooding occurred near St. Louis, Missouri (*St. Louis Post-Dispatch,* 19-20 April 1973).

3. Ellen Ducheneaux, interviews.

4. Frank Ducheneaux, Lloyd LeBeau, Aljoe Agard, interviews; Kermeth S. Engle, BIA Realty Officer, SR Agency, interview held at Fort Yates, North Dakota, 9 August 1972.

5. Ibid.; MBIAC, *Comprehensive Framework Study,* vol. 5, *Present and Future Needs,* pp. 6-8; Harland, Batholomew, and Associates, *Economic Potential of Recreation at Big Bend Reservoir* (St. Louis, 1963), p. 8; Daly and Associates, *CC Comprehensive Plan (1967),* p. 34; Donald Kritzsinger, interview; Rusty Farmer, BIA Administrative Officer, CR Agency, interview held at Eagle Butte, S. Dak., 2 August 1972.

6. *Kansas City Star,* 6 May 1972; Warne, *Bureau of Reclamation,* p. 98

7. Schell, *History of South Dakota,* p. 308; MBIAC, *Comprehensive Framework Study,* vol. 1, *Report,* p. 165, and vol. 5; *Present and Future Needs,* p. 4.

8. Ibid.

9. Schell, *History of South Dakota,* p. 361; Robinson, *History of North Dakota,* pp. 463, 465-66; Warne, *Bureau of Reclamation,* pp. 167-68.

10. Ibid.

11. U.S., DI, BIA, MRBI, *Potential Irrigation Development, Missouri River Basin Reservations,* (Billings, 1967), MRBI Rept. 185, pp. 1-3; PSG Rept. 202, pp. 56-58.

12. PSG Rept. 202, pp. 60-61.

13. MRBI Rept. 185, Appendix 10, *Cheyenne River Reservation* (1970), pp. 2, 20; Schell, *History of South Dakota,* p. 361; Cheyenne River Redevelopment Committee, *Overall Economic Plan for Cheyenne River Redevelopment Area* (Eagle Butte, 1969), pp. 41-42, 73-74; Frank Ducheneaux, interviews.

14. MRBI Rept. 185, pp. 1-30.

15. 207 U.S. 564, pp. 575-77 (1908). Other decisions which have extended the Winters Doctrine include *Conrad Investment Company* v. *U.S.,* 161 Fed. 829 (CA9, 1908), *U.S.* v. *Walker River Irrigation District,* 104 Fed. 2d. 334 (CA9, 1939); *U.S.* v. *Ahtanum Irrigation District,* 236 Fed. 2d. 321 (CA9, 1956), *Arizona* v. *California,* 373 U.S. 546, pp. 598-600 (1963). Price, *Law and the American Indian,* p. 310; William H. Veeder, "Indian Prior and Paramount Rights to the Use of Water," *Rocky Mountain Mineral Law Institute Review* 16 (1971): 656-57, "Confiscation of Indian Winters Rights in the Upper Missouri Basin," *South Dakota Law Review* 21 (Spring, 1976): 283.

16. *Stat.* 58 (1944): 887, 905, sec. 9.

17. *Act of 1 July 1932, Stat.* 47 (1932): 564

18. CE, *Water Resources Development, South Dakota,* p. 13; MBIAC, *Comprehensive Framework Study,* vol. 1, *Report,* p. 165, and vol. 2, *Historical*

Perspective, p. 56.

19. *CR Overall Economic Development Plan (1969),* p. 69; Morgan, *Dams and Other Disasters,* p. 57; Frank Ducheneaux, Lloyd LeBeau, Aljoe Agard, interviews.

20. U.S., DI, Bureau of Outdoor Recreation, *The Middle Missouri, A Rediscovery: A Study in Potential Outdoor Recreation* (Washington, D.C.: Government Printing Office, 1970), pp. 1, 28-30; Jack Merwin, "Those Dam Walleyes," *Outdoor Life* 153 (April 1973): 61-64.

21. U.S., DI, BIA, Planning Support Group, *The Standing Rock Reservation, The Recreation Development Potential, An Atlas of Sites,* PSG Rept. 203 (Billings, 1974), p. 111; *CR Fact Sheet,* p. 3.

22. Frank Ducheneaux, Kermeth Engle, Aljoe Agard, interviews; Dudley Rehder, Missouri River Division Office, CE, interview held at Omaha, Nebr., 24 May 1972; Kenneth Krabbenhoft, National Park Service, interview held at Omaha, Nebr., 22 May 1972.

23. PSG Rept. 202, p. 105; PSG Rept. 203, pp. 3, 9; *SR Developmental Plan II (1971),* p. 42; Nason, Law, Wehrman, and Knight, Inc., *Indian Island Memorial Park: Analysis and Program* (Minneapolis, 1964), p. iii.

24. Bureau of Outdoor Recreation, *The Middle Missouri,* pp. 28-30; *CR Fact Sheet,* p. 4.

25. *CR Overall Economic Development Plan (1969),* pp. 68-72; Frank Ducheneaux, interviews.

26. Ibid.; U.S., DI, BIA, MRBI, *Evaluation of the Livestock Phase, Cheyenne River Rehabilitation Program, South Dakota,* MRBI Rept. 190 (Billings, 1968), p. 13; Philbrick to author, 24 August 1972; *SR Fact Sheet,* p. 2.

27. Engel, interview.

28. Veeder, "Confiscation of Indian Winters Rights, pp. 283-308.

29. Ibid.

30. Lloyd LeBeau, Engel, interviews; U.S., DI, National Park Service, *Introduction to Middle Missouri Archeology,* by Donald J. Lehmer, Anthropology Paper I (Washington, D.C.: Government Printing Office, 1971), pp. 6-7, 9, 10, 20, 113.

31. U.S., DI, BIA, MRBI, *Employment of Indians on Missouri River Basin Projects, 2d Rept.,* MRBI Rept. 54, pp. 1-2, *3d Rept.* MRBI Rept. 68, pp. 1-2 (Billings, 1948); Agard, Kritzsinger, Frank Ducheneaux, interviews.

32. *National Environmental Policy Act of 1969, Stat.* 83 (1970): 852-56.

33. U.S., DI, Fish and Wildlife Service, "Ecological Changes During Transitional Years and Full Impoundment (1966-1970) of Lake Oahe, An Upper Missouri River Storage Reservoir," by Fred C. June, in *Twelve Papers on Lake Oahe, North and South Dakota,* Technical Papers 71-82 (Washington, D.C.: Government Printing Office, 1974), pp. 3-4, 10, 12, 40; MBIAC, *Comprehensive Framework Study,* vol. 5, *Present and Future Needs,* pp. 4-8.

34. Ibid.

35. Lloyd LeBeau, Frank Ducheneaux, Engel, Agard, interviews.

36. Schell, *History of South Dakota,* pp. 340-41.

37. Warne, *Bureau of Reclamation,* p. 166.

38. Briggs, *Rampage,* p. 196.

39. *New York Times,* 16 March 1969.

40. Bureau of Outdoor Recreation, *The Middle Missouri,* pp. 4-5; Agard, Traversie, Frank Ducheneaux, interviews.

41. Morgan, *Dams and Other Disasters,* pp. 57-63; Berkman and Viscusi, *Damming the West,* pp. 151-90; U.S., House and Senate, Joint Economic Committee, Subcommittee on Economy in Government, "Federal Encroachment on Indian Water Rights and the Impairment of Reservation Development," by William H. Veeder, in *Toward Economic Development for Native American Communities, A Compendium of Papers,* vol. 1, pt. 3 (Washington, D.C.: Government Printing Office, 1969), pp. 516-18.

42. Ibid. For a more detailed analysis of the Navajo project, see Michael L. Lawson, "The Navajo Indian Irrigation Project: Muddied Past, Clouded Future," *The Indian Historian* 9 (Winter, 1976): 19-29.

BIBLIOGRAPHY

I. MANUSCRIPT COLLECTIONS

Denver, Colo. Federal Records Center. Records of the Bureau of Indian Affairs, Record Group 75. Aberdeen Area Office, Correspondence, 1950-65. Missouri Basin Investigations Project.

Eagle Butte, S.Dak. Cheyenne River Sioux Tribal Council Records.

Independence, Mo. Harry S Truman Presidential Library. Harry S Truman Papers, Official File. Philleo Nash Papers. Samuel I. Roseman Papers.

Kansas City, Mo. Federal Records Center. Records of the Bureau of Indian Affairs, Record Group 75. Cheyenne River Tribal Council Minutes, 1946-49. Crow Creek Tribal Council Minutes, 1939-54. Crow Creek Tribal Relations, 1962-66. Lower Brule Tribal Minutes, 1948-55. Pierre Agency, Tribal Relations, 1950-70. Rosebud Agency, Tribal Relations, 1950-70. Standing Rock Agency, Tribal Relations, 1950-70.

Suitland, Md. Washington National Records Center. Records of the Bureau of Indian Affairs, Record Group 75. Aberdeen Area Office, Legislation, 1952-56. Aberdeen Area Office, Relocation Plans, 1952. Cheyenne River Agency, 1957-61. Crow Creek Tribal Relations, 1951-52. Missouri River Basin, General Programs, 1960. Missouri River Basin, Oahe Dam, Cheyenne River, Standing Rock, 1951-55. Missouri River Basin Investigations Project, Oahe Project, 1952. Pierre Agency, 1950-70. Standing Rock Agency, 1951. Standing Rock Agency, Oahe Project Contract Negotiations, 1951-55.

Washington, D.C. National Archives, Records of the Secretary of the Interior, Record Group 48. Central Classified Files, Missouri River Basin, 1937-53. Records of the Bureau of Indian Affairs, Record Group 75: Fort Randall Legislation; Missouri Basin Projects, 1950-58; Oahe Dam Legislation.

II. ORAL HISTORY COLLECTIONS

Aberdeen, S.Dak. Northern State College, American Indian Research Project, Oral History Center. Gib LeBeau, unaccessioned. Robert J. Murray, accession no. 22. Wilfred S. Parrow, accession no. 7.

Vermillion, S.Dak. University of South Dakota, American Indian Research Project, South Dakota Oral History Center. Richard La-Roche, tapes 784, 789.

III. THESES

Lamport, Nancy Lee. "Francis Case: His Pioneer Background, Indian Legislation, and Missouri River Conservation." Master's thesis, University of South Dakota, 1972.

Lawson, Michael L. "Reservoir and Reservation: The Oahe Dam and the Cheyenne River Sioux." Master's thesis, University of Nebraska at Omaha, 1973.

IV. INTERVIEWS

Agard, Aljoe. Fort Yates, N.Dak. 8 August 1972.

Ducheneaux, Ellen. Eagle Butte, S.Dak. 31 July, 1 August 1972.

Ducheneaux, Frank. Cheyenne River Indian Reservation, S.Dak. 30, 31 July 1972.

Engel, Kermeth S. Fort Yates, N.Dak. 9 August 1972.

Farmer, Rusty. Eagle Butte, S.Dak. 2 August 1972.

Krabbenhoft, Kenneth. Omaha, Nebr. 22 May 1972.

Kritzsinger, Donald. Pierre, S.Dak. 27 July 1972.

LeBeau, Lloyd. Eagle Butte, S.Dak. 31 July 1972.

Pennington, Donald. Eagle Butte, S.Dak. 3 August 1972.

Rehder, Dudley. Omaha, Nebr. 22 May 1972.

Traversie, Theodophile L. Eagle Butte, S.Dak. 31 July 1972.

V. GOVERNMENT DOCUMENTS

Many printed government documents were used for this study. Those contained in the Serial Set of Congressional Documents, including the *Congressional Record* and the many House and Senate bills and reports, are fully cited in the footnotes.

U.S. Department of the Army, Corps of Engineers. *Annual Report of the Chief of Engineers, U.S. Army.* Washington, D.C.: Government Printing Office, 1944-74.

U.S. Department of the Army, Corps of Engineers, Missouri River Division. *The Development and Control of the Missouri River.* Omaha, 1947.

———. *Big Bend Dam: Lake Sharpe.* Omaha, 1972.

———. *Fort Randall Dam: Lake Francis Case.* Omaha, 1972.

———. *Garrison Dam: Lake Sakakawea.* Omaha, 1972.

———. *Oahe Dam: Lake Oahe.* Omaha, 1972.

———. *Water Resources Development: South Dakota, 1973.* Omaha, 1973.

U.S. Department of the Army, Office of the Chief of Military History. *United States Army in World War II.* Vol. 6, pt. 6, *The Technical Services.* Vol. 3, *The Corps of Engineers: Construction in the United States,* by Lenore Fine and Jesse D. Remington. Washington, D.C.: 1972.

U.S. Department of Commerce. *Federal and State Indian Reservations and Indian Trust Areas.* Washington, D.C.: Government Printing Office, 1974.

———, Bureau of Census. *United States Census of Population: 1950.* Vol. 1, *Characteristics of Population.* Pt. 1, *United States Summary.* Pt. 41, *South Dakota.* Washington, D.C.: Government Printing Office, 1951.

U.S. Department of Health, Education, and Welfare. Indian Health Service. *Summary of Indian Health Service Reports in South Dakota.* Aberdeen, 1968.

U.S. Department of the Interior, Bureau of Indian Affairs. *A History of Indian Policy,* by S. Lyman Tyler. Washington, D.C.: Government Printing Office, 1973.

U.S. Department of the Interior, Bureau of Indian Affairs, Aberdeen Area Office, Aberdeen, S.Dak. *Preliminary Comprehensive Development Plan for Lower Brule Indian Reservation, Lower Brule, South Dakota.* Aberdeen, 1963.

———. *Preliminary Comprehensive Development Plan for Cheyenne River Indian Reservation.* Eagle Butte, S.Dak., 1965.

———. *Fact Sheet on Cheyenne River Indian Reservation, South Dakota.* Aberdeen, 1970.

———. *Fact Sheet on Standing Rock Indian Reservation, North and*

South Dakota. Aberdeen, 1970.

──── . *Aberdeen Area Statistical Data, 1971.* Aberdeen, 1971.

──── . *Fact Sheet on Crow Creek Sioux Reservation, South Dakota.* Aberdeen, 1971.

──── . *Fact Sheet on Lower Brule Sioux Reservation, South Dakota.* Aberdeen, 1973.

U.S. Department of the Interior, Bureau of Indian Affairs, Missouri River Basin Investigations Project, Billings, Mont. *Reports of the Missouri River Basin Investigations Project.* 1947-72.

U.S. Department of the Interior, Bureau of Indian Affairs, Planning Support Group, Billings, Mont. *Reports of the Planning Support Group.* 1972-74.

U.S. Department of the Interior, Bureau of Outdoor Recreation. *The Middle Missouri, A Rediscovery: A Study in Potential Outdoor Recreation.* Washington, D.C.: Government Printing Office, 1970.

U.S. Department of the Interior, Fish and Wildlife Service. *Twelve Papers on Lake Oahe, North and South Dakota.* Technical Papers 71-82. Washington, D.C.: Government Printing Office, 1974.

U.S. Department of the Interior, National Park Service. *Introduction to Middle Missouri Archeology,* by Donald J. Lehmer. Anthropology Papers I. Washington, D.C.: Government Printing Office, 1971.

U.S. Department of the Interior, Western Museums Laboratory. *Teton Dakota Ethnology and History,* by John C. Ewers. Berkeley, California: 1938.

U.S. Department of Justice, District Court, South Dakota District.

──── . *U.S. v. 9,148 Acres of Land, et al., and the Crow Creek Tribe of Sioux Indians.* Civil no. 184. 4 August 1953.

──── . *U.S. v. 7,996 Acres of Land, et al., and the Lower Brule Tribe of Sioux Indians.* Civil no. 186. 4 August 1953.

──── . *U.S. v. 2005.32 Acres of Land, et al., and the Standing Rock Tribe of Sioux Indians.* Civil no. 722. N.D. Tract R. 18251. 10 March 1958.

──── . *U.S. v. 867.5 Acres of Land, et al., and Crow Creek and Lower Brule Tribe of Sioux Indians.* Civil no. 335. 9 March 1960.

U.S., Missouri Basin Inter-Agency Committee. *The Missouri River Basin Comprehensive Framework Study.* 7 vols. Vol. 1, *The Report.* Washington, D.C.: Government Printing Office, 1971.

──── and the Missouri River States Committee. *The Missouri River Basin Development Program.* Washington, D.C.: Government Printing Office, 1952.

U.S., Missouri Basin Survey Commission. *Missouri: Land and Water,*

The Report of the Missouri Basin Survey Commission. Washington, D.C.: Government Printing Office, 1953.

U.S., President's Water Resources Policy Commission. *Ten Rivers in America's Future: The Report of the President's Water Resources Policy Commission.* Vol. 2, *The Missouri.* Washington, D.C.: Government Printing Office, 1950.

U.S., Smithsonian Institution. *Handbook of American Indians North of Mexico.* Edited by Frederick Webb Hodge. Bureau of American Ethnology Bulletin no. 30, pt. 1, Washington, D.C.: Government Printing Office, 1912.

————. *The Indian Tribes of North America,* by John R. Swanton. Bureau of American Ethnology Bulletin no. 145. Washington, D.C.: Government Printing Office, 1952.

————. "Use of Plants by Indians of the Missouri River Region," by Melvin Randolph Gilmore. In *Thirty-third Annual Report of the Bureau of American Ethnology,* pp. 43-154. Washington, D.C.: Government Printing Office, 1919.

U.S. *Statutes at Large.*

VI. NEWSPAPERS

Aberdeen (S.Dak.) *American News*
Corson County (S.Dak.) *News*
Eagle Butte (S.Dak.) *News*
Kansas City Star
Kansas City Times
McLaughlin (S.Dak.) *Messenger*
Mobridge (S.Dak.) *Tribune*
Nebraska State Journal
New York Times

Omaha World-Herald
Overbrook (Kans.) *Citizen*
Pierre (S.Dak.) *Capitol-Journal*
St. Louis Globe-Democrat
St. Louis Post-Dispatch
Sioux County (N.Dak.) *Pioneer-Arrow*
Sioux Falls (S.Dak.) *Argus-Leader*
Washington Post

VII. BOOKS

Baumhoff, Richard G. *The Dammed Missouri Valley: One-Sixth of Our Nation.* New York: Alfred A. Knopf, 1951.

Berkman, Richard L., and Viscusi, W. Kip. *Damming the West: Ralph Nader's Study Group Report on the Bureau of Reclamation.* New York: Grossman Publishers, 1973.

Bernstein, Barton J., and Matusow, Allen T., eds. *The Truman Administration: A Documentary History.* New York: Harper & Row, 1966.

Big Bend Redevelopment Commission. *Big Bend Overall Economic Development Plans.* Pierre, S.Dak.: 1964-66.

Briggs, Peter. *Rampage, The Story of Disastrous Floods, Broken Dams, and Human Fallibility.* New York: David McKay and Co., 1973.

Burdick, Usher L. *The Last Days of Sitting Bull, Sioux Medicine Man.* Baltimore: Wirth Brothers, 1941.

Cassel, John; Page, Etra; and Hogan, Gaynelle. *Economic and Social Resources Available for Indian Health Purposes: A Study of Selected Reservations in the Aberdeen Area.* Chapel Hill: University of North Carolina, Institute for Research in the Social Sciences, 1956.

Cheyenne River Redevelopment Committee. *Overall Economic Plan for Cheyenne River Redevelopment Area.* Eagle Butte, S.Dak., 1969.

Commission on the Organization of the Executive Branch of Government. *Task Force Report on Natural Resources.* Washington, D.C.: 1949.

Corwine and Doell, Consultants. *The Fort Yates Land Use and Recreation Planning Report.* Minneapolis: 1964.

Daly, Leo A., and Associates. *Comprehensive Plan for Crow Creek Reservation, South Dakota.* Omaha: 1967.

Debo, Angie. *A History of the Indians of the United States.* Norman: University of Oklahoma Press, 1970.

Deloria, Vine, Jr. *Custer Died for Your Sins: An Indian Manifesto.* New York: Avon Books, 1969.

Ellis, Richard N., ed. *The Western American Indian: Case Studies in Tribal History.* Lincoln: University of Nebraska Press, 1972.

Estes, George C., and Loder, Richard R. *Kul-Wicasa-Oyate: Lower Brule Sioux Tribe.* Lower Brule, S.Dak.: Lower Brule Sioux Tribe, 1971.

Fermin, Louis; Kornbluth, Joyce L.; and Haber, Alan; eds. *Poverty in America.* Ann Arbor: University of Michigan Press, 1965.

Fritz, Henry E. *The Movement for Indian Assimilation, 1860-1890.* Philadelphia: University of Pennsylvania Press, 1963.

Gard, Wayne. *The Great Buffalo Hunt: Its History and Drama and Its Role in the Opening of the West.* Lincoln: University of Nebraska Press, 1968.

Hagan, William T. *American Indians.* Chicago: University of Chicago Press, 1961.

Harrington, Michael. *The Other America: Poverty in the United*

States. New York: Macmillan, 1962.

————. *The Other America: Poverty in the United States.* 2d ed. Baltimore: Penguin Books, 1971.

Hart, Gerald T., and Associates. *Basic Data Report, Oahe Reservoir Valuation Project, Sioux Indian Lands.* Denver, 1951.

Hart, Henry C. *The Dark Missouri.* Madison: University of Wisconsin Press, 1957.

Hoiberg, Otto G. *Its Your Business and Mine: Missouri River Basin Development Program, A Study Guide.* University of Nebraska, Extension Division. Booklet No. 175. Lincoln: 1950.

Hough, Henry W. *Development of Indian Resources.* Indian Community Action Program. Denver: World Press, 1967.

Howard, James H. *The Dakota or Sioux Indians: A Study in Human Ecology.* Dakota Museum, Anthropological Papers, no. 2, pt. 3. Vermillion: University of South Dakota, 1966.

Hyde, George E. *A Sioux Chronicle.* Norman: University of Oklahoma Press, 1956. *Red Cloud's Folk: A History of the Oglala Sioux.* 2d ed. Norman: University of Oklahoma Press, 1957. *Spotted Tail's Folk: A History of the Brulé Sioux.* Norman: University of Oklahoma Press, 1961.

Institute of Indian Studies, University of South Dakota. *Tribal Rehabilitation Programs: Program and Proceedings, Fifth Annual Conference on Indian Affairs.* Vermillion, 1959.

Kent, Calvin A., and Johnson, Jerry W. *Indian Poverty in South Dakota.* University of South Dakota, Business Research Bureau Bulletin no. 99. Vermillion: University of South Dakota School of Business, 1969.

Keyser, C. Frank. *Missouri Valley Authority: Background and Analysis of Proposal.* Public Affairs Bulletin no. 42. Washington, D.C.: Library of Congress, Legislative Reference Service, 1946.

Koenig, Louis W., ed. *The Truman Administration: Its Principles and Practices.* New York: New York University Press, 1956.

Kristjanson, Kris. *TVA Land Acquisition Experience Applied to Dams in the Missouri Basin.* Agricultural Experiment Station, South Dakota State College. Brookings, 1953.

Lawson, Michael L. *Reservoir and Reservation: The Oahe Dam and the Cheyenne River Sioux.* In *South Dakota Historical Collections,* vol. 37. Pierre: South Dakota State Historical Society, 1974.

Lilienthal, David E. *T.V.A.: Democracy on the March.* New York: Harper & Bros., 1944.

MacGregor, Gordon, with the collaboration of Hassrick, Royal B.

Warriors Without Weapons: A Study of the Society and Personality Development of the Pine Ridge Sioux. Chicago: University of Chicago Press, 1946.

Malin, James C. *The Grasslands of North America: Prolegomena to its History, with Addenda and Postscript.* Gloucester, Mass.: P. Smith, 1967.

Mardock, Robert W. *The Reformers and the American Indian.* Columbia: University of Missouri Press, 1971.

Mead, Marvin. *The Missouri River Proposals for Development.* Citizens Pamphlet 11. Lawrence: University of Kansas, Bureau of Government Research, 1952.

Merriam, Lewis. *The Problem of Indian Administration.* Baltimore: Johns Hopkins Press, 1928.

Meyer, Roy W. *History of the Santee Sioux: United States Indian Policy on Trial.* Lincoln: University of Nebraska Press, 1967.

———. *The Village Indians of the Upper Missouri: The Mandans, Hidatsas, and Arikaras.* Lincoln: University of Nebraska Press, 1977.

Morgan, Arthur E. *Dams and Other Disasters: A Century of the Army Corps of Engineers in Civil Works.* Boston: Porter Sargent Publisher, 1971.

Mueller, Wolfgang. *Community Background Reports: Cheyenne River Sioux Reservation, South Dakota.* Chicago: National Study of American Indian Education, 1969.

Nason, Law, Wehrman, and Knight, Inc. *Indian Island Memorial Park: Analysis and Program.* Minneapolis, 1964.

Nelson, Bruce. *Land of the Dacotahs.* Minneapolis: University of Minnesota Press, 1946.

Nurge, Ethel, ed. *The Modern Sioux: Social Systems and Reservation Culture.* Lincoln: University of Nebraska Press, 1970.

Oehler, C. M. *The Great Sioux Uprising.* New York: Oxford University Press, 1959.

Olson, James C. *Red Cloud and the Sioux Problem.* Lincoln: University of Nebraska Press, 1965.

Otis, D. S. *The Dawes Act and the Allotment of Indian Lands.* Edited by Francis Paul Prucha. Norman: University of Oklahoma Press, 1973.

Parman, Donald L. *The Navajos and the New Deal.* New Haven: Yale University Press, 1976.

Phillips, Cabell. *The Truman Presidency: The History of a Triumphant Succession.* New York: The Macmillan Company, 1966.

Philp, Kenneth R. *John Collier's Crusade for Indian Reform, 1920-1954.* Tucson: University of Arizona Press, 1977.

Price, Monroe E. *Law and the American Indian: Readings, Notes, Cases.* Indianapolis: Bobbs-Merrill Co., 1973.

Priest, Loring B. *Uncle Sam's Stepchildren: The Reformation of United States Indian Policy, 1865-1887.* New Brunswick: Rutgers University Press, 1942.

Public Affairs Institute. *The Big Missouri: Hope of Our West.* Washington, D.C.: 1948.

Ridgeway, Marian E. *The Missouri Basin's Pick-Sloan Plan: A Case Study in Congressional Policy Determination.* Illinois Studies in Social Science. Vol. 35. Urbana: University of Illinois Press, 1955.

Robinson, Doane. *A History of the Dakota or Sioux Indians.* 2d ed. Minneapolis: Ross & Haines, 1967.

Robinson, Elwyn B. *History of North Dakota.* Lincoln: University of Nebraska Press, 1966.

Schell, Herbert S. *History of South Dakota.* 3d ed. rev. Lincoln: University of Nebraska Press, 1975.

Schusky, Ernest L. "Cultural Change and Continuity in the Lower Brule Community." In *The Modern Sioux: Social Systems and Reservation Culture,* edited by Ethel Nurge. Lincoln: University of Nebraska Press, 1970.

————. *The Forgotten Sioux: An Ethnohistory of the Lower Brule Reservation.* Chicago: Nelson-Hall, 1975.

————. *Politics and Planning in a Dakota Indian Community.* Vermillion: Institute of Indian Studies, University of South Dakota, 1959.

Standing Rock Redevelopment Committee. *Provisional Overall Development Plan.* Fort Yates, N.Dak.: 1966.

Standing Rock Tribal Council and Planning Staff. *Developmental Plan, Phase II.* Fort Yates, N.Dak.: 1971.

Standing Rock Tribal Council. *Programs for Progress.* Fort Yates, N.Dak.: 1963.

Steiner, Stan. *The New Indians.* New York: Harper & Row, 1968.

Stephens, Harry R. *The Government of the Indians of South Dakota.* The Government Research Bureau, University of South Dakota. Report No. 8. Vermillion: 1952.

Taylor, Graham D. *The New Deal and American Indian Tribalism: The Administration of the Indian Reorganization Act, 1935-45.* Lincoln: University of Nebraska Press, 1980.

Terral, Rufus. *The Missouri Valley: Land of Drouth, Flood, and*

Promise. New Haven: Yale University Press, 1947.

Trennert, Robert A. *Alternative to Extinction: Federal Indian Policy and the Beginning of the Reservation System, 1846-1851.* Philadelphia: Temple University Press, 1975.

Utley, Robert M. *The Last Days of the Sioux Nation.* New Haven: Yale University Press, 1963.

————. *Frontiersmen in Blue: The United States Army and the Indian, 1848-1865.* New York: Macmillan, 1967.

————. *Frontier Regulars: The United States Army and the Indian, 1866-1891.* New York: Macmillan, 1974.

Vestal, Stanley. *The Missouri.* Lincoln: University of Nebraska Press, 1964.

Warne, William E. *The Bureau of Reclamation.* New York: Praeger Publishers, 1973.

Washburn, Wilcomb E. *The Assault on Indian Tribalism: The General Allotment (Dawes Act) of 1887.* Philadelphia: Lippincott, 1975.

Water Policy Panel, Engineering Joint Council. *National Water Policy.* 2 vols. Washington, D.C.: 1950.

Webb, Walter Prescott. *The Great Plains.* Boston: Ginn and Company, 1931.

The World Almanac and Book of Facts, 1976. New York: Newspaper Enterprise Association, 1976.

Yankton Redevelopment Committee. *Yankton Redevelopment Area.* Wagner, S.Dak., 1964.

VIII. ARTICLES

Arthur, William B. "MVA—Its Backgrounds and Issues." *Congressional Digest* 29 (January 1950): 13-14.

Dollar, Clyde D. "The Second Tragedy at Wounded Knee: A 1970s Confrontation and Its Historical Roots." *American West* 10 (September 1973): 4-11.

Ferrell, John R. "Water in the Missouri Valley: The Inter-Agency River Committee at Mid-Century." *Journal of the West* 7, no. 1 (January 1968): 95-105.

Gilmore, Melvin Randolph. "Use of Plants by Indians of the Missouri River Region." *Thirty-third Annual Report of the American Bureau of Ethnology.* Washington, D.C.: Government Printing Office, 1919, pp. 43-154.

Lawson, Michael L. "How the Bureau of Indian Affairs Discourages Historical Research." *Indian Historian* 10 (Fall, 1977): 25-27.

————. "The Navajo Indian Irrigation Project: Muddied Past, Clouded Future." *Indian Historian* 9 (Winter, 1976): 19-29.

————. "The Oahe Dam and the Standing Rock Sioux." *South Dakota History* 6 (Spring, 1976): 203-28.

McCarthy, Charles J. "Land Acquisition Policies and Proceedings in TVA—A Study of the Role of Land Acquisition in a Regional Agency." *Ohio State Law Journal* 10 (Winter, 1948): 48-51.

Merwin, Jack, "Those Dam Walleyes." *Outdoor Life* 153 (April 1973): 61-64.

Meyer, Roy W. "Fort Berthold and the Garrison Dam." *North Dakota History* 35 (Summer and Fall, 1968): 220-355.

Nurge, Ethel. "Dakota Diet: Traditional and Contemporary." In *The Modern Sioux: Social Systems and Reservation Culture,* edited by Ethel Nurge. Lincoln: University of Nebraska Press, 1970.

Schusky, Ernest L. "Cultural Change and Continuity in the Lower Brule Community." In *The Modern Sioux: Social Systems and Reservation Culture,* edited by Ethel Nurge. Lincoln: University of Nebraska Press, 1970.

Veeder, William H. "Confiscation of Indian Winters Rights in the Upper Missouri Basin." *South Dakota Law Review* 21 (Spring, 1976): 282-309.

————. "Indian Prior and Paramount Rights to the Use of Water." *Rocky Mountain Mineral Law Institute Review* 16: 631-93.

INDEX

249